MW00634772

Love
Everyone

Love Everyone

The Transcendent Wisdom of

Neem Karoli Baba

Told Through the Stories of the Westerners

Whose Lives He Transformed

Parvati Markus

HarperOne
An Imprint of HarperCollins*Publishers*

HarperOne

The credits on page 378 constitute a continuation of this copyright page.

Every effort has been made to obtain permissions for photographs or pieces quoted or adapted in this work. If any required acknowledgements have been omitted, or any rights overlooked, it is unintentional. Please notify the publishers of any omission, and it will be rectified in future editions.

LOVE EVERYONE. Copyright © 2015 by Love Serve Remember Foundation. All rights reserved. Printed in the United States of America. No part of this book may be used or reproduced in any manner whatsoever without written permission except in the case of brief quotations embodied in critical articles and reviews. For information address HarperCollins Publishers, 195 Broadway, New York, NY 10007.

HarperCollins books may be purchased for educational, business, or sales promotional use. For information please e-mail the Special Markets Department at SPsales@ harpercollins.com.

HarperCollins website: http://www.harpercollins.com

FIRST EDITION

Designed by Ralph Fowler

Library of Congress Cataloging-in-Publication Data is available upon request.

ISBN 978–0–06–234299–7

15 16 17 18 19   OV/RRD   10 9 8 7 6 5 4 3 2 1

Krishna Das (Roy Bonney)

Twameva mata cha pita twameva,
Twameva bandhu cha saka twameva,
Twameva vidya dravinam twameva,
Twameva sarvam mama deva deva.

You alone are my mother and my father,
You alone are my friend and my beloved companion,
You alone are my knowledge and my wealth,
O Supreme Lord, you alone are everything for me.

Contents

Part One

In the Beginning

1968–1969

Part Two

The First Wave

1970–March 1972

Part Three

The Second Wave

March 1972–September 1973

Foreword

When I left India the first time, my guru, Neem Karoli Baba, told me not to talk about him in the West. But as I traveled around and spoke to ever larger groups, I did nothing else. It was as if I had no choice. I shared him, and some of those who heard me talk about Maharajji went to India and met him as well.

We Westerners who went to India on a spiritual quest and those of us who spent time with Maharajji experienced unconditional love and *siddhis* (spiritual powers) that we had never experienced before. Foremost was the way in which he saw us and loved us as souls. We bore witness to this exceptional soul as well as to our own true nature/selves. When we returned to the West, we carried him in our hearts and souls. All of the stories in this book, by the people who went to have *darshan* (sight of) and to bask in the presence of Maharajji in the late 1960s and early 1970s, are truly an extension of that unconditional love.

On my second trip to India in 1970, during my time with Maharajji, he would say to me simply, "Love everyone." And all I could say was, "I can't do that, Maharajji." That was because I was identified with my ego, which could not possibly love everyone. He would come up to me, nose to nose, and repeat, "Ram Dass, love everyone."

Over time this instruction took hold. My identification with ego shifted, and my perspective changed to one that came from my spiritual heart or soul. From the point of view of my soul, I was able to look at everyone as souls, and I loved each one of them. Maharajji's instruction led me to perceive myself and everyone else as loving souls.

Ego is here, in your head, which is who "I think I am." If you see those thoughts and then go down to the heart, the spiritual heart, down there you say, *I am loving awareness. I am loving awareness. I am loving awareness.* Whisper it: *I am loving awareness.*

Everything is love. Everything is a manifestation of love. Table. Tree. Yourself. Universe. The universes. They're all made up of love.

And once you bathe in that love, you dive into an ocean of love. Oh, it feels so wonderful! Love. Compassion. Love. Compassion.

We meet in that love. We meet inside.

Inside our spiritual heart.

In Hinduism it's called the *atman*. It's God, guru, and self together inside.

I'll see you inside.

Ram Dass
Maui, July 2014

Preface

In September 1971, Ram Dass and I were standing together, leaning over the balcony of the Evelyn Hotel in the "hill station" town of Nainital, looking out over the verdant foothills of the Himalayas and watching the postmonsoon clouds roll across the picture-perfect lake. Rowboats moved gracefully through the waters. Bells rang in the small temple across the lake. The sweet smell of incense wafted out from various rooms in the hotel, where some of the Westerners were meditating or doing devotional practices. Others were writing in journals or reading mail from home—missives from the other side of the world, a place that seemed far less real than the one we were now occupying.

We had come back to the hotel after a long day spent at a Hindu temple in the Kainchi valley, a half-hour bus ride away on twisty mountain roads with blind hairpin curves, where we were spending time with a holy man named Neem Karoli Baba, whom we called Maharajji (a title ubiquitous throughout India meaning "great king") or simply Baba. About twenty of us were living in the hotel as if it were an ashram. The hotel was owned by longtime devotees of Maharajji, and we were treated like family.

After a long silence, Ram Dass turned to me and said, "We are seeing Maharajji to bear witness."

That comment stayed with me over the years, and I've thought often about what he meant. In being with Maharajji, we were bearing witness to the reality of enlightenment and all that implied, and to a greater love than we had ever known. We were bearing witness to the love within our own hearts and to the realization that, as Maharajji often repeated, *Sub Ek* ("All is One"). We were bearing witness to what it meant to surrender in service to others.

This book is meant to bear witness to how a disparate group of Westerners found their way to India and to Maharajji, what we experienced there, and how the seeds of Maharajji's extraordinary love sprouted, grew, and blossomed in the West.

Introduction

We're all just walking each other home.

—RAM DASS

Neem Karoli Baba didn't come bodily to America. Instead, he sent his emissary—Ram Dass. Many of us found our way to Maharajji because of Ram Dass—either after hearing him lecture (the Indians said he had the "gift of Saraswati," the goddess of speech and poetry) or from reading his book *Be Here Now,* published in 1971. Others, who had embarked on the tantalizing journey to the East looking for adventure, good drugs, or spiritual wisdom, also found Maharajji.

This ragged band of skeptical Westerners came from a culture where it is anathema to bow down before another person and the idea of touching or, God forbid, kissing someone's feet is unthinkable. But that changed quickly in Maharajji's presence. We had come halfway around the world to experience the ancient Vedantic *sat-chit-ananda*—truth, consciousness, and bliss—as it manifested in a toothless old man wrapped in a plaid woolen blanket.

When we met Maharajji, we knew nothing about him or his history; some stories suggested that he was hundreds of years old. It wasn't until he died in September 1973 that we learned more. We discovered that, after emerging from his underground cave at Neem Karoli, he still honored his Brahminical duties to his wife, whom he'd been married to as a

Neem Karoli Baba.

young boy of nine or ten, to his children and grandchildren, and to his village. His yogic and spiritual powers were vast, but, like the wind, no one could catch him; he was a wanderer who usually spent no more than a few days in a place, which, to the amazement of his Indian devotees, changed when the Westerners arrived. But who he had been and where he had come from were irrelevant when we sat in front of him.

The Indians describe a being like Maharajji as *antaryamin*—a knower of hearts. Imagine sitting in front of someone who knows absolutely everything about you and still *loves you unconditionally.* Our thinking, rational, linear minds were quieted by the overwhelming experience of our hearts. We were *home.* We had made it to the home that's completely safe, a home built of pure love. And we were transformed.

The Path of Bhakti

For Maharajji's devotees, love is the heart of the matter. Maharajji gave no lectures, nothing for the mind to hold on to, no formal teachings other than his oft-repeated injunction: *Love everyone, feed everyone, and remember God.* And its corollary: *Tell the truth.* The only practices he encouraged were repeating the name of God (*mantra* or *japa*), singing the names of God (*kirtan*), and chanting the forty verses of the Hanuman Chalisa—a prayer to the monkey god, Hanuman, the aspect of God most closely associated with Maharajji. He didn't teach meditation; often people meditating in his presence were brought back to the here and now with a well-aimed piece of fruit.

We read the books and poetry of the great lovers of God, like Rumi. We sang all sorts of songs to Maharajji, not only kirtan. When Linda Bush was given the name Mirabai (a fifteenth-century devotional poet), she bought a tamboura (a stringed instrument made from a gourd) and sang *bhajans* (songs) to Mirabai's beloved deity, Krishna, the god of love. Rukmini, who had been involved in the Hare Krishna movement, sang such a beautiful *Hare Krishna Hare Ram* that it brought tears to Maharajji's eyes. And because Maharajji talked often about Jesus, we

Krishna Das (Roy Bonney)

Maharajji throwing fruit.

sang old gospel songs. Sometimes on bus rides back to Nainital at the end of the day from the temple in Kainchi, we would change the words to rock 'n' roll songs and Christmas carols and sing to Maharajji that way. Singing opens the heart, and the path of devotion, or *bhakti,* is all about opening the heart.

Bhakti yoga is a method of learning to live in love, much like meditation is a method of quieting the mind and expanding awareness. Ram Dass, these days, looks at everyone and everything in the universe, including the wheelchair that has become part of his life since his stroke, through the lens of "I am loving awareness."

Satsang

For Hindus, *satsang* means the community of people seeking higher truth, similar to "fellowship" or "brotherhood" in Western religious traditions and the *sanga* in Buddhism. Some of us spent no more than a few days with Maharajji, while others stayed for years, but together we formed a satsang, a family of devotees. Then he died, and we were left to deal with the rest of our lives. In the decades since his passing, we have followed and forged many different paths and studied with many teachers in various spiritual traditions, but we all hold our experience with Maharajji in the center of our hearts. And we have each other as companions, best friends, supporters, and gadflies, as we seek to merge what we learned in the East with the realities of our lives in the West.

When we left for India, there were only a few spiritual books or bookstores (such as Weiser's in New York and the Bodhi Tree in LA); there were no yoga studios on every corner, no meditation centers or teachers in every town, no one singing kirtan, no *bhakti* or *shakti* (devotional or spiritual energy) festivals. In the four decades since we came back from India, yoga and Eastern spirituality have become not only part of our lives, but also a large part of the changed landscape of America.

Some of us, like KRISHNA DAS, JAI UTTAL, BHAGAVAN DAS, and the late SHYAMDAS, brought the devotional practice of chanting (kirtan) from India to the West, while others have manifested their experience with Maharajji in ways that have little to do with religious tradition and more to do with service and changing consciousness.

DANIEL GOLEMAN wrote about the behavioral sciences for the *New York Times,* authored the revolutionary book *Emotional Intelligence,* and works with the Dalai Lama's Mind and Life Institute to explore consciousness and the brain. MIRABAI BUSH established the Center for Contemplative Mind in Society, which encourages the use of contemplative practices in college courses, the legal profession, and even high-tech environments like Google. DR. LARRY BRILLIANT has gone from helping to eradicate smallpox with the World Health Organization to directing Google's philanthropy to overseeing the Skoll Global Threats Fund. GIRIJA BRILLIANT helped found Seva Foundation with Larry, Ram Dass, Wavy Gravy, and others to use skillful means to reduce curable and preventable blindness around the world.

TOM FORRAY works with the criminally insane; SITA THOMPSON does hospice work and was a prison chaplain; ANASUYA WEIL practices Tibetan medicine; RADHA BAUM combines East and West as a nurse practitioner and acupuncturist. BALARAM DAS GOETSCH is an anesthesiologist and lawyer. RAM DEV BORGLUM directs the Living/Dying Project, helping those with life-threatening illnesses to find emotional and spiritual support. STEVEN SCHWARTZ founded the Center for Public Representation, providing mental-health law and disability law services. LAMA SURYA DAS is the founder of the Dzogchen Center in Cambridge, Massachusetts, author of many books, and a teacher of Tibetan Buddhism. KRISHNA BUSH is the producer of acclaimed documentaries, including the *Journey into Buddhism* trilogy. RALPH

ABRAHAM is a mathematician and chaos theorist. RAVI DAS JEFFERY is now retired after three decades as a Superior Court judge in Barrow, Alaska.

Others are psychologists, artists, musicians, teachers, caretakers, entrepreneurs, realtors, and web designers. These are, of course, our professional roles; in addition we have our family and societal roles. Beneath what we *do,* however, is who we *are* as souls. No matter how large or small our individual sphere of influence, we try to bring loving awareness and greater compassion to what we do and those we serve.

However, as a group we hold no single vision of who we are, who Maharajji is, and what we mean to each other. Maharajji gathers different ingredients for his satsang "stew"—all of us pungent with our array of "stuff"—and he occasionally picks up his long wooden spoon, throws in a new spice or another potato, and stirs the pot. Ram Dass used to call it the "sandpaper effect." Our conflicts, our coming together and breaking apart, our positive and negative interactions help smooth out the rough edges of our consciousness. As a group we are often as dysfunctional as many of our families of origin. But there's a difference: we are related to our family members by blood, but our satsang is a family of the heart.

Expanding Consciousness

The stories in this book were birthed in the cultural upheaval that took place in the West during the late 1960s and early 1970s. Many of the seekers who arrived in India in those days were baby boomers from comfortable middle-class homes, raised in the Jewish or Christian tradition. Most were well educated. Yet many felt as though they didn't fit into the world around them. Some felt like aliens in their families; others were uncomfortable with the religion of their youth; still others were bored in school or depressed by the materialistic postwar *Mad Men* culture of the 1950s and early 1960s. They were looking for something deeper, something with more meaning.

The social, sexual, political, and psychedelic revolutions of the 1960s brought freedom from many restrictions. It was time for sex, drugs, and rock 'n' roll! Psychedelics challenged old realities and revealed new vistas in consciousness. LSD and other mind-expanding drugs opened a generation to the existence of Spirit. As Terence McKenna, intrepid researcher and writer on human consciousness, has been attributed as saying: "LSD burst over the dreary domain of the constipated bourgeoisie like the angelic herald of a new psychedelic millennium. We have never been the same since, nor will we ever be, for LSD demonstrated, even to skeptics, that the mansions of heaven and gardens of paradise lie within each and all of us."[1]

There are many references to taking acid as the starting point for the journey of transformation that led to Maharajji. It was a time when psychedelics were the gateway to spiritual exploration; they opened the door to the possibility that Maharajji embodied. Today, spiritual teachers, books, and meditation courses are abundant, and drugs are no longer needed to open inner horizons. Consciousness, it turns out, can be expanded without drugs.

Eastern traditions fit well with the psychedelic experience. We loved the music—Ravi Shankar at Woodstock, the Beatles after their time in India; the art—Hindu mandalas and Tibetan Buddhist thangkas; and those few books that were available—Yogananda's *Autobiography of a Yogi*, the *Bhagavad Gita*, *The Tibetan Book of the Dead*, *The Gospel of Sri Ramakrishna*, Gurdjieff's *Meetings with Remarkable Men*, the Zen books of Alan Watts, the fiction of Herman Hesse and Aldous Huxley, and stories from the early pioneers who had made the fabled "journey to the East."

Eastern gurus and teachers started coming to America. Paramahansa Yogananda had founded the Self-Realization Fellowship in the United States in 1920, but in the 1960s and early 1970s the gates opened wide.

Swami Satchidananda brought Integral Yoga, one of the first initiations into the practice of hatha yoga. Maharishi Mahesh Yogi brought Transcendental Meditation (TM); Swami Muktananda awakened Americans through *shaktipat* (conferring spiritual energy); Meher Baba exhorted all, "Don't worry, be happy"; and A. C. Bhaktivedanta extolled Krishna Consciousness (ISKCON, International Society for Krishna Consciousness). Sikhs and Sufis and Zen masters—a whole retinue of holy men (but few women)—were welcomed by young Westerners seeking to understand and strengthen their emerging spirituality.

From these teachers, and from Maharajji and India itself, we learned that the best way to change consciousness was to cultivate a loving, compassionate heart, supported by methods that deepened devotion and engaged mindfulness.

About This Book

Many thousands have come in contact with Maharajji since his death in September 1973 through dreams, visions, or meditations. Others have felt a deep connection from reading or hearing stories about him. If God, guru, and self are intrinsically One, it is not necessary to have a guru in a physical body. Such devotees are no less "family of the heart" than those who were with him in India. But this book cannot even begin to contain all those stories, so we have limited this volume to the stories of some of those who were in India with "the old man in the blanket."

When interviewing the people whose stories make up this book, we asked only three main questions: What called you to India? What was your experience with Maharajji? How have you integrated that experience into the rest of your life? Despite the decades that have elapsed, most people's experiences in India, especially their time with Maharajji, remain vivid, often more memorable than what happened yesterday.

As Jack Kornfield, teacher of Vipassana meditation, says:

> One of the preoccupations of people throughout all times and all cultures has been to find that which is sacred, which is transcendental, which goes beyond the small sense of self, our jobs, our relationships, this small I. In all cultures, this search is taken as a journey, the journey of a yogi, a healer, a shaman, a seer, or a wise person. Although separated by continents and by centuries, it's always the same journey. It's the journey of going from the small self-centered view of the world to an awareness of its vastness and mystery.[2]

These stories are meant to bear witness to a time when the search for something "more" in life led young Westerners on a journey to the East and to a place, Mother India, that has been the home of great spiritual masters and the deeper mysteries of life from time immemorial. One only has to think of the great *siddhas* (perfected masters, holy men and women with great spiritual powers) of the past century, such as Ramana Maharshi, Ramakrishna, Meher Baba, Shirdi Sai Baba, Nityananda, Anandamayi Ma, and the Sixteenth Karmapa, to be thankful for these beings who, like Maharajji, lived in nonduality and stayed in a body only by the thread of their love for their devotees.

May the love stories in this book help you to remember that God/Spirit dwells within you too and spur you on to find or to further appreciate your own path that leads to loving everyone.

Part One

In the Beginning

1968–1969

1

The Call

A hero ventures forth from the world of common day into a region of supernatural wonder: fabulous forces are there encountered and a decisive victory is won: the hero comes back from this mysterious adventure with the power to bestow boons on his fellow man.

—JOSEPH CAMPBELL, *THE HERO WITH A THOUSAND FACES*

The drive from Vermont down to New Hampshire through the lush greenery of the White Mountains didn't take long on a sunny day at the beginning of summer in 1969. I had met David Hatch the day before at a party mostly consisting of educators from Goddard College. He was the one sitting in the corner playing a guitar, so I naturally gravitated in his direction. As we talked, he said, "Do you wanna go meet a saint?"

If he had asked me that question a month earlier, my immediate response would have been, "No. Are you kidding? They don't exist." But three weeks previously I had ingested my first tab of Sunshine, Owsley's luminous LSD, and experienced that extraordinary state of being in which we are all One in the ocean of love, beyond time, beyond space. As I reluctantly came down from that trip, someone handed me *The Tibetan Book of the Dead,* which I read avidly in the following days. As I turned each page, I knew I was looking at a manual for what I had come in contact with through acid. These old guys knew what they were talking about.

So when David asked if I wanted to meet a saint, I said, "Sure. Why not?"

As David's VW van pulled into the driveway, Ram Dass was standing at the front door of his father's summer house, a "gentleman's farm" called Willenrica on a lake in Franklin, New Hampshire. He was barefoot, wearing what looked like a white dress and slowly twirling a long string of beads in his hand. Light was emanating from him. I hadn't smoked or dropped anything, and yet there it was—this radiant light that seemed to arise from the depths of the startling blue of his eyes and extend in all directions. I was speechless.

I vaguely knew who Ram Dass was. During the Easter holiday in 1967, my boyfriend and I were in Manhattan looking for something to do. An ad in the paper for "An Evening with God" at the Village Theatre caught our attention. In our seats way up in the nosebleed section of the upper balconies, I caught my first-ever high from all the smoke and was thoroughly enchanted by Timothy Leary, who was sitting on stage strumming a sitar. While psychedelic slides played on a screen behind him, he chanted his mantra: "Turn on, tune in, drop out." He was so much more entertaining than the boring and pedantic Richard Alpert, who had spoken before him.

But Richard Alpert had gone to India and come back as Baba Ram Dass. Now he was living in a small cabin behind his father's summer house, and a dozen or so hippie types were living in tents on the three hundred acres of surrounding woods. I met most of them during the day. In greeting, they held their hands together in front of them as if in prayer and said a strange word in gentle tones: *Namasté*. I had no idea what they were talking about, but these folks were all so familiar to me! I asked each one, "Where did you go to school? Where did you go to camp? Why do I know you?" I didn't realize it yet, but I had found my tribe.

That evening the small group of us gathered in the barn and sat in a circle on the floor to hear Ram Dass speak. It was astounding. For the first time in my life, I felt as though I was getting answers to questions I didn't even know I had. I was completely captivated as he talked about taking thousands of acid trips and still having to come down. It certainly cut short my own brief experimentation with LSD. He told us there was a way to get high and stay high—without drugs. Are you kidding? Count me in.

The very next day David and I came back and set up a tent in the woods around the three-hole golf course in the Alpert backyard. David, who owned the first health-food store in Vermont, had all the supplies we needed. His van held sacks of rice, lentils, and flour for making *kedgeree* and *chapatis* (rice-lentil stew and flatbread, which I learned to cook over an open fire), various utensils, and a pup tent to sleep in; he also had the know-how for living in the woods. Thank goodness. (I was more at home with a desk and a typewriter.)

A few days after we arrived, I became Ram Dass's secretary. I sat in the barn and listened to the tape recordings in which he responded to questions and stories from all the people who had heard him speak since his return from India. I typed up his letters (typewriters and snail mail back in those days) while the others were out in the woods meditating, fasting, and doing yogic practices. It was the perfect way for me to learn the words and concepts of my new life.

Two years later, Maharajji would say to me, "You used to be Ram Dass's private secretary; now you're mine."

Ram Dass

Ram Dass's story—his rise through the ranks of academia, his years of psychotherapy, his meeting Timothy Leary and their dismissal from Harvard for their psychedelic explorations and experiments, the eventual despair that led him to India, and the way his life turned around when Bhagavan Das took him to meet his guru, Neem Karoli Baba (Maharajji), on a hillside in the foothills of the Himalayas—is all told in the first part of *Be Here Now,* which had yet to be written when I met him that summer of 1969.

In *Be Here Now,* Ram Dass describes how he opted to travel around India with Bhagavan Das instead of going on to Japan with David Padua and Alan Watts. With his first-class accommodations gone, he learned to move about like a barefoot pilgrim. When Bhagavan Das had visa trouble and had to go see his guru, Maharajji, Bhagavan Das commandeered the Land Rover that David Padua had left in Ram Dass's care.

Ram Dass.

The night before they came to Maharajji, Ram Dass went outside. As he stood under the stars, he suddenly thought about his mother, who had died of a spleen illness the previous year, and felt her presence. He felt great love for her and then went back to bed, telling no one what had happened. He and Bhagavan Das never conversed about "personal stuff."

The next day they found Maharajji sitting in a field in a lush green valley surrounded by eight or nine Indians. Bhagavan Das began crying tears of joy as he threw himself facedown on the ground, flat out, to touch Maharajji's feet. Ram Dass had no idea what was happening. When Maharajji looked up at him, he immediately plugged into what Ram Dass was most uptight about—his feeling of responsibility for the Land Rover—and asked if Ram Dass would give that very expensive vehicle to him or buy one for him. Everyone laughed—except Ram Dass.

After being taken away and fed, Ram Dass was brought back to Maharajji, who said, "You were out under the stars last night. . . . You were thinking about your mother." He leaned back and closed his eyes and said, "Spleen. She died of spleen."

Here is how Ram Dass describes that moment in *Be Here Now*:

> Up until then I had two categories for "psychic experience."
> One was, "They happened to somebody else and they haven't
> happened to me, and they were terribly interesting and we
> certainly had to keep an open mind about it." That was my
> social science approach. The other was, "Well, man, I'm high on
> LSD. Who knows how it really is? After all, under the influence
> of a chemical, how do I know I'm not just creating the whole
> thing?" . . .
>
> But neither of these categories applied in this situation and
> my mind went faster and faster, and then I felt like what happens

when a computer is fed an insoluble problem; the bell rings
and the light goes on and the machine stops. And my mind
just gave up. It burned out its circuitry . . . its zeal to have an
explanation. I needed to get closure at the rational level and there
wasn't anything. There just wasn't a place I could hide my head
about this.

And at the same moment, I felt this extremely violent pain in
my chest and a tremendous wrenching feeling and I started to
cry. And I cried and I cried and I cried. And I wasn't happy and I
wasn't sad. It was not that kind of crying. The only thing I could
say was it felt like I was home. Like the journey was over. Like
I had finished.[1]

Over the next six months, living in the temple in Kainchi, Richard
Alpert morphed into Ram Dass.

RAM DASS: I was staying in Kainchi, and Kainchi was very
quiet. There was a cook, a *pujari* [priest], and me. Bhagavan Das
was coming and going. Hari Das Baba came at eleven o'clock
every morning and gave me ten minutes of instruction on his
chalkboard. Then Maharajji told me that I should go back to
America for two years. He said that I was to tell nobody about
him. And he was sending his *ashirbad* [blessings] for my book.
I had no idea what book.

I was known as Tim Leary's sidekick, and when I started to
talk about Maharajji, even though I didn't name him, there was
a tremendous interest in my audience. I saw all these people who
had this great yearning, and I had brought back this great jewel, a
radiant jewel, that I wanted to keep for myself. I tried not to talk
about Maharajji, but I couldn't talk about anything else.

Bhagavan Das

Who was the giant (six-foot, seven-inch) presence named Bhagavan Das who led Richard Alpert to the man who would so radically change his life, and ours? Like so many young Americans, Michael Riggs was a teenager in despair. In 1963, at the age of eighteen, he strapped a guitar on his back and, with $40 in his pocket, left home in search of . . . something. He arrived in India a year or so later and took up the life of a barefoot *sadhu* (renunciate), studying with holy men, living a life of austerity, and doing intense spiritual practices.

One day he followed the swami he had been serving into a temple in the Kainchi valley. In a room was a wooden cot, upon which sat a little old man wrapped in a blanket. To Riggs, he looked like "a big, brilliant diamond in the sun." This was Neem Karoli Baba. As Riggs says, "I'd just met the love of my life." Two weeks later, he was back to stay.

For six months, Maharajji kept him close. So much for austerity; he was fed constantly. On the main bathing day at the Kumbha Mela—the

Bhagavan Das and Ram Dass.

gigantic spiritual festival (these days attended by over seventy million pilgrims) that happens every twelve years in Allahabad at the confluence of the sacred Ganges, Yamuna, and Saraswati Rivers—Maharajji initiated Riggs. He was given the name Bhagavan Das.

Eventually Bhagavan Das set off to live on his own and got deeply into Buddhist practices, so when he got a Quit India notice, instead of going back to America, he went to Kathmandu in Nepal, a Buddhist center that was becoming a major hippie hangout. There he met Richard Alpert, and the two of them embarked on the journey through India that culminated in Bhagavan Das's bringing Alpert to Maharajji.[2]

The seed had been planted. It would sprout in wondrous ways throughout the West.

1968: The Early Talks

The first talk Ram Dass gave after his return from India was at Wesleyan University in March 1968. A twenty-year-old student at the school, Jim Lytton (Rameshwar Das), went to hear him.

> RAMESHWAR DAS: From the grapevine and the media coverage that had been flying around about Richard Alpert and Timothy Leary, I was expecting this to be about the annals of psychedelia, coming from one of its foremost proponents. The talk was at a lounge in one of the dorms, so it was informal—people sitting around on sofas and hanging out. We were waiting for Dr. Alpert to show up, when this guy shows up in a white dress, barefoot, and with a long beard. That was just the initial shock. The talk started at seven thirty in the evening and went on until after three in the morning.
>
> After a while someone turned out the lights, and there was just Ram Dass's voice in the darkness. He was talking about his

experience in India, not about psychedelics, though there were
certainly references to that. His understanding of consciousness
and the sense of being here now with him felt very pure and
profound. I'd had an experience when I was sixteen, sitting in
the dunes at the ocean beach in Amagansett, when the horizon
opened up and I felt myself like a pinprick in the vastness instead
of being the center of my own universe. This talk by Ram Dass
was one of those figure-ground flips for me, where I went from
seeing myself as the center of the universe to feeling this vast
presence all around me.

After that talk I went up to visit Ram Dass in Franklin, New
Hampshire. He taught me the beginnings of yoga and meditation
and gave me a *mala* [a string of 108 beads], which became the
foundation of what I began to understand was some kind of inner
practice. When I got to India a few years later, I had that same
feeling meeting Maharajji that I had on meeting Ram Dass that
night at Wesleyan.

Although Ram Dass spent much of 1968 in seclusion, he did give
a few talks here and there. WBAI in New York picked up one of his
lectures for broadcast. That's how Steve and Leslie Baum (Mohan and
Radha) first heard Ram Dass.

RADHA: One Sunday there was a torrential downpour, so we
stayed home and turned on WBAI, one of the hip radio stations,
to listen to Paul Gorman's show. Gorman interrupted his usual
broadcast for a special one featuring Baba Ram Dass. Everything
Ram Dass was saying, I was nodding, "Yes, yes!" He spoke the
truth my heart knew.

We found out Ram Dass was coming to the Universalist
Church. We had seen him as Richard Alpert at the Village

Theatre in "An Evening with God." What was standing there before us now was not Richard Alpert. He had this aura of light around him; he was glowing. He talked for hours and hours, but nobody was leaving. Even the janitor was standing at the door with his broom, mesmerized by Ram Dass.

I wrote him a long letter, and he wrote back that we should come visit him. We borrowed my mother's car and headed for New Hampshire in what turned out to be the worst ice storm of the century. By the time we got there two days later, the sun was shining on the glistening snow, the ground sparkled like diamonds; it was totally magical. Ram Dass's driveway was the only one that was plowed. And there he was, standing in the freezing cold, wearing his *olfie* [a white "dress"] with his mala around his neck. (Years later he told me he had come out to see who in the world was driving up in a yellow Cadillac.)

The house was not heated because it was a summer place. He was living in what I think was the maid's quarters above the kitchen. It was a very small, intimate area with these hangings of Indian cloth all over, and on the hangings were big pictures of different people; on the floor were all these mattresses covered with Indian cloth. I had never seen anything like it.

I asked him, "Who are these pictures of?"

He said, "All these pictures are saints."

"That one is a saint? He looks like a wrestler."

Ram Dass looked at me, smiled, and said, "That's my guru." That was my first glimpse of Maharajji.

Ram Dass spent the entire day with us, teaching us how to meditate, what books to read, how to do yoga. He gave us a picture of Padmasambhava and taught us a mantra. He talked to us about becoming vegetarians, which we did right away. It felt like I had been waiting forever for these spiritual practices.

MOHAN: What I wanted to know from Ram Dass was how to get high without acid. I had been taking acid for seven or eight years by then. "How do you do it?" He gave us rudimentary concentration exercises—looking into each other's eyes or staring at a live candle flame.

I said, "Okay, thank you. Let's go."

He said, "Where are you going?"

"I'm going to go do it. I want to get high." It was strictly a matter of exploring these states of consciousness, not relevant to religion or mysticism, but hedonistically.

What happened to most people when they went to see Ram Dass in those days? Magic, pure life-transforming magic. Krishna Das (Jeff Kagel) writes about his first visit to Ram Dass in Franklin:

KRISHNA DAS: The moment I walked into the room, something happened inside of me. Immediately, instantly, without a word being spoken, I *knew* that whatever it was I was looking for— and I didn't know *what* it was—was absolutely real. In every molecule of my being, I knew that *it* existed in the world and that it could be found. I didn't know if I could find it, but this moment changed my life. . . .

For a brief moment, the lights had come on again, and I'd seen that there was a way, a path . . . that *it* was real. It made my longing for *that* a million times more intense. It also got me more depressed, because now I knew that it existed and that I didn't have it. My life got better . . . and it got worse. It got better because I understood that what I was seeking was real. It got worse because I knew that I had to find it and didn't know how to do that.

All I knew was that Ram Dass had it, and I wanted it.[3]

Spring 1969

In the early spring of 1969, Ram Dass gave a two-week series of talks at a New York City sculpture studio. Several of the talks were recorded, and the transcripts eventually became the basis for parts of *Be Here Now*. Ram Dass would play on his tamboura, an Indian gourd instrument that produced a hypnotic drone, and talk about what it meant to be present in each moment of life. He used stories that Westerners could grasp to illustrate the teachings about finding the sacred in the profane, duality and oneness, and unconditional love as he had experienced it with Maharajji.

Those in the New York area who had heard him at an earlier talk or on WBAI came to the studio to see him. Mesmerized, they showed up every night, night after night, and soaked in all they could not only of his words, but also of his magnetic presence. That's where Joan O'Connell (Anjani) met him.

Ram Dass.

ANJANI: I was working at Columbia and met Harinam and Mariam [Ed and Joanne Randall]. It was the acid days, and they were a good source of pure acid as well as good friends. Since we were all into acid, we knew about Alpert and Leary. So when he came back from India and there was going to be this talk, we thought, "Oh, here's someone who took too much acid. Now he's Baba Ram Dass; we have to go." We went to have a laugh, but we came out with our mouths hanging open, totally blown away by everything he said. That was the first touch of Maharajji, obviously.

Daniel Goleman (Jagganath Das) was a graduate student in psychology and knew of Ram Dass as a psychologist whose life had taken an interesting twist.

DANNY: In my first year of graduate school at Harvard, in the same program Richard Alpert and Tim Leary had left three years before, the halls were still ringing with that whole epic. It was a dark and dank December day, and I was writing about suicide. This woman knocks on my apartment door and says she's just come from Kathmandu. She's got two things to do: to deliver this letter to me from a friend of mine and to see this guy up in New Hampshire. She asked if I could give her a ride. We get there, and it's a big fancy house, and up in a little room there's a guy sitting with a long white beard and long white hair, wearing all white, and all these weird Indian posters all over the wall. He didn't even look at us. He's just sitting with his eyes closed. It was the most bizarre thing I'd ever encountered. After a while he opened his eyes, and we started talking.

I told Ram Dass that I was a graduate student in his old department, and he asked about people he knew. I was a member

of the graduate school program committee, so I invited him to
come back to Harvard to give a talk. It was the first time he'd
come back since he'd been fired, actually by my main professor,
David McClelland, who used to be his close friend.

When he came to Harvard, Ram Dass was full of shakti and
love and energy and talked for about five or six hours. We had
to bribe the janitor to keep the hall open. He was wearing these
white robes and had these beads and was sitting cross-legged on
the table. What he was saying was equally "different," but the
message was very heartening, very compelling.

The next day I was having lunch with one of my clinical
professors, and I told him about it. He thought Ram Dass must be
crazy.

Marty Malles (Mahavir Das), a women's undergarment salesman in
New York, had a rockier introduction.

MAHAVIR DAS: I first met Ram Dass around 1968. Eddie Fleur
[Sudhama] was my best friend. I was the one who took care of
him when he was taking LSD, because I didn't take drugs. He
told me that there was this guy who was saying some really
incredible things, and I should go see him.

My first wife, Pauline, and I took a cab from my office in the
garment center all the way up to the Ethical Cultural Society,
arguing all the way. We walked into this big room, and there
is this guy with a beard sitting in the middle of the room, with
about twenty people around him. These people are filthy; they
are sitting on the floor. And I didn't like this guy. Ten minutes
later Pauline and I took a cab back to Brooklyn, arguing all
the way.

In the springtime Eddie said, "Listen, the same guy is going to be at a sculpture studio on the Upper East Side. You have to see him now. You're going to see him differently."

"No. I had enough of this filthy guy and the people he hangs out with."

Eddie said, "If you don't see him, I won't be your friend anymore." He actually said that. So I went.

Everybody was sitting on the floor. I said, "There is no room for me, number one, and number two, this is a very expensive suit." Someone guaranteed that I would be comfortable. I said, "I better be, or I'm leaving in five minutes."

I sat down on the floor and looked in front of me, and on a little elevated place was Ram Dass. I think he spoke for three or four hours that night. I didn't move and went back every night after that. I fell in love with this guy, just fell in love with him. That beautiful silken voice with that New England accent, and his beautiful eyes. I don't know what I missed the first time, but I got it all the second time.

I didn't have the nerve to speak to him except the last night. He looked at me and said, "What can I do for you?"

"Take me with you."

He told me to leave him my address. About six months later I got this envelope that had in it a mala and instructions on how to say *Ram*. There was a little thread in the mala from Maharajji's blanket. I thought about Ram Dass every day, every single day. I said that mantra over and over again, not having any idea what it was. I just did it because he said so.

When Ram Dass later stayed at Eddie's house for a visit, I said, "Listen, what can I do? Give me something to do."

Maybe eight, nine months later, Ram Dass gave me this box of beads with a roll of very thick thread and a piece of Maharajji's blanket. He said, "If someone asks you for a mala, string 108 beads plus the big bead in the front and make a knot and put a thread of Maharajji's blanket in there. I am going to tell people to write to you." And he did. I was the East Coast mala guy. I made hundreds and hundreds of malas. It was great work.

Getting Tuned In

There were those who heard Ram Dass lecture in person and those who heard him on the radio. In the late 1960s, radio was the social media of the counterculture. In this "golden age" of radio, FM stations were the alternative to AM stations, which played nothing but teeny-bopper music, the pop "Top Forty." The disc jockeys for the FM "underground" rock stations, on the other hand, were playing whatever they wanted—songs that ran six or seven minutes long, even whole albums, often without commercial breaks. If the DJ wanted to throw in some blues, classical, jazz, or whatever, that was fine too.

In 1969, Mitchell Markus (Raghvindra Das, or Raghu) was the program director of a major alternative rock 'n' roll radio station in Montreal.

RAGHU: I was a pretty unhappy young man, and the only thing that meant anything to me was music. If not for Dylan, I don't know what I would have done. When I got involved with the radio station, basically it was all about music and getting high.

I'm sitting at my desk one day, and the receptionist calls and says someone wants to talk to me. When I talked to this person, she said, "We would really love your help. We are promoting a lecture by a man named Ram Dass."

I went, "Ram Dass—who's that?"

"Richard Alpert? Tim Leary?"

"Oh, God, yeah. I love them." I was deep into the psychedelic movement at the time, and they were heroes. They sent me a lecture, all about the transformation of Alpert from his and Leary's Harvard days, to India and what happened with Maharajji, talking of his foibles, allowing us to understand that we could let loose for a moment and be whoever we are; you know, "Be here now."

It was everything I had been waiting to hear for years and years. I'd been feeling lousy about myself, my family, society, about the culture (even though we were in Canada, which was a little less pernicious than the United States, especially regarding the Vietnam War). I was so taken with this lecture that I went to whoever was deejaying at the time and said, "Put it on." It was the middle of the week around noon. The switchboard lit up. Nobody had ever heard anything like this. After that we played his lectures over and over again.

In the winter of 1970, Ram Dass came to Montreal. It was mucky and slushy, the usual Montreal horror, but he came to the station and did this wonderful interview. As soon as we met in person, I had a knowing and a connection and a gratitude that I hadn't felt in my whole life. I didn't know what I was being grateful for. I was just happy; I didn't even know why. I became some kind of missionary. I wanted everybody else to feel what I felt.

1969: Spiritual Summer Camp

As more people found their way to Ram Dass's front door in Franklin and the weather warmed up, one by one they started to stick around.[4] After the sculpture studio series, Ram Dass invited Jeff (Krishna Das)

Ram Dass in the summer of 1969.

to work for his father during that summer, so Jeff was the first to move in. Jim, Danny, Joan, Leslie, Steve, and others soon followed. They set to work building wooden tent platforms to keep out the damp from the ground.

Since many of them had come to Franklin during the past year and met with Ram Dass privately, they were already doing yogic practices— meditation, *japa* (saying a mantra with a mala), hatha yoga, reading spiritual books, fasting. They were yogis-in-training who were having some deep inner experiences. I was happy to be typing in the barn or working in the kitchen of the main house, helping George, Ram Dass's father, make raspberry jam.

Radha (Leslie) had set up an altar space in her large tent that accommodated pictures of every saint for the last three centuries and many of the Hindu deities. She was determined to get enlightened.

RADHA: The summer of '69 was really special. There were these meditations in the morning and all kinds of singing and chanting. The boys built a meditation hall in the middle of the pine trees, and it smelled fantastic. I wanted to be like Hari Das Baba, who had been Ram Dass's teacher in India. Ram Dass told us that Hari Das did a lot of meditation, was on silence, and took only two glasses of milk a day, nothing else. So for six weeks I drank only two glasses of milk a day just like Hari Das. I got constipated, not enlightened. I was also on so-called silence, although I had a chalkboard that I wrote on continuously. Later when I was in India, Maharajji was talking about being silent, and he looked at me and said, "And you don't write either."

After a particular Zen sitting, I had some kind of opening where I saw that I was going to go to India, which was the last place I wanted to go. Why did I have to go to India? Ram Dass was enough for me. We had all the tools we needed; we just had to do them.

On weekends, many came from near and far to hear Ram Dass. Some of us would prepare *prasad* (consecrated food) to distribute. We'd all sit on the lawn, soaking up the sun and Ram Dass's words. The warmth of his presence carried the words straight into our hearts. Westerners easily related to his humor and his ability to use his less than stellar traits as teachings. His incredible storehouse of stories turned him into a spiritual Pied Piper; soon hundreds were coming on the weekends. There was much going on—Sufi dancing on the golf course, hatha yoga classes, chanting. Spiritual summer camp, indeed. Woodstock was happening down the road, but only a few left to attend the music festival. Lifelong friendships formed, and the kernel of Maharajji's Western satsang was born.

Lama Foundation, *Be Here Now*

After the "summer camp" in New Hampshire, Ram Dass went out west to lecture, then went to see friends who had started a spiritual community in New Mexico called the Lama Foundation—a place where all spiritual traditions are honored and their practices taught. It's still there—sitting in a stunning setting at 8,600 feet above sea level in the beautiful and rugged Carson National Forest in the Sangre de Cristo Mountains, the southern tip of the Rockies. You can see the gorge of the Rio Grande River from the front porch.

Joe Bonner (Dwarkanath), a young artist, spent a considerable amount of time at the Lama Foundation, where *Be Here Now* was designed and put together.

DWARKANATH: I was eighteen when I first went to Lama Foundation in the summer of '68, inspired by people I knew who were good friends of the founders, Steve and Barbara Durkee [now known as Asha Greer and Nooruddeen] and Jonathan Altman. Meanwhile, I had heard Ram Dass in California when he first lectured there. He came to Lama in the late fall of '69 to do this month-long "ashram experiment," as it was called. Participants had private spaces to stay in and went through various *sadhana* routines [spiritual practices]. I was there for the second half.

Then in early spring of '70 I moved back up to Lama to work on the *Be Here Now* production. I was there for seven or eight months working on a team doing the illustrations. Steve and I went through the core book manuscript and broke it up into 108 units, and then the team of about five of us worked on illustrating those 108 units, page by page.

Be Here Now turned out to be the spiritual catalyst for a generation and beyond. It would go on to sell over two million copies and be called the "counterculture bible." No one had ever seen or read anything like it, and it was responsible for turning untold thousands onto the spiritual path, including such diverse people as Steve Jobs, Wayne Dyer, and Michael Crichton. The book didn't come out until 1971, by which time the first Westerners had arrived in India. How they got to India was often an integral aspect of the journey to the East.

2

On the Hippie Trail

Europe used to be just one colour: white. It used to have one religion: Christianity. The West believed that world history began with Greece and Rome. As you say, the hippies were curious for different cultures. From us, they learnt that Mesopotamia—here in Turkey and the Middle East—was the mother of all civilization. They carried home with them a kilim woven from different beliefs: threads of Islam, sky-blue of Buddhist prayer flags, silver from Hindu temple bells.

—RORY MACLEAN, *MAGIC BUS*

f you were to go to India from the United States today, it would be a fairly simple and somewhat costly trip. You get on a flight in New York and arrive in New Delhi a little more than fourteen hours later—nonstop. In the early 1970s, however, that wasn't even close to possible. India was halfway around the world, and travel and communication links were sketchy, but Westerners who were heading to India did have a number of options for getting there.

The "Hippie Trail."

There were some inexpensive ways to fly. I traveled with two friends from a meditation group in New York who were going to see Sathya Sai Baba in southern India. We took a charter flight from New York to London, which cost around $50, and hitchhiked around Europe for ten days before returning to London to catch the last of the cheap Arab charter flights that would take us to Bombay (now Mumbai), with seven dust-choked stops along the way at places I had never heard of, like Abu Dhabi and Dubai, which were far from well-heeled bustling cities at the time.

We had a seven-hour layover in Cairo, so we relinquished our passports and boarded a tourist bus to go see the pyramids. I was wearing a Star of David necklace that someone had given me, not realizing that Egypt and Israel were having overt hostilities since Anwar Sadat had become the new Egyptian president. As the bus rolled out of the airport, there were heavy coils of barbed-wire fencing all along the route, guarded by soldiers carrying machine guns. It was all worth it for the spectacular moments spent gazing up at the pyramids and the Sphinx. All in all, the trip from New York to Bombay cost me around $300.

But there were those who wanted more adventure or a cheaper way of traveling. These brave souls flew from the United States to Europe and then went overland to India—via train, bus, private car, or hitchhiking—on what would become known as the "hippie trail."

The journey started in London or Amsterdam or Luxembourg, wound through western Europe, and then followed the "northern" route through Istanbul, Tehran, Herat, Kandahar, Kabul, Peshawar, and Lahore—the ancient cities of Turkey, Iran, Afghanistan, and Pakistan—before crossing the border into India. There were cheap hotels, well-known hostels, restaurants, and cafés that catered to Westerners along the way and gathering spots, like the Pudding Shop in Istanbul, where messages pinned to a bulletin board were a way to find your next ride.

Jeffrey Miller (Lama Surya Das) attended the State University of New York (SUNY) in Buffalo in the late 1960s. Jeffrey met Ram Dass when he talked there after returning from India as well as other emissaries of the journey to the East, such as Allen Ginsberg, Gary Snyder, R. D. Laing, Ken Kesey, and Wavy Gravy. He sat through a *sesshin* (meditation session) at the Rochester Zen Center with Philip Kapleau Roshi, the first American Zen master, and was very impressed by the clarity, peace, and power of meditation.

In a strange set of circumstances, Jeffrey's friend from high school in Valley Stream, New York, had a girlfriend, Alison Krause, who was shot and killed by the Ohio National Guard during an antiwar protest at Kent State in May 1971. He was running with her, holding her hand, when she got shot in the back and died in his arms. One of the others who was killed in that tragedy was a Jeffrey Miller from Long Island, so for one terrible night Surya Das's family thought he had died. That turned his head around about the contradiction inherent in "fighting for peace," and he started to think about the Gandhian concept of "becoming peace." He thought, "I am going to go to India to see the Dalai Lama and find out about this."

LAMA SURYA DAS: After graduation, I flew to London, hitchhiked across France and Italy, took a smelly old boat to Greece, went to Turkey, got a public bus to Istanbul, then went to the Pudding Shop, where everybody met in Istanbul. There was a note on the bulletin board: "Volkswagen bus with Canadians. Need riders to share gas and driving to go overland to India." Perfect. I met the Canadian hippies, ten of us in the Volkswagen bus, nine or ten days to Kabul. We slept outside or in the cheapest flophouses we could find in Turkey, Iran, Afghanistan. Adventures all along the way: dangerous broken roads, bandits, and difficult border crossings.

A buddy I had met in Greece, Ken Humphrey, from St. Louis, a former medic in the Green Berets, and I did a little visiting around Afghanistan. We went up inside the tall standing Bamiyan Buddhas, two of the biggest buddhas in the world, the ones that were blown up later by the Taliban. There used to be a big caravansary in that area, a real traditional Asian crossroads. Now it is a dry desert valley, but in olden days it was like the Euphrates valley, very rich. The desert was so hot that, after a walk one July day, my chukka boots, which were only about a month old, had a hole burned right through the sole of each foot.

Krishna and Mirabai's journey was epic. John and Linda Bush met at SUNY–Buffalo. John, a young poet and playwright, was a lapsed Catholic who had served at Mass in a cathedral as an altar boy; he identified with the Beat poets until Richard Alpert came to the university in 1965 and turned him on to LSD and the potentials of human consciousness. Linda, a teaching fellow in the English Department, had been married to an aeronautic engineer and had lived at Cape Canaveral. She worked on the first manned launch to the moon, Apollo 8—the first woman issued a hard hat and a jumpsuit at the Cape, where she watched launches from underneath the launching pad. Although it was the time of the "right stuff," the marriage wasn't right for her. After her divorce, she went back to school for her PhD.

Both John and Linda were very involved in antiwar activism and the civil rights movement. Then in the late 1960s, a group of very creative and intellectual graduate students started taking psychedelics and began to glimpse, as Mirabai put it, "the truth of the interconnectedness of all life on the planet." They left the university and formed a commune in British Columbia, where they lived in tepees, cooked over open fires, washed clothes in the stream, and fished for salmon with the Kwakiutl Indians. John and Linda left when the rainy season hit and flew to Luxembourg, where they found out about the "hippie bus," or the "magic bus"—the longest bus ride on the planet, two months on the "Green Turtle" to get from London to Delhi.

KRISHNA: It started to feel very biblical as we got into eastern Turkey. People were wearing traditional dress, whereas Istanbul was quite Western. From eastern Turkey we went into Iran to Tehran. The bus broke down, so we were there for almost two weeks. The Shah, our puppet, was still running the country. The northern suburbs of Tehran felt like southern California—women wearing miniskirts, hair dyed blond, lots of makeup, people driving convertibles. This was a certain time in that region when many people were Westernized in their approach to dress and habits and thought. Hard to believe now.

Of course, we also were very aware of the dark side. We would go into cafés and talk to other students, but when the conversation would veer into politics, they would get very nervous, start looking around, and say they really couldn't talk because the *savak* [the secret police] were everywhere. Being involved in the peace movement, we had had a lot of government infiltrators, double agents, and agent provocateurs, but this seemed like a whole other level of control. As we went farther east into Iran, there was no remnant of any Western influence except maybe in the trucking areas.

We were traveling through Iran and Afghanistan during Ramadan. People were very observant. There were no restaurants open during the day, but there were stores where we could buy apricots and hazelnuts and soft drinks, so it wasn't really a hardship for us. A cannon shot would go off at the exact moment of sunset, and that was the trigger for everyone to feast. During the day it was austere, but at night it was remarkably celebratory.

This was in the days before there was any sort of East-West tension with Islam. We saw it as another spiritual tradition that we honored. I wasn't particularly attracted to Islam as something I wanted to do, but I was impressed by the piety people were living. Both in western Iran and certainly all through Afghanistan, the call to prayer would go out and whatever you would be doing—talking to someone in the store, bargaining over some article of clothing you wanted to buy—people would say, "Excuse me," and right in front of you they would take out their prayer rug and do their prayers. It would take about ten minutes five times a day, and I thought, "Wow, that's quite the spiritual practice, every day of their lives." It was a level of devotion that I hadn't seen before.

I got sick in Afghanistan and wound up in a hospital in Kandahar for a week, completely unconscious with this delirium fever. There was blood everywhere on the floor, excrement, really filthy—the last place in the world you would want to be if you had a health issue. [Mirabai stayed near him praying, "Please don't die, please don't die."] Through some blessing, I ended up with a doctor who had been trained in America, spoke perfect

English, and was a lovely guy. He monitored my progress and
gave me medicine. He felt like this angel of mercy in the middle
of Kandahar.

From there we crossed into Pakistan. We came through the
infamous Khyber Pass, which was this wild lawless place where
you could buy every drug in the world, a complete no-man's-land
filled with smugglers. Total arms bazaar, from infantry pieces to
small handguns. They were famous for creating knockoffs of any
kind of gun. You'd go through the pass and descend from there
into the subcontinent. Pakistan at the time had no identity of its
own. It was still really India, but the way they defined themselves
was to turn against all things Indian with these giant signs
everywhere that said, "Hate India."

Mirabai remembers going through the mountains of the Hindu Kush
in the back of an open truck that was hauling a grindstone for a mill.

MIRABAI: Pakistan was so green, and all the women had oiled
black hair, bright saris, and dark eyes that looked right into ours.
In those days Pakistan wasn't so different from India. It wasn't
that long after partition, and Lahore was beautiful, with those
wide green lawns. It was still very British there: tea served in
white pots on silver trays, poured slowly into china cups. Then
we were in Amritsar. I fell in love. I hadn't had any desires
or dreams about India. I didn't have any Indian friends. Yet I
thought, "I am home. I have come home."

Dangers of the Road

There were other dangers on the overland route besides getting sick.
You could wind up catching a ride in a vehicle loaded with drugs.

Jacques Achsen left Montreal in 1968 and went to Jerusalem right out of high school. His parents were religious Jews, so he knew enough Hebrew that he didn't have to take the language program before entering university. Instead, he partied for six months, indulging in some of the 1960s' favorite activities, and ended up living in the Arab village of Bethany (where Jesus resurrected Lazarus). He started school, but got fed up with it after a couple of years. Then he and his girlfriend at the time decided to hit the road.

JACQUES: We were going to join Allende and the revolution. We got to Amsterdam intending to go to Rotterdam to get on a boat to Chile. We were sitting around in one of those famous hotels in Amsterdam, when this American guy started talking to us. He was on his way back from India. I had never thought about India. No Ram Dass, no *Be Here Now*. Nothing. He mentioned Benares and India, and I turned to Vicki and said, "Honey, we are going to Benares."

We headed east with not much money, figuring we'd hitch-hike. Couldn't even get through Austria. My brother, who was coming with us, looked like a hippie. The Austrians would drive by and yell "Manson," so we took a train to Yugoslavia, and from there we hitched or did buses or trains. In Afghanistan we met these four Americans, one of whom had lived in India for a while and spoke some Hindi and Punjabi. We jumped in their Land Rover and went with them to India, along with a good supply of Afghanistan's finest in the cushions of the car. The spare tire on the roof was heavy with hash. Every time we hit a bump it was like *boom*. "Take it easy, man."

We get to the border at Pathankot. The land border was not Amritsar yet. There was this famous woman border cop there who says, "I am channeling the Hindu goddess Durga. I can read your mind. If you have drugs with you, I will know." She used to freak everybody out. They would give up their drugs and get in trouble. But we're in a car. She doesn't do cars. She does buses. We're cool.

We ended up with a Sikh border guard who welcomed us. He was happy when he was addressed by this foreigner in Punjabi. Good, but he still had to do a cursory search of the car. He picked up a cushion and asked, "You have any weapons? No weapons. Okay, you can go."

We got through the border into India.

There was also the ever present possibility of violence.

When Meenakshi was in high school in the suburbs of Chicago, she took care of children for a woman who had studied Indian dance with a famous Katak dancer. India fascinated her. When she graduated, Meenakshi drove a cab in Chicago to earn the money to go. She hadn't heard about Ram Dass or Maharajji. She and a friend flew to London, but when they got to Turkey, Meenakshi went on alone.

MEENAKSHI: When I got to Tehran, I met a man from Switzerland named York. We spent a long time together in Tehran. I was always very well dressed, but I could not walk outside without having the veil that the women wore—these half-moon-shaped pieces of material that went down to the ground. They held them with their teeth. Young girls had those on, but the veils were translucent, and underneath you could see that the girls wore miniskirts.

I asked the one Iranian man who was staying in the hotel if he could take me to get one of those things so I could be on the street, and also to get a Bible. I wanted to read it from beginning to end on the way to India. He took me to get the cloth and the

Bible, and we spent the whole day together. Then he wanted to take me to this restaurant in the mountains. I felt very trusting of him, so I said, "Okay, fine."

At the restaurant he drank a lot. When we got back in his car, it was pitch-black, because we're way out in the middle of nowhere. He drives up to the edge of a cliff and says, "I could drive off this cliff and kill us both right now, and nobody will know what happened to you. And I love my mother." He pulls a knife, holds it to my throat, and says, "I could cut your throat and throw your body over there, and nobody would find you, and I love my mother." He hands me the knife and says, "No, you kill me." I drop the knife on the floor. Then he pulls out a gun, holds it to my head, and says the same thing. By this time I was like, "Okay, this is not my time to die." I was not afraid at all. He's ranting and raving, and then he puts his hands around my neck to strangle me. I didn't know this at the time, but he was the champion wrestler of Iran.

Suddenly a car was coming down the road, and the lights distracted him. I jumped out of the car and stopped this VW van that was full of Iranian men. I went like this, putting my hands around my neck, and pointed at him, trying to show them that he was going to kill me. They shoved me in the van and sat there trying to figure out what they were going to do to this man. Kill him? Finally they let him go, drove up into the mountains, and dropped off all but two of the villagers; then they took me back to Tehran. I had no idea what the name of the hotel was or where it was. Somehow, because there weren't that many places where Westerners could stay, they figured it out. We got there at dawn. That man was gone from the hotel. York and I stayed there for a week longer; a couple of those men would come every day and call up from the street to see if I was okay.

Douglass Markus (Laxman) also had some heavy encounters with violence and thievery on his overland journey. Like his brother Mitchell, Douglass had retired from the radio station in Montreal. Mitchell had already gone to India. Douglass sold his motorcycle, car, and all the rest of his worldly goods and took off for India with a friend, Peter Brawley; Shelly, a fellow announcer from the radio station; and her boyfriend.

LAXMAN: Our trip was fraught with the good, the bad, and the ugly, sometimes very ugly. In Yugoslavia, we got into an altercation with some locals who wanted to steal our car. Peter got beat up and had his teeth knocked out. That's when I had my resolve about nonviolence confirmed. Even though they also beat me, I could have fought back, but I didn't. And the guy realized that and didn't really hit me that hard. He walked away after a couple of punches.

Farther along on the trip we're with a couple of American guys in a VW bus in Afghanistan. We arranged to give them some money to help pay for gas. About twenty or thirty miles later they picked up a couple of young Afghan guys on the road who turned out to be real hustlers, trying to sell us hashish. In the back of the van was a U-shaped table that we all sat around, and Shelly and her boyfriend were in the front. Shelly's boyfriend started to flip out. A lot of people flip out moving from West to East; they become totally disoriented. The two Americans were straight guys, right out of the army with buzz cuts, and they weren't very appreciative of how he was behaving. They were thinking about dumping the four of us on the side of the road.

I had a little hippie pouch that held my passport, all my important documents, and money. Suddenly this Afghani hitchhiker had his hand in it. I looked him straight in the eye, slid out from under the table, went up to the front, and told the two buzz-cut guys we had a problem, but the buzz-cuts didn't pay attention, because Shelly's boyfriend was freaked out and they thought we were all a bunch of drug-crazed hippies.

As I was standing in the middle of the van, all of a sudden I was lifted out of my body and had this unbelievable vision telling me, "You're heading home." I was crying like crazy. I couldn't believe what was happening in the middle of this little hell realm! I was filled with such joy and comfort and awe. "I'm going home! India, here I come."

One of the exciting aspects of this type of travel was networking with other Westerners along the way. Those who were heading to India specifically to find Maharajji never knew where their next lead might come from.

Peter Goetsch (Balaram Das) was a very smart but lackadaisical student in New York, nominally going to New York University, when he heard a Ram Dass lecture on WBAI. In the early spring of 1969, someone told him Ram Dass was in New Hampshire. After visiting Ram Dass there, Balaram had dreams about Maharajji. In one, he says, "Maharajji was sitting on the deck of this big, golden ship with sails, and I was in the water. There was a big rope that came from the ship to me. It was attached to my stomach, like an umbilical cord. It still feels like that."

BALARAM DAS: I flew to London and hitchhiked successfully all the way through Europe. Once I got to Yugoslavia, hitchhiking didn't work anymore, so I got on the Orient Express train to Istanbul and another train out of Istanbul across Turkey to the Iranian border. In the compartment on the train, I met a British girl named Pat who was also on her way to India. She said, "I met someone last night in Istanbul who was on his way back from India, and he gave me a list of five big saints in India, like where they are." She pulled out this little scrap of paper and at the top of the list, number one, it said "Neem Karoli Baba" and, in parentheses, "Ram Dass's guru." So that was a real breakthrough. Then it said, "Kainchi, between Nainital and Almora." I had everything I needed to know.

Maharajji and the Indian-Pakistani War

The Westerners who crossed into India from Pakistan were aware of the tension at that border crossing. War broke out in November 1971, and the border was closed for the duration of the conflict. At that time Balaram was in Vrindavan with Maharajji.

BALARAM DAS: Maharajji sent most of the Westerners up to Nainital to get away from the war. I was in Vrindavan throughout the whole thing, seeing Maharajji almost every day. A man came to raise money for the troops, the Javans. It's a word that means "young men." Maharajji said, "Balaram, give him 200 rupees." So I gave him 200 rupees. "Get the receipt." The guy wrote out a receipt and gave it to me. Maharajji said, "Let me see that." He took the receipt, read it very closely, gave it back to me, and said, "Now we'll win. India will win." It was like, "It's okay now. Balaram Das has donated. Balaram is Krishna's older brother. He's in the fight. It's going to be fine." Everyone cracked up.

The one thing I can't communicate sufficiently was how incredibly funny Maharajji was, and what a joy it was to be with him because of all these wonderfully lighthearted ways he had of talking about everyday things. You can see in some of the pictures that everyone has these huge grins on their faces.

Krishna and Mirabai were also in Vrindavan at the start of the war when the Pakistanis were bombing Agra airport, only eight miles away. Maharajji said everyone should get out of Vrindavan, so they went to Delhi.

KRISHNA: Maharajji also came to Delhi briefly, and we found out he was staying in the home of a wealthy devotee. There is Maharajji in his blanket surrounded by all these top generals, who were kneeling in front of Maharajji in their military uniforms with star-encrusted epaulets and lots of brass. He is giving them the blessings of a saint. It felt like the *Bhagavad Gita* come to life. These guys were going into battle, and here was Maharajji talking about how to do it in a dharmic way and bring God into it.

Mirabai and I were the only Westerners there along with all this top brass from the army and a couple of top ministers from Indira Gandhi's government. They were all seeking his counsel. I thought, "Hey, I might as well ask him a question too." I was in the antiwar movement in America, and one of the reasons I came to India was to leave it behind; now I was in another country at war. I asked, "What am I supposed to learn, Maharajji, by being in this country during wartime?"

He looked at me, shook his finger, and said, "Learn to be peaceful."

It was a deeply profound transmission.

Part Two

The First Wave

1970–March 1972

3

The Early Ones

Summer / Fall 1970

The minute I heard my first love story,
I started looking for you, not knowing how blind that was.
Lovers don't finally meet somewhere.
They're in each other all along.

—RUMI (TRANS. COLEMAN BARKS)

At first, the trickle of Westerners arriving in India to see Maharajji was small. Frank, who had a number of degrees in religious studies and philosophy, had made a strong connection to Ram Dass in the States and had arranged his talks in the Santa Barbara area. Ram Dass told him to go meet Maharajji. "Go to the Evelyn Hotel in Nainital and talk to M. L. Sah." He also gave Frank K. K. Sah's address in Nainital.

As Ram Dass said, "So many people wanted to know about India. Some of them were very 'shifty.' Krishna Das and Danny and Ramesh, Radha and Mohan—when they started to question me, I finally gave them K. K.'s address in India. I was saved. I was putting K. K. in the driver's seat."

During Ram Dass's first trip to India, Maharajji had K. K. (Krishna Kumar) Sah take Ram Dass to his home, and the two began a lifelong friendship. K. K. had a special relationship to Maharajji, having known him since he was a young child, and often served as the interpreter for Westerners with Maharajji. So getting K. K.'s name and address was a boon that led directly to Maharajji.

K. K. lives in Tallital, the southern part of Nainital, one of the most popular "hill stations" in India, set in the Kumaon foothills of the Himalayas in northern India. At almost 7,000 feet above sea level, Nainital has served for centuries as a place to escape the broiling heat of the plains. It's set in a valley that surrounds pear-shaped Naini Lake—one of fifty-two sacred sites in India where, according to Hindu mythology, parts of the goddess Sati's lifeless body fell while being carried by her distraught husband, Lord Shiva, after she incinerated herself from the inside out by yogic means. One of her eyes (*nain*) fell in the place that came to be called Nain-tal, "Lake of the Eye." Despite the somewhat gruesome story behind its origins, Nainital is a beautiful lush valley and a popular tourist location for Indians, many of whom go there to honeymoon.

Called First

Frank and his wife, Jan, flew from Santa Barbara to Delhi.

FRANK: I'll never forget landing in India, looking out one window at the full moon and out the other window at the Ganges. I felt like I'd come home. We got there in the summer of 1970 and stayed at the Evelyn Hotel. When we first got to Nainital, we hadn't slept in forty-eight hours. Our room was right above the kitchen, and the first thing I said was, "Can anything come out of that hole in the floor?"

The manager said, "Oh no, not a chance."

I'm sitting on the toilet, and this giant scorpion comes out of the hole and starts walking toward my bare feet. That's the only time I've ever levitated. I literally lifted off the toilet seat. We changed rooms at once.

Over the next three months, K. K. Sah took us twelve times to darshans with Maharajji alone, privately. We had time to ask him all our questions. It was beyond, beyond, beyond belief. What a blessing! It was us, K. K., and Maharajji. He never asked for anything. Not a dime, not a commitment, not anything. They gave us tea in those little clay cups; and when we'd leave, they'd give us those pink cardboard boxes filled with greasy *puris* [deep-fried flatbread] and potatoes. We'd eat all we could and then give the rest to the monkeys on the way home or to the staff at the Evelyn.

As the darshans progressed, I'd ask a technical question from a Patanjali yoga *sutra* [a written aphorism or a collection of precepts], and he'd either answer technically or sit in silence while we floated in the space. Then he'd pound his fist and go, "Questions, questions, I know you have questions!"

I asked Maharajji, "When am I going to meet Christ?" He indicated I would meet Christ when I was ready and the time was right. There always seemed to me to be a parallel between Maharajji and Christ. It's like the Narnia books. At one point Lucy is told that she is not coming back to Narnia, and Aslan says, "The reason I brought you here is so that you can know me back in your world."

Every time I was with Maharajji, all I could see was light and love. I kept trying to see his physical eyeballs when his eyes were open, but I never could; I'd just be blinded by the light. Answering before we could get our questions out and all of the miracles meant nothing. They had absolutely zero impact on me. The true miracle was his state of consciousness, his being, that infinite love, that oneness with God, that beyond the beyond. That is so priceless. His presence—that's the whole thing.

In Sanskrit, *darshan* means "auspicious sight" and usually refers to seeing a holy person, the image of a deity, or even a sacred site that inspires you with reverence and devotion. For those of us who were with Maharajji while he was in the body, darshan meant being in his physical presence. We called the time we spent with him darshan, but as Maharajji said, "You don't need to meet the guru in a physical body." You can also have darshan through a dream, vision, or deep meditation. You have darshan whenever you connect with the presence of the divine. Darshan is a gift, the moment when you are allowed to "see," like when the clouds blow away so you suddenly get a clear view of the awe-inspiring Himalayan peaks.

JAN: I have one fun story. Frank had met Lama Govinda in Big Sur, and Lama Govinda said, "If you're ever in India, come and visit me in Almora." So one day we took a bus up there and went to visit him. We're climbing up this hill that was totally infested with leeches. There were all these signs: PRIVATE PROPERTY. KEEP OUT. THIS MEANS YOU. SCRAM! I'm going, "Are you sure we should be up here?"

I'm feeling more intimidated by the moment, but Frank said, "He said I could come to visit . . ." So we go up, and there is the lama's wife. Big woman—quite tall, big boned, very imposing. Maybe it was just her personality. There I am, barely five two, in my twenties. I'm already intimidated by all the signs, and she's standing there in her Tibetan dress. But then the lama came out and remembered Frank, and we had a nice visit.

The next time we saw Maharajji, he leaned over to me and had this little smile on his face. He said, "Did you meet his wife?" as though we had been two matrons meeting at the bridge table or a cocktail party.

That's classic Maharajji. He knew Jan had been intimidated by the lama's wife and subtly let her know that he'd been with her, in a way that was both fun and reassuring.

It was on their second trip to India, after Maharajji had left his body, that S. L. Sah, one of the owners of the Evelyn Hotel (who were all devotees of Maharajji), told them that Maharajji had said, "I called a thousand. I could have called ten thousand, but I called Frank first."

Permission Granted

Right before Frank and Jan left India, Danny (Jagganath Das), Jeff (Krishna Das), and Jim (Rameshwar Das) arrived in Nainital in mid-September 1970. The three of them knew each other from "summer camp" in Franklin, New Hampshire, in 1969. Ram Dass had given them K. K.'s address. All three wrote to K. K., who brought their letters to Maharajji and said, "Ram Dass's students want to come to see you."

Maharajji said, "No! Tell them not to come." K. K. pouted like a small child until Maharajji finally relented, "All right. Tell them what you want."

Maharajji with Rameshwar Das and Jagganath Das (Danny).
Krishna Das is seated at bottom left.

K. K. wrote back: "As you know, Sri Maharajji does not encourage the devotees to come to him. But his doors are always open. So if you are traveling here in India, you can come and see him."

That was all the permission they needed. The three of them flew to India.

RAMESHWAR DAS: We tried to find K. K. in Nainital, finally tracked down his office, and were told he was at Kainchi. We got a taxi and were going down the switchbacks on the hills past Bhowali. There was a point where you would first get a view of Kainchi on the floor of the valley from way up above. I began to get this extraordinary feeling of coming home.

He sent us to eat almost immediately: "Take prasad." I ate seventeen puris and three large helpings of potatoes. Those leaf plates, which are about fourteen inches wide, were heaped high. I think that was probably the only factor that grounded me a little bit. Later, sitting in front of him was like absorbing the love and energy that I felt from Ram Dass originally. It was simply extraordinary to be in his presence.

K. K. introduced us as Ram Dass's students from America. Maharajji said, "Oh, they come from good families." He was playing with this soft sweater I was wearing that my mother had given me. It was a sweet and intimate welcome, very welcoming. I felt like I was being absorbed into his family in some way.

DANNY: For me, that first darshan was really wonderful in all the ways that Maharajji is wonderful. He was very loving. He said, "Do you have sweaters? It could get cold." He told someone to get us food. It was a very sweet encounter. In the West I had been in the heart of American psychology, and here was a sea of love—totally off the map of Western psychology. It was so clear that we had missed something really important about human abilities, human potential, about the heart. Here was a being who was endless love and presence. It wasn't some temporary state; it was who he was. That's what really got me.

KRISHNA DAS (from *Chants of a Lifetime*[1]): I'd been dreaming about this moment for the last year and a half, and now it was here. I was actually seeing him with my own eyes! My friends and I had only seen old black-and-white photos, so it was unbelievable to see him moving around, in full color, and to hear him speak! The atmosphere was filled with incredible sweetness. His voice was soft and intimate, yet seemed to come from far away, as if he were seeing us and our whole lives in that very moment. A thrill ran through me as I bowed to him for the first time in this life. I put the apples I'd brought next to him on the *takhat* [the wooden platform, covered with a blanket, that he sat on]. He immediately took the apples and threw them to the other people in the room. I was shocked, thinking that he wasn't accepting my offering. He looked at me and asked, "Is it right to give it all away at once?"

I hesitated, "I don't know."

"The prasad [anything, usually edible, that's first offered to a deity or holy person and then distributed to others] comes from God and goes back to God. When you have union with God, you don't need anything." I looked up at him, confused. He continued, "When you have God, you don't have any more desires." Now *that* was clear![2]

Just One Darshan

Govind and Gayatri met on the road in Afghanistan in 1970. They traveled together to India, where Govind learned to make jewelry according to traditional Indian methods. Their one encounter with Maharajji shows just how powerful even a single unexpected darshan can be in changing the course of a life.

GOVIND: We got to India just before New Year's Eve, 1970. There were six or seven of us together in the Volkswagen van. After going to the Kumbha Mela in Allahabad in January, Gayatri and I left our group of friends. I was to meet them later in Bombay, where they were going to put together a hash deal, but since she and I had only recently met and wanted to be by ourselves, we got on a train heading to Bombay. It was our first train ride in India. Anyone who's been in India knows what it is like to get on a third-class unreserved train—the overflowing crowds and the chaos. We were lucky and got seats right on the aisle, near the door where you get on the train.

After it was totally full—literally, there was barely room to breathe—at the last minute this guy walked onto the train. He was so big it was unbelievable; he wasn't that tall, more sort of wide. But it wasn't the physical size; his presence was so big that he felt huge. We were transfixed and couldn't take our eyes off him. He went to a row where you couldn't possibly fit one more person; the seas parted and everybody moved over. He sat down cross-legged in the middle of the bench. As soon as he got on the train, all of a sudden everybody went from wanting to kill each other to get a seat to passing out *chikus* [a tropical fruit] and bananas.

He just sat there, not talking at all. We kept looking at him for hours and hours. He would send us a sideways glance every once in a while, and each time he gave us that twinkle we got even more mesmerized.

As the train moved slowly through the desert, he called the conductor over and whispered something in his ear, then gave us that sideways look again. In another hour or so, the conductor walked up to us and said, "The train is going to stop in a few minutes at a place that isn't in fact a stop, and *he* said that you two are to get off the train and go up to Mt. Abu and spend the night there, and then come back to this same place. Tomorrow's train, which also doesn't stop here and has never stopped here, is going to stop and pick you up so that you can continue your journey."

We didn't even question it. The fact that "he" said it was all that mattered.

The train suddenly stopped in the middle of a vast emptiness. The conductor said, "This is where you get off." We picked up our bags and were about to get off the train when the conductor added, "You are very fortunate. He is one of our most esteemed saints in all of India."

Somehow we got up to Mt. Abu—a holy mountain that rises out of the desert with a big glittering lake at the top, lush and beautiful. We wandered around the woods and the lake, but nothing significant happened. The next day, we went back down and were sitting out there in the middle of nowhere when this train came up and stopped. The exact same two seats were empty and waiting for us in what was otherwise a madhouse. Countless hours later, the train pulled into Bombay station.

I said to Gayatri, "I have no idea who that guy was, but I know that he just reset our karmic destiny."

Within a few minutes of arriving at the hotel in Bombay, we bumped into the people I was supposed to meet. In the meantime, they had put together some sort of deal. They said, "Oh, man, too bad you weren't here. You could have been part of it." I remember feeling relieved, as if I somehow knew we were now on a different path than those friends. And in the next few weeks we had our first contact with the teachers who became the other major spiritual influences in our lives.

Around ten months later we were back in the West when *Be Here Now* came out. When I saw Maharajji's picture, I thought, "That's the guy from the train." But in all the pictures I would see of him over the years, he had on a plaid blanket, and the guy on the train had been wearing a beige *khadi* [homespun silk or cotton] shawl. I always had a kind of *knowing* that it had to have been him on that train, but I never told anyone.

During the next few years, we were back in India as *sanyasins* [seekers]. The two times that we wanted to go see Maharajji, before I opened my mouth my teacher would say, "Next week I want you to do this or that in Bombay." "Okay," I thought, "we're not supposed to go see Maharajji for whatever reason."

We stayed in India for most of the next eleven years, and when we came back to the West to live, we started going to the Hanuman temple in Taos every year for *bandhara* [a celebratory feast].

Many years later, one of the friends from that trip showed up and told me that three of them had spent some time in jail at one time or another over the years. If we hadn't visited Mt. Abu, I might have been at that meeting and been part of some deal, either then or in the future, but that world no longer held any appeal.

During the same week that I saw this old friend for the first time in many years, someone had a picture of Maharajji wearing a beige khadi shawl. I finally trusted what I'd somehow known all along.

4

May All Beings Be Happy

Winter 1970

May all beings be happy.
May all beings be peaceful.
May all beings be liberated.

—METTA MEDITATION

t seems that one of the essential initiations for Westerners in India was taking at least one Vipassana meditation course, taught by S. N. Goenka. Born and raised in Burma (now Myanmar), Goenka spent fourteen years studying Vipassana meditation with Sayagyi U Ba Khin before settling in India. He began teaching in 1969, just around the time Westerners were starting to journey to India.

Krishna Das (Roy Bonney)

S. N. Goenka.

The technique of Vipassana goes back two and a half millennia to the Buddha, who taught *dhamma*—the universal way to liberation. Vipassana is a totally nonsectarian approach and thus appealed greatly to Westerners. In a speech he gave at the Millennium World Peace Summit at the United Nations in New York in 2000, Goenka said: "Rather than converting people from one organized religion to another organized religion, we should try to convert people from misery to happiness, from bondage to liberation, and from cruelty to compassion."

Vipassana courses not only served as fantastic instruction and practice in this ancient and powerful meditation technique, which today has spread across America as the practice of "mindfulness," but also created a marriage for many of us between Buddhist meditation practice and the heart-wisdom lovefest of Maharajji. We met and became friends with the people who would eventually bring these practices to the West— Sharon Salzberg, Jack Kornfield, and Joseph Goldstein. In Bodhgaya, we also befriended Lama Tsultrim Allione, the first Western woman to be ordained a Tibetan Buddhist nun by the Sixteenth Karmapa; she now heads Tara Mandala, a Tibetan Buddhist retreat center in Colorado.

Today this marriage of "kissing cousins"—Hindu bhaktas (lovers of God) and Buddhist meditation practitioners—is seen in the Open Your Heart in Paradise retreats led by Ram Dass and different Vipassana teachers on Maui or in videos like *Cultivating Grace and Transforming Suffering* with Ram Dass and Jack Kornfield. As Ram Dass said to Jack, "Doing that mind training allowed me to be so much more open in the heart and really expanded my connection with bhakti."

Back in the early 1970s in India, Vipassana courses also served as a crossroads that led many to find Maharajji.

MIRABAI: Our first week in India, I met Sharon Salzberg on the street in Delhi. She and I both had been at Buffalo; I hadn't known her there, but we knew of each other. Bhagavan Das had told her there was a meditation course being taught for the first time by Goenka for Westerners and it was going to be in Bodhgaya, where the Buddha had been enlightened. It seemed almost like having wine and cheese in Paris. Let's go learn to meditate! I was clueless. I had never sat with my legs crossed, let alone closed my eyes and looked within. The only related thing I remembered was Allen Ginsberg *Om*-ing at the Pentagon.

I met Ram Dass right outside the gates to the Burmese *vihara* [monastery], standing there with a couple of the others. They were trying to figure out how many cookies they should buy to take in, because once we got inside the gates, there wouldn't be any sweets. I liked him immediately.

From the beginning, I was deeply moved by Goenka, by the practice, and by the dedication of all of us students. Forget *zafus* [meditation cushions] or carpets—we were on the floor sitting cross-legged in our hippie clothes. We did one ten-day course, and then we did another and another, so we were there for a couple of months, sitting in silence, meditating our little hearts out. It was wonderful to simplify and just sit. In graduate school I had read a thousand books and my head was full of ideas and words. Letting it all go and looking to see what was really inside changed my life.

We would have a day or two in between the ten-day sessions when we would be able to go out and get more cookies and talk. Ram Dass would make fun of us. He called us the "used-to-bes" as in "What did you used to be?" He thought it would be better to be here now. I still didn't know anything about Maharajji. A couple of times Ram Dass would lead kirtan in the Buddhist monastery, singing *Sri Ram Jai Ram,* and I loved it, but I was pretty much in the moment with the whole Buddhist practice.

One night I was on the roof with Ram Dass looking at the stars. Ram Dass was talking about being connected to everything. I remember looking at the stars and *getting it,* getting that we were all part of one great whole and there was a reason we were here. It was one of those moments after which nothing was ever the same again.

KRISHNA: I had done a lot of psychedelics, which is certainly inner work, but I had never done meditation. I knew I couldn't take psychedelics for the rest of my life, but it was the only way

I knew to dissolve the ego and contact these higher planes of consciousness. After about the third day of the course, I started having these profound experiences that I only had before through psychedelics. I always knew it was my consciousness I was experiencing, but now I was scientifically proving it, and it was very exciting to me.

LAMA SURYA DAS: Almost by chance I met up and trekked on pilgrimage with Mirabai and Krishna to Lord Shiva's icy Himalayan Amarnath cave after the full moon of August. It was great going over the snowy 12,000-foot pass with Krishna in his flip-flops, smoking a *chillum* [a pipe with a mixture of tobacco and hash], and shouting, *"Hari Om!"* and *"Bolo Shivanath!"* to the sky. When we came back, there was a letter waiting for them from Goenka's secretary, saying Goenkaji is giving a ten-day Vipassana meditation course in the state of Rajasthan, near holy Mt. Abu. They left. After a few days, Ken and I decided to go sit in that course as well. Later that winter in Bodhgaya I did three courses in a row and met a bunch of the satsang who'd already been with Maharajji.

After Bodhgaya I heard people were going to Allahabad to see Maharajji. He moved around like the wind, and people learned of his whereabouts through the grapevine: in this season he is in Kainchi; in that season he's in Vrindavan; in the winter he is often at Dada's. I said, "What's a Dada and where's a Dada?" That's how I got to Allahabad. I had the magic words: 4 Church Lane.

At Dada's, I was always trying to find a place to do my one-hour silent and introspective Goenka meditation, twice a day if I could, because that's what you were vowed to do. I was sitting in my white pajama clothes from the Khadi Bhavan in Delhi, maybe

five or six people away from Maharajji, when I felt something
go *squish* in my lap. It was a very ripe peach. Maharajji was like,
"Wake up. What are you doing looking for your breath? Here,
have God's prasad."

Bruce Margolin (Badrinath Das, or Badri) was a lawyer, well known
in Los Angeles for defending those on drug charges, including Timothy
Leary. He had "made it" in a worldly sense. However, he was troubled
by the premature passing of his father and brother when he was a teenager. He felt compelled to see more of the world and search for meaning
in his life, so at age twenty-nine he "retired." As he said, "I left my home,
I left my dog, I left my car, I left my relationships, but I *had* to go. I sat
in my driveway and cried for an hour before I left town. I didn't know
what was going to happen or how long I'd be away." After taking a long
and winding road through Greece, Turkey, Israel, and Africa, he finally
felt ready for India; he flew out of Addis Ababa in Ethiopia and landed
in Bombay.

BADRINATH DAS: Shushila, whom I met in Bombay, said she'd
take me to Goenka's meditation course. When we got off the
train in Rajasthan, it was like a cowboy town from a hundred
years ago, with no cars, just horses. There were around a
hundred people in this ashram, about half of them Westerners.
There was no fee involved in the course; Goenka never asked for
anything. But you had to promise not to use drugs, not to speak
unless spoken to, not to play music, and not to interfere with
other people. This code of conduct was called the *shila*. This was
ten days in meditation. You woke at four in the morning and
meditated until nine at night.

The first three days he teaches you to keep your thoughts on your breath. You freak out because your mind wants to get out of that situation: "I gotta go. I've got other things to do in my life. I can't be sitting here contemplating my breath." But Goenka was sitting there with you with strength and compassion. He said your mind is like an elephant. If you train an elephant, it can do anything for you—lift rocks, move trees, move mountains. Your mind can do anything too, if you control it and it doesn't control you. He constantly reassured us along the way. He explained the life of Buddha and his teachings. Goenka also spoke about himself when he lived in Burma and had been addicted to heroin. After the first three days he teaches you to concentrate on your body sensations. Finally, the last day Goenka teaches *metta* [loving-kindness] meditation, and how you can travel in your mind to anybody anywhere and meditate on them with love.

While there, I heard that Ram Dass was in India and that he had taken courses with Goenka. When the course was finished, we took a train to New Delhi and when we checked into the hotel, on the register was Richard Alpert. Fantastic! I left a note saying I had a message for him from Goenka. I had shown Goenka *Be Here Now,* and he had said, "If you see Ram Dass, tell him that I have more to teach him."

Ram Dass said, "Now what are you going to do?"

I said that as far as I was concerned, seeing him was the pinnacle of my experience.

"No way. The ultimate is the guru. He happens to be thirty miles from here, and I'll go with you first thing tomorrow. I want you to experience him before he possibly vanishes." Then he said, "No, you better go tonight, because he may leave tomorrow, and I can't leave right now."

That night I went to Vrindavan.

JACQUES: During the [Indian-Pakistani] war we were at a course in Bikaner, on the border with Pakistan, and they were having tank battles nearby. We were there to meditate. We had a ten-day course pretty much in the dark, because the whole time was a blackout, with sirens and thuds in the background. I can hear Goenka saying, "E-q-u-a-n-i-m-i-t-y. Never mind *boom boom boom.* We don't care about *boom.* Watch your sensations."

The Word Spreads

Sunanda Markus was "made in India" when her Middle Eastern parents lived there during World War II before coming to New York, where she was born. She had always wanted to go to India, since her parents had such good feelings about the country. She too found her way to Maharajji from connections she made at a Goenka course.

SUNANDA: When I was in college, my boyfriend broke up with me and I was flattened, totally flattened; it made me get into the spiritual thing. I read *Siddhartha* and was intrigued, so I saved my money, after graduation flew with my girlfriend to Europe, and hitchhiked as far as Afghanistan. I flew to Nepal to visit a boyfriend in the Peace Corps, and then I went to Benares, where I became friends with Krishna [David] Dobrer. We went to Bodhgaya together, and I sat my first meditation course at the Burmese vihara.

   We stayed for the second course in February 1972. At that course there were a bunch of people who had been with Maharajji. Parvati and Raghu kept looking at me and saying,

"Where do I know you from? What city, what town did you grow up in? How do I know you?" They were very, very insistent. Raghu said, "Come to Maharajji and bring prasad, an offering of some kind."

When I look back, I see that I needed that kind of heart opening and mindfulness development, as scanty as it was at that age, as my way of being prepared to meet Maharajji.

Of course Raghu and I felt like we knew her; Maharajji later married Sunanda to Laxman, Raghu's brother!

Krishna Dobrer went to North Africa, because his brother had been in the Peace Corps in Tunisia. Disappointed because it was so modern, he traveled through the south of Tunisia, through Algeria into Morocco, and got the culture shock that he was looking for. He next did the infamous hash-smoking bus trip from London to Kathmandu and then trekked in Nepal, which he felt was his initial opening—being with the Tibetan people, who were really living their religion, not just doing the rituals.

KRISHNA DOBRER: When Sunanda and I went to Goenka, during the course I was dealing with all of my negativity. I wanted to kick people because they sat so straight and were so perfect. Then one day Goenka says, "We're going to practice universal loving-kindness." Yeah, right. Here I am dealing with all of this dark, negative stuff from my childhood, anger and resentment, and I hated Goenka. He's supposed to ring the bell so I could move. He's probably feeding his face in the other room. I had such incredible negativity. Then he started doing the *metta* meditation, and it was like the room filled up with this thick, thick honey and my heart opened; I fell apart and cried. That was at the end of the first ten days.

At the end of the second ten days when we did metta, I had this profound experience. Everyone had left the meditation hall, and I couldn't stop laughing and crying, pounding on the floor and going, "My God, the only reason to be in a body is to remember this." So I took myself and my meditation very seriously.

We met some Maharajji people who said, "Well, if you like metta, he *is* metta, and you're probably one of us." Sunanda and I decided to go and meet Maharajji even though Goenka had said, "No gurus. Avoid gurus please."

Florence Klein (Krishna Priya) had been very political in high school—Black Panthers and SDS—and would have taken to the streets if she hadn't hit the road. When she was eighteen and could get her own passport, she headed for India. Her parents, both with PhDs, didn't support her travels; they believed she should be in college. But having been the most popular babysitter in the neighborhood, she had several hundred dollars saved up. She got to India a year before she met Maharajji.

KRISHNA PRIYA: I did my second Goenka course in Bodhgaya in February of '72. Maharajji had sent a whole bunch of his devotees to that course. One day during feeding time, when you were actually allowed to do something other than meditate on your breath, there were all these people in their whites huddled together looking at something and whispering to each other. As any curious teenager would, I peeked over to see what they were looking at. I did a double take, because as soon as I saw this picture, I remembered I had a dream of that person the night before, so this was terribly interesting.

I elbowed my way into the huddle. I said, "Who is that?"

"Neem Karoli Baba. Why are you asking?"

"I had a dream about that guy. Does he really exist?"

"You had a dream about him last night?"

"Yeah."

"You never heard of him before?"

"No."

"Did you ever see a picture of him before?"

"No."

"What about Ram Dass? You know Ram Dass?"

"No."

"What about *Be Here Now*?"

"No."

I'm thinking, "These people are hysterical. What is the matter with them?"

The course went on day after day, and I found to my distress that I could no longer think about the sensation of my breath on my upper lip. All I could think about was this guy I had never heard of that I had had a dream about. By the end of the course I asked those people dressed in white how I could find him.

Sometimes it seemed that we found Maharajji. At other times it was clear that he found us, as the people who were "on the bus" found out.

5

On the Bus
January / February 1971

When love beckons to you, follow him . . .

—KAHLIL GIBRAN, *THE PROPHET*

After doing numerous back-to-back Goenka courses in Bodhgaya in the winter of 1970–71, it was time for the original group of Westerners to move on. Ram Dass had promised to meet Swami Muktananda in Delhi for the celebration of Shivaratri, the big Hindu holiday that is an all-night festival to Lord Shiva. Everyone was anxious to find where Maharajji might be. The bus was headed to Delhi, but Danny convinced Ram Dass that they should take a detour to see where the Kumbha Mela had been—the huge spiritual gathering held at the confluence of the three holy rivers in Allahabad. In a surprise encounter, there was Maharajji! It was a massive lesson for Ram Dass about who was actually in control. After all, hadn't he "made the decision" that the bus would go to Allahabad?

RAM DASS: I went back to India after the conclusion of Muktananda's world tour. I went to Nainital and to all of the different places in the hills where Maharajji would hang out. I couldn't find him, so I went to Bodhgaya because all the Westerners were going there. I said, "Well, I can't find Maharajji, so the best thing to do is meditate."

One day after doing a bunch of courses I said, "I'm going to find Maharajji, because I can't meditate any more. I just want to

On the bus. Seated, left to right: [unknown], Loren, Sita, Ram Dass, Rameshwar Das holding Muffin, Jai Shri, Richard Kurz and his girlfriend Beverly, Danny, and Little Joseph. Standing, left to right: Dwarkanath, Tukaram, Tenny, Russell (now Swami Shankarananda), Mariam, Pema, Mirabai, Harinam, Krishna (Bush), Krishna Das, John Travis, Gerard (from Belgium), assistant bus driver, and bus driver Gino.

Rameshwar Das

know where he is." The rumor in Bodhgaya became that Ram
Dass was leaving to meet Maharajji, so when we got going,
we were twenty-four meditators on the bus. Tenny's little girl,
Muffin, wanted ice cream. It was a straight road from Bodhgaya
to Delhi for ice cream.

Danny came up to the bus driver and said, "If you turn right
here, you'll reach Allahabad, one of the most sacred cities." I
was just, "Ice cream straight, sacred city right . . ." I was really
deciding, and the others were helping me decide. The bus driver
asked if he should turn right or go straight. Well, we were
spiritual people, and Danny said we should see this place where
the Kumbha Mela is held, where the holy rivers come together.
I said to Danny that the *mela* [gathering] had passed, but Danny
insisted that the space itself was holy.

"Okay, we'll go right."

We came to these big grounds by the rivers, which were
all empty since the mela had ended. Danny said, "There's a
Hanuman temple, so why don't we go over by that?" We drove
over a sandy field where people were walking two by two and
dogs were running around.

Then Rameshwar Das shouted, "There's Maharajji!" He was
walking with Dada.

Dada told me later that Maharajji said, "They've come," as if
he expected us.

He was standing in sand, and I touched his feet with my
forehead. I was crying, completely out of it.

I didn't know where we were going. The big bus went through
the streets to Dada's house. Didi came out of the house and
said that Maharajji had told them that morning to make lunch
for twenty-five people. I realized that was before I had "made a
decision," that my decision was obviously his decision. Clearly he

was expecting all these people, even though he had told me not to bring anyone. That was the beginning of me and the Westerners with Maharajji.

After the initial shock, and first darshan for many of them, the busload of Westerners followed Maharajji to Dada's house. Dada Mukerjee, an economics professor at the University of Allahabad, and his wife, Didi, were longtime devotees, having been with Maharajji for forty years at that point (more about them in Chapter 10).

DANNY: Between two Goenka courses I had gone to the Kumbha Mela in Allahabad and loved it, so when we were going to once again pass through Allahabad, I said we should go over to the mela grounds because it's pretty amazing. I directed the bus where to go, and when we got to the grounds it was absolutely empty. Then I remembered there was a little Hanuman *mandir* [temple] over on the edge of the grounds. I said, "Let's go to the temple at least."

Maharajji was standing there with Dada Mukerjee as though they were waiting for us. When I saw him, it was the only time I ever laughed and cried at the same time. It was like there was no emotional package for the impact, because it was very miraculous: it seemed to me that he was there out of nowhere. We stayed several days at Dada's and then the whole group started to try to follow him, wherever he was.

DWARKANATH: There was a two-day break between courses and a group of us Westerners were sitting at a *chai* [tea] shop in the village of Bodhgaya when the bus on which Tenny, her daughter, and I had traveled overland to India drove up. The bus was coming down a narrow street, going relatively slowly; we jumped up and waved to Gino, the owner/operator, and he stopped. Gino was biding his time in India waiting for his next busload of people scheduled to go back to London. Ram Dass negotiated with him to drive us to Delhi for Shivaratri.

Then Rameshwar Das cried out, "Stop the bus! There's Maharajji!" Everybody piled out.

That was my first darshan. I didn't know how to put together this person standing before me with the relationship I had cultivated with the little picture of Maharajji that Ram Dass had given me. I knew Maharajji as a concept, and then there was this person. People were laughing, crying. Dada gave directions for how to find his house. Gino is so masterful that he managed to get us to Dada's house as it was getting dark, where a meal was ready and waiting for us.

On the second night we were there, we were called to come in from the living room for the meal. Everybody was complying, but I turned around and went back in the darshan hall to pick up the blanket that I had used as a shawl, figuring I should fold it neat and tidy. Just then the doors burst open, and Maharajji came in from his room across the front hall. He sat down; I sat at his feet. He bent over and tapped me on the back or on the head and said things. I didn't know what he was saying. I felt so happy to be getting that attention that I figured there wasn't any conflict between this external person and the sort of internalized guru that I had cultivated. Joy and love seemed to bridge that. It totally disrupted dinner plans, because everybody else came back into the room.

KRISHNA: When we were ready to leave the final retreat, I was in a really clear space. Goenka had been a really good teacher, and doing meditation in the same place where the Buddha had been enlightened and visiting the Bodhi tree in between sessions were great too. My idea now was to go to Darjeeling and see Kalu Rinpoche, especially after all this Buddhist meditation. I kept hearing about Maharajji, but Goenka had been very strict about not getting involved with any gurus. "You don't need a guru. They are all just after your money or your mind." He was very antiguru. These friends on the bus were into gurus, but I had the dharma; I didn't need a guru.

The publisher's proofs of *Be Here Now* had arrived, and they opened the box on the bus. I was sitting behind someone who was looking at the page where it said in giant type, "The guru." I am looking over his shoulder and thinking, "*Hmm,* the guru. Not my thing." Then Ramesh said, "There he is!" I am looking at the picture that says "the guru," then I look out and see this old man in a blanket standing on the side of the road in front of this Hanuman temple. There were a lot of synchronicities happening all the time, but this one was unmistakable.

Everybody gets out, and people are doing *danda pranaam* [full prostration] to Maharajji, so I thought, "Okay, I'll get into it." I did a danda pranaam to Maharajji, and it felt really good. I felt touched that I had this opportunity to meet him.

Then we are in Dada's lovely home, and we have darshan with Maharajji. I decided that I would meditate, because I didn't know the protocols. At this point my practice was pretty deep. I started doing metta practice, and all of a sudden my heart opens up like it never had before. I felt this energy coming in through my crown and going out through my heart. I had had this experience before, but now it was like somebody opened up a hydrant and the water was shooting out. "Okay, I get it. There is really something going on here."

I found that all I needed to do was meditate with Maharajji. I would do metta and old boundaries would dissolve, and I would be in this ocean of love with him. Not the stillness of Buddhism, much more of an active dynamic process.

MIRABAI: Just about everybody had read *Be Here Now* before I got it, as I was very much toward the bottom of the hierarchy of who got to read next. In those hours on the bus before we got to Allahabad, I was reading the part about Maharajji. I was thinking about Goenka, because he discouraged his students from going to Hindu gurus.

Buddhism had come out of a rejection of certain kinds of Vedic *pujas* [worship rituals], which the Buddha thought were empty. Hinayana Buddhists teach that it is all within and all you need is a spiritual friend or elder who will teach you the practice; you didn't need a guru to tell you what to do with your life. It was very convincing—until I read the book. *Be Here Now* is a really loving introduction to Maharajji. I thought, "He must be a wonderful person, although obviously I don't need a guru, but how wonderful that he exists and that he is Ram Dass's guru. I'll never meet him anyhow, because it says right in the book that it is impossible to find him."

I was looking at a full-page picture of Maharajji when all of a sudden Ramesh said, "Stop the bus!" The bus came to a screeching halt. And sure enough, there was Maharajji! Everyone scrambled to get to him. Ram Dass leapt off the bus. "Maharajji! Maharajji!" The others followed. I was the last person off the bus. I was a PhD student, an intellectual, and political New Yorker. I never imagined I would bow in front of someone. But as I got off the bus, I looked at Maharajji. In a flash, I thought in an embarrassingly self-centered way, "Maharajji, you didn't have to do this for me. I would have believed . . ." Then I was off the last step of the bus and flat down at his feet. There was nothing else to do except a full prostration. My heart broke open in that moment, just from seeing him, and it's never been the same. I'd never had such an experience with anybody or anything else.

We went to Dada's house, and we were in Dada's rose garden chanting *Sri Ram Jai Ram*. We didn't know many chants at the time, but we knew that one. Everyone was floating around in white clothes that we all had made in Bodhgaya. I had grown up as a Catholic girl, and I remember thinking that this is what they said heaven would be like. This is heaven.

Jean Nantel (Tukaram) and his girlfriend, Susan McCarthy (Sita), were from Montreal and heard several of Ram Dass's tapes that Raghu played on the radio. They were riveted and decided to go to India, where Sita's brother Jim (Kabir Das) was already a sadhu, living in a small hut in a remote village above Almora.

TUKARAM: Sita and I went to Delhi to change money. We were headed back to Almora and said, "Let's splurge. Let's stop in Nainital and have a hot bath before we go back to our hut."

As the bus pulled into Nainital, a guy walks up to us and says, "Do you know Ram Dass? He is landing today in Delhi. He'll be here tomorrow. Come with us. We're all at the Evelyn Hotel." This was Rameshwar Das. Ram Dass shows up the next day. He takes one look at Sita and me, and his mouth drops open. We'd had a difficult encounter in Franklin, New Hampshire. He figured, "They'll never find me. It's a big country. They've got no clues."

So a bunch of us all went to Bodhgaya and did five ten-day courses in a row. Then Ram Dass chartered that bus. I was sitting next to Ramesh when Maharajji suddenly appeared. I had never bowed or knelt before anybody, but when I got out of that bus, I fell flat on my face and that was the best fall of my life. A moment like no other before or since. It was the no-mind quality. There was nobody in the mud. There was nobody above. There was no nothing. There was no *other* at all. It was effortless, and it was instant.

SITA: We got to the Evelyn Hotel and, oh my gosh, everybody was just like these saints floating around. They were so open-hearted; they didn't mind that we knew nothing about *karma* [the cycle of cause and effect], dharma, or bhakti. Ram Dass arrived the following day, and everyone was going to leave on the train to Bodhgaya. My brother Kabir lived several hours away north of Almora. We went to tell him we had found our tribe. Kabir had been in India for years and had read all the books; he considered himself quite "enlightened." He dismissed our group of newcomers as novices. Tukaram and I left to join the others on the Bodhgaya trip.

When it was my turn to read *Be Here Now,* I got cozy in the back of the bus, lying atop the stack of luggage. When I came to the page about "the guru," I was admiring Dwarkanath's sketch of Maharajji, when Rameshwar Das said, "There's Maharajji." I saw him standing under a peepul tree beside the Hanuman temple, as though he was waiting for us to arrive. I must have hopped, almost flew, to the front of the bus. Touching Maharajji's feet was everything. *Everything.* I stayed with Maharajji from that day until the day he died.

On a Different Bus

The Westerners didn't spend all their time with Maharajji, who often couldn't be found when they first arrived in India, or disappeared without warning, or sent them on their way for a short or long period. Many had met other holy men who had toured in America, like Swami Muktananda, or they had been introduced to Sathya Sai Baba by Hilda Charlton, a spiritual teacher in New York, and thus wanted to meet him. So during the times they couldn't be with Maharajji, they had darshan with other highly esteemed spiritual masters in India, like Anandamayi Ma or the Mother from Pondicherry, or visited the ashrams of Ramana Maharshi, Ramakrishna, or Meher Baba, great siddhas from an earlier era.

The other masters were all great beings, but there is such a thing as *lineage*. You "belong" to a particular master, and when you meet him or her, you are "home." For those who "belonged" to Maharajji, these other masters were wonderful teachers, but didn't quite feel like "home."

For example, I had spent quite a bit of personal time with Swami Muktananda in the United States before I left for India, even meditating alone with him in his room. And because I had been close to Hilda in New York, when I first arrived in India, not knowing where Maharajji was to be found, I went to Sai Baba's ashram in Whitefield. I spent three months there and then another few weeks at his ashram in Puttaparthi. It happened to be during a time when Sai Baba was not giving private or group darshan to Westerners, and the only interaction I had with him was his saying to me, "Your husband is waiting for you," and, "Do you have a son?" (I met my husband-to-be in Nainital and later had two sons.)

I kept wondering what was wrong with me. Why wasn't I comfortable bowing at the feet of either the Paramahansa (Muktananda) or the Avatar (Sai Baba)? Why couldn't I open my heart to these spiritual masters? But when I finally met Maharajji, it was a true coming home, the surrender that was no surrender. There had been nothing wrong with these other masters or with me; I simply wasn't theirs.

After Maharajji *jaoed* (pronounced "jowed"; from Maharajji's frequent command *Jao!* "Go!") the Westerners from Dada's in Allahabad, the bus deposited them in Delhi, where Ram Dass had promised to meet Swami Muktananda for Shivaratri and then to go on tour in South India with him.

DWARKANATH: Shivaratri was a big event, lots of people, big, big home with an outdoor tent, all-night chanting of *Om Namah Shivaya*. After that Ram Dass got this VW van. He had made arrangements with Muktananda to travel on a *yatra* [spiritual pilgrimage] that Muktananda was making in South India. Ram Dass, Rameshwar Das, Krishna Das, and I first went to Haridwar and had darshan with Anandamayi Ma. Then we drove to Hyderabad, where we met up with Muktananda, and from there we traveled as part of his fleet of vehicles. Ram Dass got permission to take a little bit longer route, and we stopped for a night in Tiruvannamalai [Ramana Maharshi's ashram at the foot of the holy hill Arunachala].

Then we continued on with Muktananda to Whitefield, where I had darshan with Sai Baba. It was a little crazy. I had already met Maharajji, and I was not in the least interested in these other guys. When we finally got to Ganeshpuri [the location of Swami Muktananda's ashram], which was the final destination, I stayed for a couple of weeks. I appreciated Muktananda when he sent me away with his blessings.

Dale Borglum (Ram Dev) was all done with his PhD in mathematics at Stanford except for writing his thesis, but he just wasn't able to focus on it. He had heard Ram Dass talk at Stanford, and when Ram Dass came to northern California with Swami Muktananda, Ram Dev helped put together Muktananda's tour—the kingly thrones, peacock feathers, bushels of flowers, the radio spots, the church rooms. When Ram Dass and Muktananda left for Australia (as part of Muktananda's world tour), Ram Dev finally finished his thesis in six weeks flat. Then Ram Dass invited Ram Dev to come to India.

RAM DEV: I got to Bombay in the spring of 1970. My very first day in India turned out to be Holi [a wild Hindu holiday celebrating the divine love of Radha for Lord Krishna, which ushers in spring]. I didn't know this wasn't a usual day, but everybody was drunk or stoned and throwing colored powder at each other. I was overwhelmed, jet-lagged, and exhausted; I realized I needed to go somewhere to get it together. Ganeshpuri was half a day's train ride away. Why not go there?

At first it seemed fantastic, quiet and meditative. A few weeks later, Muktananda and Ram Dass show up, along with literally ten thousand devotees from Bombay who hadn't seen Baba for six months or so. Most of them left after a few days, but the place was now very different. A lot of people were affected by the shaktipat. You'd see somebody bouncing into the walls or dancing some strange dance.

I was always trying to do the good thing, so I could get enlightened. I rigorously followed whatever Muktananda in his talks said was important—meditation, saying God's name, serving the guru. He also said don't eat any more than you absolutely need to stay alive. I was there for six months, totally disciplined. By the time the monsoon came, I had chronic diarrhea, weighed 113 pounds, and had blood coming out of my feet and my anus. I couldn't digest food. The thing in Ganeshpuri is that you were either well enough to work in the fields or you were sick enough to go to Bombay to the hospital. I finally go to the hospital, look in the mirror, and freak out. There had been no mirrors in the ashram. I had shaved my head already and looked like I had just escaped from a concentration camp.

I thought that this couldn't be what enlightenment was about. When I came back to the ashram, I said, "I've really appreciated, Baba, what you've given me, but I'm going to want to see other parts of India."

I went to Bombay and bumped into Mohan, who was there taking care of Radha, who had a bad case of hepatitis. We had met each other when they followed Ram Dass and Muktananda out to California. Mohan would take me to the luncheon buffet at the Taj, the big fancy hotel, and almost like a Jewish mother would force me to eat. I'd go back to my hotel and throw up because I couldn't digest the food. After a few days Mohan said, "Why don't you go to where Ram Dass is, up in Kausani?" What a great idea!

I got to Delhi, went up to Nainital, and came walking up to the Evelyn Hotel. There's Danny on the veranda with his *lungi* [a sarong-style piece of cloth men wear instead of pants] pulled up, sunning himself, eating white bread toast with jam on it, and reading a novel. What is this scene about? I mean, this guy is sitting there sunbathing, reading a nonspiritual book! Something is wrong here.

I went up to Kausani. At first the people there didn't recognize me because I looked so different. Less than a week later a telegram came from Nainital saying, "Maharajji has returned to Kainchi. Come immediately." Everybody was so excited, saying,

"Oh Maharajji, Maharajji, he's so great." I'm thinking, "Well, Ram Dass said Muktananda is the same being as Maharajji, and I hadn't really felt a connection to him at all."

The bus stops at the Kainchi ashram, and even though I was telling myself I was feeling very blasé, I was the first person off the bus. I went running in. There was a place you stop to wash your feet, but I didn't stop. There's all of these temples, and I went, *whoop,* right by them. I made all of the turns, almost as if I knew where to go, and there was Maharajji on his takhat. He sees me across the courtyard and gets all excited. The feeling was like we were five-year-olds, best friends, and I had been off to summer camp for two weeks, which seemed like forever, and he was so glad to see me again.

I have these apples, which I drop at his feet, and he starts whacking me on the head, saying, "Bramananda Yogi, Bramananda Yogi." I still don't know what that means. Krishna Das said that there was some yogi up in the Kumaon hills who had that name a long time ago. Who knows. He never explained; I never asked. But as he's hitting me, words begin to fail me. I felt that for the first time in my life I was home, that my life was not a mistake. No matter how hard or how easy the rest of my life was going to be, its meaning, its completion, its everything had been found in that moment.

MOHAN: When Radha and I first got to India, we spent a few nights in Muktananda's ashram in Ganeshpuri. The conditions in the ashram were quite austere for Western aspirants. We were given preferential VIP guest treatment. We'd had a luncheon for him at our home in America, and Radha was quite close to him before we went to India.

One day we were kneeling right in front of him. Swami Muktananda had a large collection of hats, and he wanted this hat I was wearing—a wacky hippie skullcap, multicolored, with hanging things in the front. I had been wearing this hat since Europe. I had gotten it in a very bizarre manner. I was in Amsterdam, naked in a sauna, and I saw a tattoo on some guy's butt that I recognized. His girlfriend was the sister of a woman I was going to marry before I was with Radha. They were hippies living in Amsterdam, and she made this hat and gave it to me. Tied in with my '60s lustful, promiscuous lifestyle, it wasn't a saintly hat with any religious significance. I wouldn't give it to Muktananda, and instantly it felt like psychic spears were being thrown through us.

From the outside, it looked like all the devotees at the Ganeshpuri ashram were doing very strict practices. They were up at four thirty in the morning doing the thousand names of Vishnu, the Vishnu Sahashranam. It was a very rigid program. We were exempt from that, and here the guru wanted something and I refused to give it to him.

The next morning I said, "Let's leave." We're up way before dawn. There is only a narrow one-lane road that goes past the ashram to the town of Ganeshpuri before it turns and goes back out to civilization. The ashram is on this dead end, a beautiful marble palace in the middle of an intense tropical jungle, completely remote. The buses would not stop. Finally around seven the good swami comes out, and we pranaam. He gives us his blessings to leave, and the next instant a bus stops.

I wore this hat all the time. That day I first met Maharajji, we didn't know we were going to meet him. We were coming down from Kausani, and no one expected him to be in Kainchi. We were just stopping to pranaam to Hanuman. It was a complete shock. There were no crowds, no one around. I am kneeling in front of Maharajji, and I am hoping I have something worthy of giving him, to influence him, to manipulate him to like me. I came from the world of manipulation. He took the hat off my head. He lifted it up. Ah, I felt so blessed that he wanted something I could give him! I was overjoyed. "Oh, take it." He put it on his head. Fantastic.

Then he asked, "Muktananda? He liked your hat?" He winked at me and put the hat back on my head.

So I knew he knew. We hadn't told anyone about this embarrassing incident. Once I knew he knew, that's it, check-mate. That whole scene meant nothing to the other people who were there. They didn't know the history of the hat or what it meant to me. They just saw him take a hat and put it on his head. It was a silly, stupid hat. I am sure they just saw some goofy thing.

Everyone had these intimate experiences in front of each other, totally intimate, that were meaningless to everyone else. It was pretty mind-blowing. I knew he knew. I have no explanation of how he knew that stuff, but it was very freeing.

We all had that experience of Maharajji's saying something or even just making a gesture or winking in our direction at the perfect moment, so that we knew he knew—everything. You'll hear this again and again in Westerners' stories, because it made such an impact, at least at first. After a while, we understood and even expected, in the very core of our being, that Maharajji did indeed know everything. Our past, present, and future were all available to him like an open book.

At times this was wonderful. Your heart was full of love and suddenly a place would open up in front of him, and you could touch his feet while he patted your head. Or you hadn't heard from home in a while, and he'd tell you not to worry, that they were all right. Or he would bring up something you were angry about in the past and diffuse it with humor. We had never experienced such overwhelming love in our lives.

But then you'd be having a bad day. Another devotee pushed your buttons, and you were ready to explode. You were getting ignored by Maharajji, who threw fruit to everyone but you. You'd see your desire for attention, your reactivity, your anger, your greed, your sexual secrets . . . and you knew he saw it all. Nowhere to run, nowhere to hide. Many tears were shed while facing your inner darkness.

And still he loved you. This is unconditional love—where there are literally no conditions for receiving that love. You don't have to be "good," to be "pure," to be "holy." You are worthy of being loved just as you are.

What teaching could be greater than that?

6

Christ and Hanuman
Are One

Spring 1971

Ask, and it shall be given you; seek, and ye shall find; knock, and it shall be opened unto you: For every one that asketh receiveth; and he that seeketh findeth; and to him that knocketh it shall be opened.

—MATTHEW 7:7–8

W hile I was in South India with Sai Baba, in the spring of 1971, others had already found Maharajji and were having sporadic darshans, some in Vrindavan in February and March and by April and May in Kainchi, although they would then be sent away with some frequency. Some joined Ram Dass on his tour with Swami Muktananda, while others went here and there for meditation courses or to see more of the endless array of holy places in India.

Krishna Das, Dwarkanath, and Danny picked up Ram Dass at Ganesh-puri to drive back up north, and they stopped in Vrindavan to see if Maharajji was there. They had learned about the ashram in Vrindavan from Dada and had stopped there at the beginning of their trip, but Maharajji hadn't been there. Again, Maharajji wasn't there. They sang kirtan and hung out in the front around the temple for a while, then decided it was time to leave. Just as they were going out the gate of the ashram, a little Fiat skidded to a stop, and Maharajji got out and went into the ashram. That's when Ram Dass gave Maharajji acid again.

RAM DASS: Maharajji said, "Did you give me some pills, some medicine last time?"
"Yeah."
"Did I take it?"
"I don't know." I'd had some doubt.
"You got any more?"
I got my medicine bag and held out three tabs of strong LSD, and he clearly swallowed one pill at a time. I sat at his feet as a psychologist would to watch his behavior. About halfway through he pulls his blanket over his head and then brings the blanket down and makes a face like a madman! He was kidding. He didn't react at all. He just said, "These medicines, these plants, were well known in ancient times. They let you go into the room with Christ, but you can't stay. You can't stay."

DANNY: That was the second time Maharajji blew my mind with an unexpected arrival. It was also the time that he said to Krishna Das, "You like horses," and he said to Dwarkanath, "And you like cows." Then he said to me, "Your favorite animal is an elephant, but you must never go near elephants," and he repeated and repeated it. He started yelling, "Ram Dass, come over here. Tell him he must never go near elephants." What was that about? You never knew with him.

Fast forward to Sri Lanka, my postdoc years. I'm back in India with my Harvard professor David McClelland after Maharajji's passed away. There was a guy who had raised an orphan elephant from the time it was a baby. This elephant was now big and had been trained to do tricks. The guy says to me, "We have a custom here in Sri Lanka to show how brave you are: you go under the belly of an elephant and then we pluck a hair from the elephant and make a bracelet from it for you as a sign of your courage." I declined.

Six months later I'm back in Cambridge, and the McClellands get a letter from this guy's daughter, saying, "Oh, it is so sad. My father was having the elephant do tricks for a busload of German tourists, and the elephant grabbed the arm of a tourist and wouldn't let go. My father was trying to get him under control, and the elephant turned on him, picked him up in his trunk, threw him down on the steps, and killed him on the spot."

When Anasuya (Teresa Weil) went to India, she didn't think Maharajji was findable, so she wasn't looking for him. At one point she went to Bombay to pick up her mail and found it was cheaper to go to a Goenka course than to stay at a hotel because it provided meals. "I thought, 'I don't have to sit Vipassana or do this meditation if I don't want. I'll just be quiet. No one will know I'm sitting there doing my mantra, right?' That's how I took my first ten-day retreat, but I got totally hooked on Vipassana."

ANASUYA: Danny didn't go on the Muktananda yatra with the other guys; he had gone to Bombay to do another course, and that's where we met. While I did the second ten-day meditation retreat, he went to do an isolation retreat. When he came back we met Krishna Das in Bombay and went to Ganeshpuri. Then I went to Bhopal, where I found that Ram Charan Das, who had given me mantra initiation, was off helping the villagers do their harvest.

Danny and I had decided to meet up in Delhi. In the meantime, Danny had seen Maharajji in Vrindavan, who was giving them the talk about "women and gold" being impediments to liberation.

Danny said, "Maharajji, I met this girl in Bombay."

He asked Danny if he had a picture of me. When he said he did, Maharajji asked to see it. He asked my name, where I was, and what I was doing.

Danny said, "She is in Bhopal with her guru."

The next day Maharajji said, "Do you still have that picture? She's in Bhopal, but she is not with her guru." Then he said, "She loves you, and she loves you in the proper way, like Sita loves Ram, and you will marry her."

When I met Danny in Delhi, he told me that story, and I said, "Well, I want to meet this person who is planning my future for me."

Danny said that they were going up to Nainital to see Maharajji. I wanted to go too. Ram Dass said I couldn't ride up with them in the VW van. *Hmm,* I thought. *Okay, then I'll take a regular bus.* A day later he relented and said I could come in the van. He hadn't wanted a woman in the van. He still hadn't realized things were never in his control.

The first time I met Maharajji I thought, "Wow, such a nice man, such a nice old man." I knew he was supposed to be some great guru, a great siddha, but I didn't feel that at first. He was just very sweet and kind to me, personable and open, leaning in, looking directly at me, asking me questions, really engaged. The second or the third time I saw him, I felt a strong connection. I was like, "Whoa, I really like this guy, but I just took initiation with this other guru. What does this mean?" It was all so new to me. I had no understanding. Was this a bond that I had created that was going to last lifetimes? Is it bad karma to find someone else who you thought was your guru? It was rather confusing.

I'd get up early and sit for an hour. We'd go to Maharajji's temple and then come back in the evening, and I would sit again for another hour. After a while when I would sit, I would be talking to Maharajji in my mind and praying to him, saying, "I am so confused. Am I doing the right practice? I'm doing this Buddhist practice, and I met this Hindu guru and I took a mantra from him, and now I met you and I feel so connected to you." I just kept asking him in my mind, "Am I doing the right practice?"

One day we were sitting in the room at Kainchi we called his "office." Ram Dass had brought the blanket that he had carried from Australia; finally Maharajji and the blanket were in the same place, so he could offer him this beautiful blanket. Maharajji picked it up and immediately handed the blanket to me. I thought he was giving it to me to put somewhere, so I placed it on the ground next me. Maharajji looked at me and said, "That's for you. I'm giving you this blanket." I looked at Ram Dass like, "Whoa . . ." I'm really the last person he'd want to give the blanket to. I was the only woman there with the group of guys. I didn't want Ram Dass's blanket.

Maharajji had such a twinkle in his eye; he looked over at Ram Dass and said, "Is that okay if I give her the blanket?"

Ram Dass kind of laughed and said, "It's perfect, Maharajji. It's perfect."

I never asked Maharajji what he had said to Danny about marrying me. What was I going to say? I thought maybe he knew something I didn't. Danny and I hadn't started staying in the same room, but we were definitely spending a lot of time together.

At some point in the darshan Maharajji told everyone to leave, and then he said to me, "Not you. You stay. You have a question for me." Everybody got up and left, looking at me enviously.

When I was alone with him and K. K., I could barely remember what my question was. Then I said, "Am I doing the right sadhana?"

He just said, "*Thik hai.* Yeah, it's okay." That was his answer, "It's okay."

Then he stopped and looked out the window. He said, "Do you think that by coming to temples like this it brings you closer to God?"

It was such an interesting thing to ask me, because it acted like a koan. I realized I didn't know. I don't know how to explain it, but I had the deepest experience of *not knowing.* It was like my mind stopped for a second, completely stopped, and my heart burst open. I started weeping and weeping; I wasn't unhappy, but I started to cry uncontrollably.

At first he didn't say anything, but I could not stop. He said to K. K., "What's wrong, what's wrong? Ask her what's wrong." I couldn't speak. He'd wait for a few seconds, and then he'd ask K. K. to ask me again what was wrong.

Finally I could speak, and I said, "I feel so much love." He sent K. K. out to get me some hot milk to drink.

I don't think Maharajji ever set out to give people an initiation or said, "I'm your guru," but for me that was it.

BALARAM DAS: I finally arrived in Nainital on May 5, 1971, and checked into a hotel. I dropped off my big backpack and went walking into the bazaar down in Tallital, the lower part of Nainital, where K. K. lives. There was this photography shop, and I saw pictures of Maharajji in the window. I couldn't speak a word of Hindi, but I stopped when I saw the picture, walked in, and said, "Neem Karoli Baba."

The man knew some broken English. He said, "Kainchi, he's in Kainchi. Come tomorrow and get a bus to Kainchi." I knew you couldn't go empty-handed, so I got a little package of puffed rice with raisins and almonds, Indian trail mix.

The next morning at the bus station, there must have been three hundred people assaulting the one ticket window. No lines, it was just clawing, and there was no way I could cope with that. I couldn't speak the language. I was feeling very depressed, and it must have showed, because an Indian family came up to me and said, "We are going to Almora. You can ride with us in our taxi." They took pity on me because they saw there was no way I would be able to do this on my own.

They dropped me off at Kainchi. There was the ashram. I walked over the bridge. I could see Maharajji sitting on his takhat on the side of the courtyard. I went through the gate, kicked my shoes off, and walked over to him. It was like the expression "walking on air." I actually experienced it that time. I had no sense of my feet touching the ground. I was just looking at him and walked straight there. I put the prasad at the edge of the takhat. He looked at me and said a few things, but I had no idea what he was saying. I went and sat at the edge of the group of Indians.

He called one of his people over and pointed at me; the guy disappeared and came back with a straw mat for me to sit

K. K. Sah and his niece Kiran.

on, because I was sitting on the concrete. He was always so
concerned about your physical well-being. Sitting on the concrete
was not part of the program, so he gave me the mat. He didn't
say anything else to me. I was there for maybe twenty, thirty
minutes. I got my box of prasad—the puris and potatoes—and I
sat there with my jaw hanging open.

   Then he called me and through a translator said, *"Aab jao, phir
aana.* Go now, come again. And on the way out, bow in front of
each temple." I had not done that on the way in. I had walked
right past all three of them, and obviously he had noticed. So
of course I did. I had never done that before. It was the start of
a whole transformation. I bowed in front of him, got my shoes,
crossed the bridge, and started walking back to Bhowali. It was
still early, nine probably, and I was feeling very exhilarated.

   I hadn't gone very far when this young Indian man runs up to

me and says, "When you get to Nainital, you have to meet with
K. K. Sah. He works in the government building, up in Mallital,
the top. Everybody knows K. K. Sah." Then Maharajji drove by in
an Ambassador car; he was looking at me out the window.

I walked up to Bhowali, caught a bus to Nainital, and spent
the rest of the afternoon tracking down K. K. He wasn't home,
but his sister Bina gave me tea and little snacks, and after a while
Rameshwar Das came. He told me I should come to the Evelyn
Hotel. I got my luggage and switched over to the Evelyn. That
first day is still really vivid in my memory.

RAGHU: I managed to get over to India by November of 1970,
just as I turned twenty-five. Ram Dass didn't know where
Maharajji was when I arrived, so I went to Pondicherry, a French
colony seaside town from the eighteenth century—very exotic
and enchanting and the home of another saint, Sri Aurobindo,
and his shakti, simply called Mother.

It was arranged that I could have a short visit with the
Mother of the ashram. She was very old, and I had heard she
had some sort of muscle disease that affected her motor control.
I wondered, "Geez, it'd be terrible if all I saw was a decrepit
old body instead of a holy woman." I was ushered into a room
that was full of light. Mother contacted me with her eyes, and
I never noticed her body. It was my first spiritual experience
with a human who had gone beyond duality. It was a very deep
experience.

I then went to Muktananda's ashram, where Ram Dass finally
gave me the info to get up to Maharajji. Even all these years
later, I can hear the clang of the doors in Kainchi as Maharajji
used to smack them open to come out from the back room onto
the porch where his takhat was. As soon as I saw him, the first

thought was, "Oh, that's what Ram Dass was all about. Wow!"
And the second thought was that *knowing* that you always knew
him, always will, knowing that presence was always there.

Maharajji said, "Where were you before you came here?"

I was going to say, "Well, I've been at Swami Muktananda's."

But before I could say anything, he looked at me and in English
said, "Mother, Mother."

The second I saw Maharajji, I absolutely knew I was home.

Jesus on the Main Line

The small group of Westerners had some very powerful darshans with
Maharajji during this time, especially when Maharajji started talking
about Jesus. This prompted the Westerners to start wearing crosses,
even those who were not raised in the Christian tradition. During the
last few years of his life, when Westerners were with him, Maharajji
spoke often about Jesus and about how Hanuman and Jesus are one.

Hanuman is the Hindu deity most closely associated with Maharajji—
a monkey god who is an incarnation of Lord Shiva. Hanuman is noted
for his devotion to Lord Rama; his only desire was to serve Rama always, and his greatness stems from his complete merger with Rama.
He plays a significant role in the Hindu epic the *Ramayana*. When the
chapter called "Sunderkand" ("The Beautiful") was recited—which details Hanuman's exploits in his quest to help Rama find his wife, Sita
(who was abducted by the evil Ravana)—Maharajji would cry. There is
a picture of Hanuman tearing open his chest, revealing that Rama and
Sita live in his heart; it's very much like the Sacred Heart of Jesus—a
representation of divine love within.

Jesus was always coming into the conversation. Maharajji once talked
about Abraham Lincoln, saying that Lincoln was president, but he knew

LSR Foundation Archive

The Taos Hanuman.

that Christ was really the president. He told us to see the reflection of Christ in everyone.

When one Westerner asked, "What can I do to gain pure love for Sri Rama?"

Maharajji replied, "You will get pure love for Ram by the blessings of Christ."

ANASUYA (from her journal):

May 14, 1971
Asked for crosses. Should wear them out. Gave them to him. Touched them to his head.

Isha [Jesus], Hanuman, Ram, and Krishna are all one. Sweeper came and touched his feet. Maharajji said everyone is God, see God in everyone. Maharajji said we should love everyone as God and love each other.

Asked me to sit in front of him and said, there is one Guru. I must take pity on all creatures. Repeated to everyone that

God is *one*—Isha and Ram are one. Love is God. See no differences, love all the same. Christ felt no pain when they stuck the nails in him. Asked us all, especially Mitchell, if we understood. Told him we understood, but haven't experienced it. Asked me if I understood. Told him that I did with my mind, but not yet with my heart. He said Nay! All is one, must love all as God. Closed his eyes, hand on his heart. When he opened them, he said the mind travels thousands of miles in the blink of an eye. Said all religions are the same, we shouldn't think there is any difference between Ram and Christ and Hanuman, all lead to God. Jesus made a great contribution to the world.

Mitchell asked what was the best method of meditation. Maharajji said to do as Jesus did and see God in everyone, then said that Jesus on the cross felt only love. Take pity on all and love all as God.

If you love God enough, there will be no separation. Jim asked how to get rid of separation. Maharajji said there is no separation. Said not to have evil thoughts of others, not to see evil, hear evil. Can't realize God if you see differences. We must learn to find the love within.

RAGHU (from his journal):

May 30, 1971
Ram Dass: How did Christ meditate? After this question was asked, Maharajji began to cry, and two teardrops came from his eyes. It seems when Maharajji was crying that he turned right into Christ and his powerful love for mankind and was then so moved to tears. A very powerful experience for those of us in his presence. Christ appearing in form.

He then said: Christ was lost in love. He was one with all beings. He had great love for all in the world. He was crucified so that his spirit could spread throughout the world. He was one with God. He sacrificed his body for religion. He never died. He never died. He is *atman* [the essential unchanging self or soul]. He lives in the hearts of all.

Ram Dass: Does he reincarnate in form?

Maharajji: He is the whole world.

Ram Dass: Why was he maligned so?

Maharajji: It is so with all saints, but he sees only love in all. One should not speak, hear, or see evil. One should see love everywhere and in everyone. *See the good in all.* When Christ was alive, they ignored him. After he was crucified, they worshipped him. *He is in the heart of every being.*

RADHA (from her journal):

October 24, 1971

The second time he called us down, he had us sing a Christian song to him.

Maharajji to RD [Ram Dass]: You shouldn't fear anyone. If you live in truth, God will always stand with you. No fear.

RD: Christ feared nothing.

Maharajji: Christ didn't fear death.

Maharajji began to cry and held his hand to his head. Said, the body passes away. Everything is impermanent except love of God. If you have a pure heart and mind, you love God. How can I keep you from making puris if you love God? Some places only let sadhus prepare the food. But here I let all bhaktas make food, because they have pure hearts and all are equal in the eyes of God.

RD: We feel so impure.

Maharajji: (twice) I don't believe you're impure. I know you're pure and you love God.

Ram Dass cried.

Maharajji: If you love God, you overcome all impurities. The blood in us all is one, the arms, the legs, the hearts are all one. The same blood flows through us all. God is one. No fear. People didn't believe Christ until he died. Ram Dass is a yogi and should fear nothing. The heart never grows old.

KRISHNA DAS: At that time of my life, I was very interested in methods, trying to find a meditation practice that would liberate me. In those days we were thinking you had to sit up straight for like four hundred years and breathe. I noticed one day sitting with Maharajji that my idea of happiness—which I equated with enlightenment—was someplace where I wouldn't be. Unconsciously, my belief was that this space—enlightenment, freedom, nirvana—was somewhere else, and it had nothing to do with me.

When Maharajji said to meditate like Christ, that Christ lost himself in love, everyone was included in that. It wasn't somewhere else. It was all-consuming and included me. It was love. And love is what we were experiencing in those moments with Maharajji—unconditional, spacious, all-inclusive love. The pope never said Jesus lost himself in love. For my friends who were brought up Catholic, it was guilt and shame and sin. When Maharajji said that, it changed my thinking. Love, all-inclusive, nonspecific, involving each person, including yourself. Lost in love, he became the supreme atman. He recognized the oneness of it all as love.[1]

Much later, when the group was considerably larger, Maharajji one day sent the Westerners scurrying, looking for crosses. After checking the homes of the *angraisies* (foreigners), they came back to Maharajji without having found even one cross. One devotee recorded the rest of the story.

IAIN (from his journal):

> We trembled into his room to report our failure, only to find him shining in mirthful glory and pulling out a *whole box* of beautiful, loved, and worn crucifixes and saints' medallions. In giggles of delight, he passed them out to all the satsang, enough for everyone there. He looked at us quizzically.
>
> "Where did these come from? Oh, where did I get these? [giggle, giggle] Christ sent them to me! He sent them parcel post!"

It is difficult to express the extraordinary space that was generated each time Maharajji talked about Jesus, which he did often. It was as if he was there with Jesus, as if we were all there with Jesus. He talked about how Jesus helped the poor, and all are poor until they are one with Jesus. Always, always, he came back to *sub ek*—it's all one.

Maharajji's devotees came from every religion and social class. As a siddha, an enlightened master, he had long ago thrown away his Brahmin thread and recognized no difference between the highest or lowest in the social order or caste system. And for us Westerners, there was never any push for us to change our beliefs, only to recognize the reality of *sub ek*.

7

Kausani:
The Monsoon
Retreat

Summer 1971

*In order to understand the world, one has to
turn away from it on occasion.*

—ALBERT CAMUS

Kausani is a hill station thirty-two miles north of Almora, famous for its spectacular panoramic view of the high Himalayan peaks Trisul, Nanda Devi, and Panchchuli. Anashakti Ashram (also known as Gandhi Ashram) sits on a ridge overlooking this powerful Himalayan range. It was here in 1929 that Mahatma Gandhi spent time writing his commentary *Anashakti Yoga*. He called the area the "Switzerland of India."

Rameshwar Das

Eating on the floor at Kausani. Left to right: Dwarkanath, Iain, Tenny, Krishna Das, Ram Dass, Balaram Das, and Raghu.

In the summer of 1971, Ram Dass went to Kausani not for the view, but because it was the perfect place to do a meditation retreat.

RAM DASS: I said to Maharajji, "I know this teacher, Munindra. He's going to teach me meditation up in Kausani."

Maharajji said, "If you desire." That's the kiss of death. *If you desire.* He never liked me meditating.

I went to Kausani and took a few of the boys—Dwarkanath, Raghu, Danny, Ramesh, and Krishna Das. Tenny was there. We got up on the hill, and Munindra sent a note saying his mother was sick and he wouldn't be there this summer. A lot of us felt sad. I said, "Guys, let's just stay here."

One of them went down to Kainchi and told Maharajji what was happening. He started to send more people up to Kausani to "meditate with Ram Dass." Of course I was mad. I was always getting mad. We moved into the Gandhi Ashram and had a retreat. I didn't meditate, because I was the teacher. We were having fun. Singing and stories and sitting in the sun looking at the mountains. When we got back to Kainchi in the fall, I came in and Maharajji said, "Here's the meditation teacher. Here's the meditation teacher." I was so mad at him, but you couldn't stay mad.

Ram Dass may have been upset about the change in *his* plan for the summer in Kausani, but for others it was an incredible opportunity.

LAXMAN: After I arrived in Delhi and hooked up with my brother, we left for the foothills. Maharajji was not in Kainchi, so we made our way to Kausani. There I see all of these saintly looking satsang people in white, and here I am with my hippie bell bottoms. Certainly not part of their club. I mentioned it to Ram Dass, and he told me it was just the look and we'd get some white clothes.

I was brought into a small room made of wood; there was a two-inch-thick mat on the floor and that was it. We lived simply, ate simply, didn't talk, and just sang. On weekends we would chant *Sri Ram Jai Ram* and maybe some spiritual American revival songs. I was so light of being and naturally high all of the time. Food was very limited and very simple. I must have lost about thirty pounds. The big test for me was to get from my room across the courtyard to the dining room over crushed stone that was pretty sharp. I had very tender Western feet, and it took me over a month to be able to walk barefoot across those stones without feeling a thing. As an aspiring yogi, I felt extremely accomplished.

How those three months shaped all of us was unbelievable. I totally surrendered and was opened up. Once a week everyone would get an interview with Ram Dass. It was fabulous. He would do eye contact with me, and his question would be, "If there is some secret or anything inside that bothers you, or disturbs you, or needs to get released, tell me now."

I'm inside looking all over my mind, my body. I'd think, "What am I holding on to? What secrets do I need to let go of?" I'd say, "Well, I don't think I have any."

"That's okay. Maybe something will come up the next time." He had the most beautiful smile.

I couldn't wait for the next week when we'd meet again, I'd get lifted up by Ram Dass's gaze, and I'd think about what might come out of it the next time.

Murari and Rukmini (Tom and Linda Spiritoso) came to India in June 1971 from Philadelphia. They had heard a Ram Dass tape and then a lecture. In the years it took them to get it together to go to India, Rukmini became involved with Krishna Consciousness.

RUKMINI: The first month in India was an emotional, psychological, and physical disaster—culture shock. To preserve some semblance of sanity, Murari and I had been heavily indulging in "sense gratification" (to use a Krishna Consciousness term). We were sleeping a lot, eating a lot, and buying things. It was during the latter occupation that "it" happened. We wandered into a clothing store and *bam!* Hanging near the ceiling was a large picture of Maharajji. Since Ram Dass in *Be Here Now* had discouraged any attempts to find Maharajji, we had made none.

It turned out that the clothing store owner was a devotee. He told us that Maharajji would be found in Kainchi. Within two days we were there, but to our disappointment and crazy kind of relief, Maharajji had just left for Vrindavan that morning, and no one was there except for Krishna Das and Balaram. I say "relief" because, remembering Ram Dass's advice not to seek out Maharajji, we of course were absolutely freaked out at the thought of seeing him and possibly being thrown out. We felt that his rejection would have been like God throwing us out of the kingdom of heaven.

So we didn't get to see him in Kainchi. Luckily Krishna Das and Balaram Das advised us to see Ram Dass, who was in Kausani. We didn't need any persuasion. The next morning we were there, and we remained for three weeks, to cool out. It felt

Rameshwar Das

Front row, left to right: Tukaram, Mariam, Peter Brawley, Raghu, Vishwambar, Murari, Annapurna. Back row, left to right: Ravi Das, Carlos Vishwanath, Dwarkanath, Sita, Danny, Ram Dass, Rukmini, Iain, Harinam Das.

so right! We began to realize that Maharajji had sent us to be
with Ram Dass before we could be ready to see him.

ANASUYA: Ram Dass and the boys were going to go up to
Kausani to do a retreat with Munindra. One day Maharajji looked
at me and said, "What are you going to do?"

"I just want to stay here with you."

I thought, "Why are they going up to Kausani when they
could be here with Maharajji?" At that point I was totally in love
with Maharajji.

He said, "There is a *kutir* [a small hut] up the stream. You can
stay in the kutir. You can meditate up there. I will have someone
bring food to you. Can you cook your own food?"

"Yes, I can cook my own food."

He was taking such an interest. So that was my plan, to spend
the summer in the kutir up the river, just do my practice, and
come down to see Maharajji every day.

Then Danny and I went to Delhi. I think he had a visa issue,
and I probably went to get my mail. Maharajji gave me 100 rupees
to buy a sari because I was wearing *kurta* [a man's long shirt]
and pajama pants. I bought one sari and one Punjabi outfit.
Danny and I had a near sexual encounter there—we slept in the
same bed.

When we came back from Delhi, Maharajji called me into his
room and said, "You and Danny decided to live together."

"No, we didn't."

"Yes, you did. You talked about it. You decided you were going
to stay together."

"No, we didn't, Maharajji."

"Don't lie to me." Then he said, "You should live together. You
should go to Kausani with him and live with him." He arranged

for Mr. Soni, who was the head of the forest department, to have us stay in the forest guesthouse up there while we looked for a place.

Suddenly I was going up to Kausani and staying with Danny. I was really sad that I wasn't going to stay in the kutir for the summer, but on the other hand I loved Danny. Anyway, Maharajji told us we had to go live together, which is really wild for a Hindu. Most Hindu gurus would not be telling people to do that. He was not your average Hindu guru, which is why I think we ended up with him. He was so outside of any limits and boundaries, cultural or perceptual. So that's how I ended up going to Kausani.

Coming Down from Kausani

From time to time, someone would come down from Kausani for some reason—to go to Delhi for a passport issue, for example, or go to the Evelyn Hotel in Nainital for a break from the "meditation retreat." On the way from Kausani to Nainital, the bus passes the Kainchi ashram. Occasionally, when someone would stop in Kainchi, Maharajji would be there!

RAGHU: I came down from Kausani to go to the Canadian Embassy in Delhi to get my passport renewed. On my way I stopped in Kainchi. Maharajji was sitting outside on the takhat. He looked at me, and the first thing he said was, "Are you married?"

"No, I'm not married."

"Sure you're not married?"

"Nope. Don't want to get married. Just want to marry God." That sent him into peals of laughter.

Then he said, "Did you have darshan of a Tibetan lama? Did you get teachings from him?"

"No, I've never met a Tibetan."

"*Jao.* [Go.] "

I went down to Delhi, and it turned out the High Commissioner at the Canadian Embassy was a friend of my former boss at the radio station, Jeff Sterling. The High Commissioner was James George, a noted Buddhist scholar. He invited me for lunch at the embassy mansion. I said, "Is it true that they are letting Tibetan refugees into Canada?"

He said yes. Then he went, "As a matter of fact . . . ," and in walked Kalu Rinpoche and a retinue of monks from another room on their way to join us for lunch.

I was stunned. All I could think was, "Wow, Maharajji knows the future. He knows everything that is going on." I was really, really stunned.

I went in for lunch and sat right across from Kalu Rinpoche, one of the great Tibetan siddhas of the last century. It was a huge honor, never mind a spiritually transformative experience, to be with this venerable Rinpoche.

At one point I said to him, "Meditating up in the Himalayas where I have been is so easy, but now that I am in Delhi it is difficult to get any kind of center. Do you have to be in the mountains to really transform?"

Kalu gave me a whole discourse on the seven siddhas of India from ancient times. One was a spinner. One made clay pots. They became one-pointed through their work, became one with what they were doing. He said it's not necessary to be in a cave. It is here, and you've got to do it right here, which is a tremendous teaching. I felt like I was on acid all the way back to Kausani.

And yes, Maharajji did get me married.

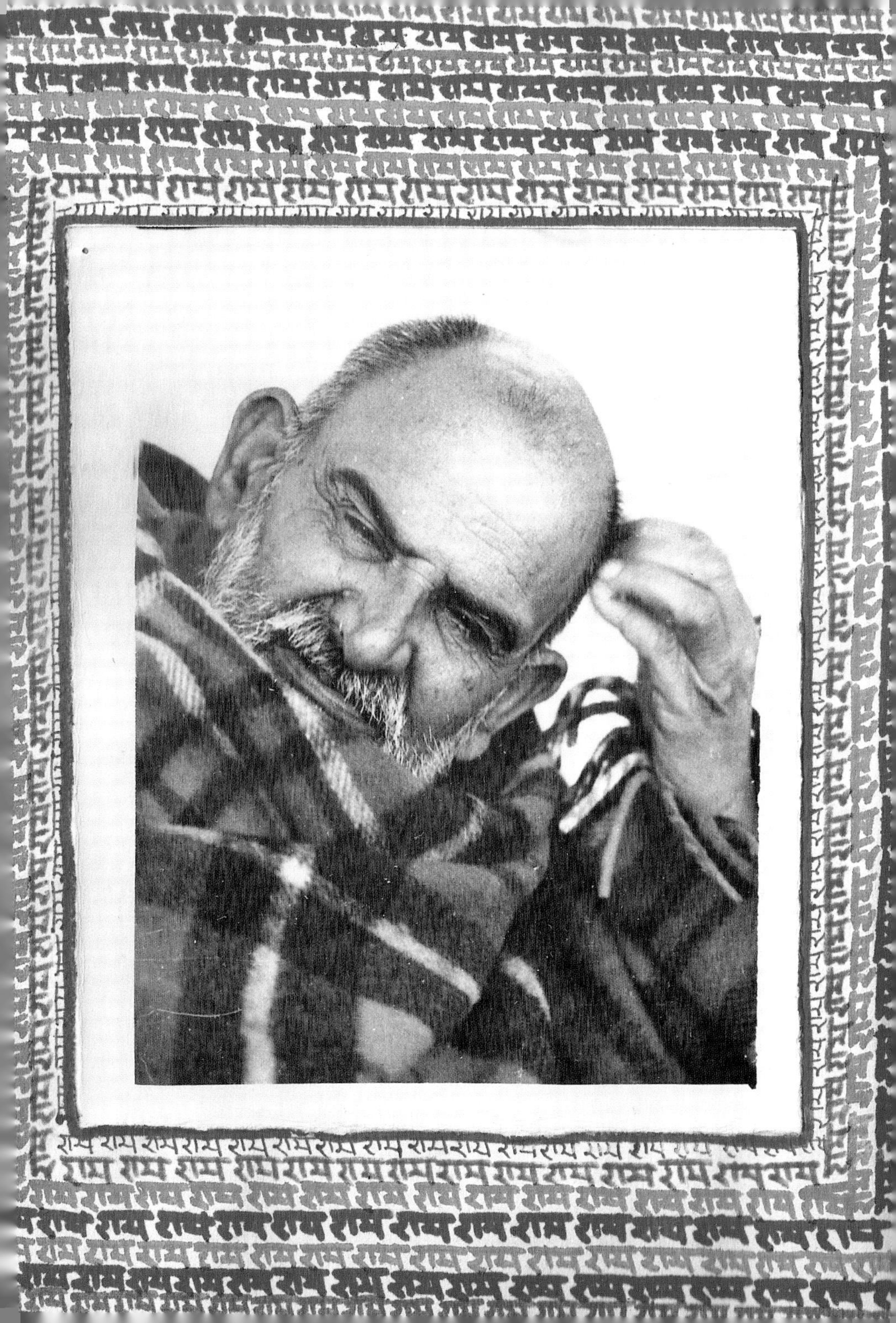

- See all beings as the reflection of Chri...
- You will get pure love for Ram by the
                              blessings of Christ.

- Everyone is a reflection of my face.
- A saint doesn't need money. All the
  wealth in the world is mine. Even the
  money in America is mine.
- Give up money, sex, and attachment.
- Birds and saints don't collect.
- Help everyone who throws sticks at you
  and calls you names.
- A saint's heart melts whenever anyone
  else's heart comes near the fire.
- The guru is not eternal.
- It is not necessary to meet your guru
  on the physical plane.
- The body passes away. Everything is
  impermanent except love of God.
- Maharaj-ji once asked a girl, "Do you
  like sorrow or joy?" (He asked this four
  times). The girl answered, "I've never
  known joy, I've only known sorrow.
  I love sorrow - It brings me close to His...
- You get gyan from suffering. You are
  alone with God when sick, when in the
  cremation ground & when in the hospita...
  You call on God when you suffer.
  GOD IS...

There is only one. Christ, Hanuman, Krishna & Ram are all one. You can't realize God if you see differences.

- See everything in the universe for good.
- Love all beings as God even if they hurt, shame you. Be like Ghandi and Christ.
- THE WORST PUNISHMENT IS TO THROW SOMEO OUT OF YOUR HEART.
- <u>I SEND PEOPLE AWAY BECAUSE ATTACHMENT HAPPENS BOTH WAYS.</u>
- I CAN'T GET ANGRY WITH YOU - NOT EVEN IN A DREAM.
- If YOU ARE ANGRY, YOUR HEART GETS TURNED OFF.
- <u>IF YOU LOVE GOD, YOU OVERCOME ALL IMPURITIES.</u>
- THE HEART NEVER GROWS OLD.
- THE BEST SERVICE YOU CAN DO IS TO KEEP YOU THOUGHTS ON God.
- KEEP God IN YOUR HEART LIKE YOU KEEP MONEY IN A SAFE.
- <u>I AM ALWAYS in communion with You.</u>
- A suffering MAN is HIGHER than God. One should help him.
- IF You REMEMBER God, he takes CARE of everything.
- TRUTH is the most difficult TAPASYA.
- Men will hate you for telling the truth
- If You Live IN TRUTH, God will ALWAYS
STAND ...

...SS should not be taken in the [cold?]
climate. It should be taken in the [cold?]
cold, in a quiet place, alone, with
shanti. It allows one to come into
the room and *pranam* to Christ, bu[t]
after two hours you must leave. The b[est]
"medicine" is to love Christ.

- Money brings anxieties.
- <u>Clinging to money is A LACK of tRUST IN God.</u>

- Keep only as much money as you nee[d]
for daily needs. Distribute the rest.
- Money should be used to help others.
- Give up money and all wealth is yours
- Money is around a saint, not through [?]
- THE JADE elephant will NOT bRing you
CLOSER To God.
- If you have enough faith you can gi[ve]
up money & possessions. God will gi[ve]
you everything you need for your spirit
development.
- <u>HOLD ON TO NOTHING.</u>
- All women are mothers. Serve all wo[men]
the way you'd serve your mother.
- a pure woman (sati) takes you to God i[n a]
moment. A pure woman is better tha[n a]
hundred yogis.
- LOVE IS The only [?]

Never act out of desire. When you get thirsty you forget god.

If you want to see god, kill desires. Desire are in the mind. When you have a desire for something, don't act on it and it will go away.

All is the blessing of god. But if you desi the puris (Indian breads), don't take them. A if you don't want them, don't take them.

- MAHARAJ-JI: Does YouR teacher have desir
  R.D. - Yes, but he told me NOT to have desir
  M: Do you have desires?
  R.D.: Yes.
  M: Then he didn't teach you. How can h teach what he isn't?

- THE mind goes a thousand miles in the blin of an eye. The BUDDHA SAID THAT.
- It is difficult to sacrifice thought. It comes through GRACE & the blessings of Christ. PuRify & wAit for grace.

- YOGA is nothing. You CAN AttAin so much without it.

- HATHA YOGA is okay if you ARe STRICTLY brAHMACHARYA. Otherwise it is dangerous. You can raise Kundalini by devotion & by feeding people. You need the grace of the guru for devotion. Kundalini can be awakened silently; it goes up the spine to the Ajna. Kundalini rests below the navel. It can be raised by the guru's grace, by the gentle, simple touch of the guru's hand.
- Devotion to God is

...a wife must serve god by serving her husband. The greatest husband is God. Women are more open to love God. They have higher status than men. It's a woman's _dharma_ to serve her husband & that is most pleasing to God.

- Eat simple food. Lead a simple daily life. Don't eat wine, meat, eggs, hot spices. They lead to an impure heart.
- It's good to fast three days a month.
- If you feed everyone, you'll never starve.
- **FEED EVERYONE & LOVE EVERYONE.**
- Work is God. Making food is a service to god, because people need food to live. Work is worship.

TALK LITTLE. READING & TALKING CREATE interFERENCE in tHE MIND. TOO MUCH dISCUSSION NOT THE WAY.

- Better to see God in everything than to try to figure it out.

1/72 - One morning in Allahabad, Mahara turned to Ram Dass & said "The whole universe is blind. How can I make them see?" Kabir said that.
- BE HAPPY ALL the time!
- All religion...

his
deny

ople
ople,
ot
ne
ing or

ti ke loga;
injog
rang
up and
eting
boat !

.....A saint's heart melts whenever
anyone else's heart comes near
the fire .....

Previous pages: Snapshots of Naima's journal pages. This page: Mira's journal.
Following page: Aarti being done to Maharajji.

BALARAM DAS: The monsoon started, and it was cold as anything in Kausani. I didn't do the meditation, because I hadn't done the Vipassana course. I wasn't really fitting in with the program. While everyone was meditating, I was lying around reading, going into the bazaar, and drinking tea. I read pretty much every book they had there—the *Ramayana*, the *Bhagavad Gita*, the *Mahabharata*, Sri Krishna Prem, the *Yoga of the Katha Upanishad*. I got the most mileage with Maharajji from the story of Nachiketa and Yama from the Katha Upanishad. He loved that one. I started getting the cultural reference grid. I spent hours staring at the map of India. I had this wonderful map from Britain that folded out and had every little town, every little railway. It was a huge amount of information, which was fascinating.

Since I wasn't doing the meditation, I came back from Kausani to Nainital in July or early August. At the Evelyn Hotel were Harinam and his wife, Mariam, and this girl, Pat, whom I had met on the train going overland. Harinam had an appointment to spend the night at Kainchi. It had all been set up. Maharajji had told him, "Come on this day, and you'll stay here." This was huge, because it was the first time one of the Westerners had stayed there.

The next morning Pat, Mariam, Harinam, and I all shared a cab to Kainchi. Maharajji was in his little office. What happened next was really the big shift for me, the big mental swing, where I didn't care about anything but having darshan. We were sitting in the office; we had our tea. Dada was there; it was the first time I met him. Maharajji tells Dada to take Harinam and Mariam to the forest rest house a little bit upstream, and then he asks me, "Do you want to stay too?"

"Yes!"

"*Thik, thik.* Dada, send them all up there."

So all four of us were going to stay. Harinam was a little put out, because he thought that was going to be his special thing, but what are you going to say?

Then Maharajji asked me, "What's your name?"

I said, "Peter."

He was going "Pecar," the way they say their *T*s. "Peter, Peter."

I went to touch his feet when I was going to go up to the rest house, and he said, "Peter *accha hai,*" which means "Peter is good."

I mean, it sounds nice, but the effect it had on me was unbelievable. I had this pain inside my chest. It was heart-wrenching, and it hit me like a thunderbolt. I was in a daze. Opening your heart hurts. It's like that picture of Hanuman tearing his chest open. It was literally like that. It was an amazing experience of being loved and being worthy to have love.

That changed everything. From then on, I just wanted to be with Maharajji, to be in his physical presence as much as I could. He'd say to go and I would get up and go, but maybe I'd have a cup of tea and come back in ten minutes. I even got to the point when I could hear the *jao* coming, and I would get up and leave and not even be there when he'd send everyone away. Then I'd come back after everyone had departed.

While "the boys" (and a few women) were having their retreat in Kausani, I was dealing with hepatitis at the Evelyn Hotel, where I was taken care of like family. As the nonstop monsoon rains went on, the walls of my room turned green with mold, but I was comforted by visits from people on their way to and from Kausani. Toward the end of the six weeks I was sick at the hotel, Radha and Mohan arrived from

Bombay, where she had also had a bad case of hep. Mohan went to join the folks at Kausani, and Radha and I recovered together. Just as we were able to walk up the many steps of the hotel, we heard the news: Maharajji was back in Kainchi!

The time we call "Nainital High" was about to begin.

8

Nainital High
Fall 1971

Life is short, but it comes with a great blessing:
it is thy turn to meet God.

—SANT KIRPAL SINGH

A s the monsoon season was coming to a close, word went out that Maharajji was back in Kainchi. My first darshan on the physical plane took place in Kainchi on September 7, 1971, but I actually had first experienced darshan after the summer of 1969. I'd taken some acid with an old college friend and had flown off to an inner temple on a journey of initiation. The next day I was still too high to sleep, and I was getting frightened of the lower astral realms I was being pulled into as I started to come down. I sat in front of the little black-and-white photo of Maharajji that Ram Dass had given me, clutching my New Hampshire wooden mala, and repeated and repeated a heartfelt mantra: "I'm

Rameshwar Das

Nainital High. First row, left to right: Ram Dev, Raghu, Danny, Dwarkanath, and
Vishwambar. Second row, left to right: Carl, Uma, Annapurna, Anasuya, Parvati, Radha,
and Mohan. Third row, left to right: M. L. Sah, Ravi Das, Surya Das (behind Ravi Das),
Sita, Laxman, Carlos Vishwanath, Krishna Das, Tukaram (behind Krishna Das), Ram
Dass, Rameshwar Das (behind Ram Dass), K. K. Sah, and Balaram Das.

scared, and you have to help me. I'm scared, and you have to help me."
And there he was. I could see him moving in the photo, within a ball of
blue light. I knew everything would be all right.

After that I got a bigger picture. I talked to it all the time, and I would
see him in there from time to time. Never told a soul. After all, who
talks to pictures? When I finally came face to face with Maharajji in
Kainchi, one of the first things he said to me was, "You used to talk to
my picture all the time. You asked many questions!"

With Maharajji in Kainchi, the retreat in Kausani was over, and suddenly the Evelyn Hotel in Nainital became a mini ashram. We had bell
ringers to wake us in the morning. On Sundays, we'd gather on the

front patio, and Ram Dass would read from the Bible, one of the Hindu holy books, *The Aquarian Gospel of Jesus the Christ,* or *The Lazy Man's Guide to Enlightenment.*

We loved the fairy-tale land of Nainital. In the fall, it's all dressed up for the Hindu holidays, with little white lights sparkling everywhere. We could walk around the lake and visit the Naina Devi temple, the Shiva cave, and the Hanuman temple. We could go for boat rides and shop for Indian clothes and items for our personal pujas, like bells, pictures, and incense. But most of our time was spent at Kainchi.

According to Maharajji's longtime Indian devotees, this was the first time he had ever stayed in one place for such an extended period—seven weeks! Our days were filled with Maharajji, and our nights with dreams of him.

What was it like going to Kainchi? First came the ten-and-a-half-mile ride from Nainital, winding along the hairpin turns of the mountain roads. The road was barely two lanes, and in some places it was so narrow that a vehicle would have to honk its horn loudly before proceeding around a blind switchback turn, so a car or truck coming from the opposite direction could stop in a wide enough place to let the vehicle pass by. On one side would be the rise of the mountain, which frequently sent rocks and mud and trees tumbling down onto the road following the heavy monsoon rains, and on the other side would be a dangerous drop-off. As you rode along you could see "dead grasshoppers"—cars and buses that had gone over the edge and lay on the valley floor like rotting carcasses.

But then, tucked into a bend of the river that flowed through the Kainchi valley, you suddenly caught sight of the red spires of the temples and the white buildings that comprised the Neem Karoli Baba Ashram. Ah, home again.

We'd arrive for morning darshan around eight via bus, taxi, or Ram Dass's VW van. We'd sit around Maharajji until we'd be sent across the

Krishna Das (Roy Bonney)

Kainchi, as seen from the road.

courtyard to eat—massive amounts of spicy fried potatoes and puris. I remember sitting next to Ram Dass as I stared at the leaf plate in front of me, wondering how, after having hepatitis, I could possibly eat the vast pile of spicy fried food and the box of sweets Maharajji had given me. Ram Dass laughed and said, "This isn't food. It's prasad." So I ate it. Needless to say, many of us lived on charcoal pills for digestion and Liv 52, the Indian herbal liver medicine.

At some point after we were fed, Maharajji would send us up to the back part of the ashram, to Indra kutir (where Ram Dass had stayed during his first trip to India), to rest. We'd nap, write in our journals, or go sit on one of the rocks in the river to sing, meditate, or cry. Why the tears? What we came to see was that Maharajji's bright, shining light was illuminating our inner darkness, and our impurities and desires would sometimes seem totally overwhelming.

Then we'd be called down to the front part of the ashram for our second darshan, which would last until the final bus of the day arrived to take us back to the Evelyn Hotel. We'd have our last chai and sweets and be given boxes of prasad potatoes and puris to take with us. Many of us ate dinner together at the hotel, and on special evenings K. K. came to teach us *aarti*—a song of praise to the guru, accompanied by waving a light in front of the guru or the guru's picture. K. K.'s beautiful voice and the deep devotion of his heart made these evenings memorable.

RAMESHWAR DAS: We used to do all kinds of touristy things when we were hanging out in Nainital. We'd go out boating on the lake, walk up into the hills, or hike up to a ridge called Snowview, where you could see the Himalayan peaks off in the distance. We went to old movies at the Ashoka Talkies. Mostly we ate at the hotel, although there were a few restaurants in town. The prices were pretty low then, even though the rupee was about eight to the dollar.

One day Danny, Krishna Das, and I were out in a boat on the lake talking about Maharajji. Then we went to the bazaar and stopped at a photo shop near K. K.'s home, where they had photos of local saints. The next day at Kainchi, Maharajji said to us, "You were out on the lake? What were you doing?"

"Oh, we were talking about you, Maharajji."

He made this sort of puffing sound.

Okay, yes, we had had a toke of *ganja* [marijuana] while boating.

He wasn't commenting in a negative way; he was just letting us know he knew what we were doing.

Then he said, "You were looking at photos of me." We acknowledged that too.

Knowing he knew what was going on every moment was one aspect of it. Another is that we were so gently taken care of all the time. We were enfolded in his family around Nainital, getting to know K. K.'s family, going over there to have meals. I decided we needed a group photo, the one we call "Nainital High." I went to Kala Mandir [the photo shop] and set it up. The photographer brought a huge view camera to the porch of the Evelyn Hotel. There was no shutter on the lens; they took off the lens cap and counted. I still have the gigantic 11-by-14 negative.

RAGHU: Rameshwar Das had been taking photos of Maharajji, and he made stamps with Maharajji's picture on them. Sheets and sheets of stamps, and he gave them out to all of us. Somebody started giving them to Maharajji, and he was delighted with them. You'd give him sheets of stamps, and he'd give them out. One time he was asking for stamps. I only had half a sheet left, so I took my half a sheet and ripped it in half. I didn't try to hide it or anything; it was right in front of him. It was so unconscious it was unbelievable. I went up and gave him the half I had ripped off.

He looked at me and threw it back at me. *"Nahin!* [No!]"

That took me a week to live down. I thought I was going to die. We used to go to the river when anything happened. I don't know how much time Krishna Das and I spent on the rocks in the river bemoaning how useless we were. It was just awful to see yourself in that light.

A few days later he was asking for stamps again, and I had the same stamps. This time I gave them all to him. He turned and gave them to somebody, and then he looked back at me and gave me the finger *mudra* [the raised forefinger gesture that meant either *sub ek* ("It's all one.") or "Watch it!"]. That was the end of that.

ANASUYA: Danny and I were spending the summer together in Kausani, and at some point we thought we should get married. We came to Kainchi and asked Maharajji if there was an auspicious time that he could recommend for us to get married. He said, "Where there is love, there is marriage. Nothing more is needed."

He said, "In America when people get married, do they exchange rings?"

We said, "Yes."

He told Danny, "Get her a ring. *Shaadi ho gaya.* [You're married.]"

He called us back down a little while later, and there were some Indians there. He said, "Tell them what just happened."

I said, "Maharajji married us."

He thought that was the biggest joke for days. He loved to see the expression on the Indians' faces when they heard that story.

At one point in September, after we all had come back from Kausani and were in the Evelyn Hotel, he said, "You can come and spend the night at the ashram. You're still angry at me because I didn't let you stay in the kutir."

Maharajji stamps.

In the meantime, months had gone by, and I had had a beautiful summer in Kausani, so I said, "I'm not angry, Maharajji."

"Yes, you are. Tomorrow you can come and stay."

We came back the next day, and we couldn't stay for some reason. He was playing with me.

The next week we did stay overnight in one of the rooms in the back. Danny was on a bed on one side of the room, and I was on a bed on the other side of the room. I had this really intense dream in which I woke up on my bed and walked outside. Maharajji was standing there with a couple of Indians, and he was holding a child. I thought to myself, "That is really unusual. I've never seen him holding a child." He motioned for me to follow him. He walked around the front of the building, still holding this child, and came in the front door of the room where we were sleeping. The Indians stayed outside. It was just him and Danny and this child and me. Then I woke up.

Danny woke up at the same time across the room, and I told him this dream. At five o'clock the *chaukidar* [ashram gatekeeper] knocks on the door and offers us some tea. Then a little while later he calls us down to see Maharajji. Maharajji is sitting with some Indian people and a little child, and he looks at us and says, "Will you take this child to America?"

"If you want, Maharajji."

"Yes, that's what I want."

The parents were kind of delighted, actually. Maharajji was asking Danny questions. "How much money do you make in America? Do you have enough money to buy milk for this baby?"

The parents tried to give the baby to us, and the baby started crying. Maharajji said "No, no, no, *thik hai,* you don't have to go."

But then he continued asking us questions. He said, "If I give

Balaram Das

Maharajji, Parvati, and Anasuya.

you a child, would you take it?" We said yes. "Would you give it lots of milk? Would you raise it to be a scholar?" Yes.

He was like, *"Thik hai,"* and that was that.

I got pregnant two weeks later.

When I found out that I was pregnant, I asked Maharajji, "Is having a baby going to keep me from God?"

He said, "When you have your baby, are you going to be attached to it? Be like a lotus rising above the mud. Don't be attached to your children. Love them, but don't be attached."

I thought about that all night—it was a really tall order! How was I not going to be attached to this baby? The next day, I said, "Maharajji, I don't know how to not be attached to this baby."

He said, "Just remember God and have faith, and it will happen." I'm still waiting.

BALARAM DAS: I'd like to say something about how we were received, not only by Maharajji, but by the Indians there. In spite of the fact that we did offensive things culturally, somehow they didn't care. I guess they said, "Well, first of all, they're not doing it on purpose; they're ignorant. Second of all, Maharajji doesn't seem to mind." So they didn't mind either. They certainly were generous and tolerant to an extreme degree.

I'd go to the temple and watch the way that the Indians would express their devotion. I saw that some would take an apple, peel it, slice it, and put it on a leaf plate. I saw them do that several times and thought, "I could do that." So I got an apple. I had my Swiss army knife and my leaf plate, and I peeled and sliced the apple. Maharajji was sitting there talking with a few gentlemen, and he looked at me holding the plate of apple slices toward him. When I would do something like this, he would get this look of amazement. It was as if your dog sat up and talked to you, and you'd say, "My God, he talks! Look what he can do. He's so cute." Maharajji looked at me with this beautiful look, so much love you can't even describe it.

He picked up an apple slice and started chewing on it. Then he grabbed a handful of apple slices and gave them to the Indian men. "Will you eat this food that he brought?"

This is a tricky thing in Indian culture. I had prepared this food. I was probably not qualified to cook food generally for these gentlemen, but on the other hand it was coming straight from Maharajji's hand and he had eaten it. They said, "Oh yes, Baba, we'll take it."

Maharajji took the rest of the apples, gave them back to me, and said, "With these apples I am going to give you great wealth." Great. *"Aab jao, phir aana.* Go now, come again." That was one of the first things I learned in Hindi.

Maharajji got up and went inside, and these Indians came running over to me and said, "Oh my God! That was the greatest thing ever. Do you know what just happened?"

I said, "Well, yeah, he gave me the apples."

They were very excited; it was a great boon. Of course, it has been.

I remember during that time every day having darshan; then we'd come back and everyone was dreaming about Maharajji all night. It was an amazing time, and I was totally transforming. When I went to India I had the big beard and the big pony tail. After I realized that I wanted to be with Maharajji as much as possible, I thought, "Well, how am I going to do that? What's the best way to conduct myself to make that happen?" I had to fit in, blend in, and maybe he wouldn't notice me to send me away. I lost the beard, I got the hair cut, I got the mustache that young Indian men like. Everything's clean now. Then I got the vest. The *dhoti* [a man's garment made of one long piece of cloth, wrapped around the hips with one end brought up between the legs and tucked into the waist] and the long white shirt with the tails hanging out of the vest, with the pen in the pocket. That was the new me.

Also at this point I got this urge to understand what was going on. I wanted to learn Hindi. I got a couple of books in India, but they were terrible. I wrote to my father back in New Haven, Connecticut, and said, "Go down to the Yale Co-op, where they sell all of the textbooks, find all the books on Hindi, and send them to me." A couple of months later I got this big parcel of materials that I used to learn the language. I learned to read the writing system. That was an ongoing process the whole time I was there.

RADHA (from her journal):

October 10, 1971

I was very unhappy this day and saw that one could be affected by the sorrows of this world if one's mind is not on God. I cried

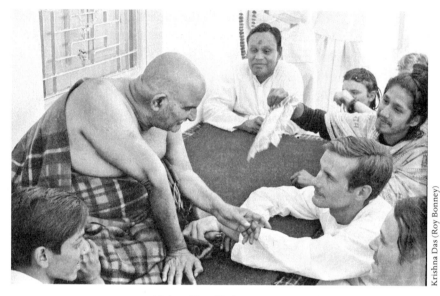

Maharajji and Balaram Das.

Krishna Das (Roy Bonney)

the whole day on and off. I got upset at Maharajji because he did not seem to care. I went out to the river, chanted *Ram*, thought I was no Radha and that God is the only guru (in your heart).

Maharajji told someone to get me, that I was crying. He put his foot out for me to rub, asked who my guru is. I gave a snappy answer, "God."

He asked, "Who's greater, guru or God?"

I said, "They are one, the same. Perhaps guru is greater, since he has taken a human form and we could talk to him."

Then he asked if I was angry with him. I burst out laughing, and he was laughing. Then I started to cry again and said, "I just want to remember and adore Maharajji always."

He asked why I was crying. I said, "There can be no happiness for one who forgets God. I don't remember God always, and therefore there's suffering." Maharajji granted me the boon of never forgetting him. He said that I should try to remember him every moment, and he would help me.

Before this, when I was crying, he took my hands and pulled me up, so that I had my head and hands on his lap, and I cried in his lap. His kindness and love cannot be expressed. I've never seen anything like it.

KRISHNA: There were a lot of hippies in India who subsidized their life there by sending a few ounces of hash back and getting money for it. My funds were getting quite low, and I thought maybe this was something I could do. But I was really kind of tortured by it, so I said something to Maharajji. He looked at me and said, "Always tell the truth, and you'll never be afraid." I had been paranoid about this. What if I got caught? I was entertaining a criminal act. When he said that, I realized I wasn't going to do it. It was very freeing.

Maharajji in the "office"; Radha outside the window. (The bars are to keep monkeys out.)

MIRABAI: One thing he said to Krishna that has always stayed with me was, "Always tell the truth, and you'll never be afraid." I realize that when you develop that quality of openness that comes when you are honest and transparent, you're more likely to live in a world that is wholesome and safe. There are things to be afraid of, of course, but that kind of deep honesty builds a strength in you, so that you're not afraid of what can come. That was deep for me.

Kabir Das (Jim McCarthy) sailed into Bombay harbor on New Year's Day, 1970. He had visited forty countries by that time, most in the third world, but knew very little about India. He was soon hooked. Eventually he settled in Dinapani, up in the Himalayan foothills near Almora, until he was bitten by a snake and the bite got infected. He taxied down to the English hospital in Nainital at the same time the retreat in Kausani was ending and his sister, Sita, had met Maharajji in Kainchi. After a few days in the hospital and hearing about Maharajji, he checked himself out.

KABIR DAS (from his writings):

"Guru Nanak has come! Guru Nanak has come!" Maharajji shouted across the courtyard. These were the first words he spoke to me, as I rounded the corner by the Shiva temple. A strange sight I may have seemed, carried in the strong crossed arms of two young Americans. A small figure from the distance, Neem Karoli Baba sat on a wooden cot on a veranda, wrapped in a plaid blanket against the early morning mountain chill. He quickly assumed larger proportions as we approached the takhat. He was rocking back and forth, calling me "Guru Nanak," and directing my handlers to bring me up the steps to the edge of the bed.

Maharajji sat surrounded by a dozen or so Indians and Westerners. He asked what had happened, but he did not wait for or seem to expect an answer. He proceeded to ask more questions. In any case I was tongue-tied. After a few minutes of solicitous concern about my as yet unexplained condition, he began to talk about the sick, making one beautiful statement after another: "God comes to us in the form of the sick and ill so that we can serve." He spoke that morning for a long time about the importance of doing *seva* [service] to the sick.

People came, singly or in groups, in a nonstop procession. Except for moments of beatific quiet and stillness, he was continuously talking and moving about on his takhat. He took note that I was Canadian and that Sita was my sister. No mention was ever made again about "Guru Nanak." Three months later in Vrindavan, he gave the name Kabir Das to me. That name stuck.

Kausalya (Karen Pettit) was nineteen years old, living in Seattle, and working as a figure model for a group of artists. When *Be Here Now* came out, it became her bible. She was determined to meet Maharajji. Her boyfriend was interested in the "left-hand path"—Aleister Crowley, tantra, hanging out with yogis in caves. Together they went to India, spent one night in Delhi, and the next day were on a bus to Nainital.

KAUSALYA: My story of being around Maharajji at the beginning was totally about wanting recognition and not getting it. I was probably the youngest person there at the time and straight out of the whole teen queen thing [Kausalya had been Miss USA]. The majority of people were in very contemplative, meditative places, and I was, "Okay, just show me what to do."

Maharajji seemed like he went out of his way to ignore me. It went on and on for weeks. Everyone had a name. Everybody was having their special little routine with him. Every day it would be, "Well, I traveled this far, and he is not my guru obviously, because he would be acknowledging me or bringing me into the roost. I'm leaving." And yet I would stay.

Charlie left and went to Darjeeling to sit in caves with the yogis; he came back in about three days and said, "I've had enough of India. I'm leaving." I was not. He gave me $200 in traveler's checks, and that lasted me ten months in India through the grace of God and all those wonderful Indian devotees who took care of us constantly.

How do you get into the inner sanctum? One day I thought, "Well, I'm going to trick the system." Everyone would go off to Kainchi on the bus, and I thought, "I'm going to go late. I'm going to take a cab. All by myself. He has to at least say hello or give me a pat or something." I got there, and Dada said, "I'll tell Maharajji you are here." I was outside on the porch; Maharajji was in the office. He opened up the shutters on the window, took one look at me, and slammed them as hard as he could right in my face.

"Okay, I get it. Never mind." I sat at the river and cried. I gave up. I said, "This is not the purpose of being here. Whether he gives me a name or pats me on the head or not, it is not about what I can get *from* him. The purpose is being *with* him."

One day many weeks later in Vrindavan, I was daydreaming. Dwarka hits me and goes, "Maharajji just gave you a name." He did? Maharajji patted me on the head, gave me roses and prasad. He asked me questions. My time had come. The tiara just had to break first.

LAXMAN: My relationship with Maharajji—and this is personal because everybody sees him differently—was he's not in the body. Somebody so omniscient, how could he fit in that body? I could not wrap my mind around it. I'd always stand in the back of the darshan crowd. I loved being away from him, because I felt his presence everywhere around me and we were much more at one. When I saw him, I saw duality. How could it be? You can't be there and I'm here, and when I'm all alone we're one.

In the fall in Kainchi there's this big *havan*, fire ceremony, as part of Durga Puja [also called Navratri, a nine-day festival to worship the Divine Mother and celebrate her victory over evil]. So I'm walking around the fire, throwing my coconut in, which represents killing my ego. (It's going to take more than that.) All of a sudden my swallowing is becoming very laborious and heavy. Now I'm getting very uncomfortable, because I can't pull my tongue forward; it keeps sliding back. My throat is thickening, my tongue is compressing, and I'm getting really frightened, so I start talking to Maharajji. "Maharajji, how could you do this? You know how much I love you. How could you let me die here in your ashram? Why are you doing this?"

I kept trying to pull my tongue forward, trying to undo this very uncomfortable situation. And somehow I was still managing to breathe, although I was full of fear. I went over to Ram Dass, completely freaked out, and told him what was happening.

Ram Dass looked at me and said, "Unbelievable. Of all of the low-life useless folks in this entire satsang, how is it that *you* get *kechari mudra?*"

Well, now, my self-esteem started to soar; all of a sudden I'm special. So what is kechari mudra anyway? He explained that yogis practice for this for eons, and then finally their tongue goes down their throat, and they stop breathing and go into bliss. Yep. Got one on you, Ram Dass. It was very sweet. For three months I kept tasting nectar on the back of my tongue. *Mmm,* it was good. And it was a constant reminder of my connectivity with Maharajji. That's what it really was for me.

RAM DEV: Mohan and I and a couple of Westerners were with Maharajji and a bunch of Indians. He and Mohan were talking about the price of skim milk in America, and they were going on and on and on. He asked Mohan, "How much is a kilo of milk in America?" and Mohan would say *x* number of rupees, and Maharajji would say, "Can you believe it? Can you believe how much the milk costs in America?"

"Wow, Maharajji. No."

They were doing this for the longest time, and I'm in the back thinking that maybe this guy isn't quite who I think he is. Maybe he's a little senile after all. I had only been there for a very short period of time, I had just gotten my PhD from Stanford, and I felt pretty smart. I'm thinking, "Why are we talking about the price of skim milk in America endlessly here?"

All of a sudden I have this thunderbolt in my mind that was clearly coming from Maharajji. It's hard to explain to someone who did not have that experience how it wasn't just my imagination. It was as if Maharajji said to me, "We can talk about important things. We can talk about God and love, but that just makes the mind busy. There's this ocean of love that's always available, so if you talk about something trivial, we can just dive into the ocean of love." I felt this intense bliss wash over me. I was in this blissful state for many hours after that darshan. That was really a lesson for me.

RUKMINI: Our first meeting with Maharajji was in Vrindavan after Murari and I left Kausani. We were totally unprepared for his presence. Maharajji was lying/sitting on his wooden bench like a gigantic mountain. He wore a white sheet and was really, really big, ominous, awesome. He looked fierce. We, the only Westerners, sat at his feet, hearts pounding, answering questions about where we'd been, what we did in the States, and what our relationship was. Then he *jaoed* us away.

After the first time, he didn't say anything else to us and was sending us away with prasad almost immediately. We were determined this fifth day to ask him a question about spiritual life, and on that day he left Vrindavan!

A few weeks later Murari left India. We were both confused about gurus and our relationship to Maharajji. After taking a Buddhist meditation course with Goenka, on Ram Dass's advice, I was alone in India and didn't have any idea what my trip was all about anymore. Any thought of joining the Krishna Consciousness movement was gone.

My sense of confusion, however, was still there and had to do with conditioning and clinging to bhakti models. Taking the Buddhist course was a groove, but totally different as a technique. No forms, no focus, just watch your body sensations. All my astral devotional props had to be laid aside. At the end of the course, I spent the entire train ride writing about the pros and cons of Vipassana meditation and bhakti devotional practices.

In this state of absolute confusion, I arrived at Kainchi. In a little room, he sat wrapped this time in a blanket and appeared very small, although he bubbled over with love. He asked my name, gave me some prasad, and sent me to Ram Dass, who was on the other side of the courtyard with the whole satsang, at that time about twenty people.

Since everyone had already eaten, Maharajji called them over. I sat alone with what seemed like mountains of potatoes and puris. From time to time Maharajji would say something, and everyone would laugh and look at me. Here I was, knowing nothing, totally dependent on someone else's word whether to eat, sit, or come over, and everybody seemed to be laughing at me.

Then *bam,* he called me. I leapt up like a happy puppy and bounded over. He called me "Ram Dass *chela* [disciple]" and told him to take care of me. He pointed out my letter writing, which of course, no one had told him. He also read the confusion in my mind and said, "You came to India looking for a guru, and now you don't believe there are any saints." Two days before, in the depths of the loss of faith, I had written Murari, "No one knows anything." I felt as if Maharajji opened up my brain and reshuffled it for clarification. He hit me on the head several times, tweaked my nose, and sent me back to eat.

For that whole month of October I stayed with Ram Dass and the satsang in Nainital. For the most part Maharajji ignored me, sometimes saying my name, which was Linda, very lovingly and laughing. Maharajji had begun naming people, so everyone was on a desire-jealousy-attachment-attention trip from time to time. During one of my downs, feeling incredibly impure and convinced I wasn't worthy of a name, I felt propelled down to see Maharajji. I had been thinking the night before about asking for a mantra, because I read about the divine quality of receiving a mantra from your guru. During this month, a feeling of surrender had been growing in me. I wanted nothing else than to remain with Maharajji and was slowly giving up plans to return to the States in December.

I ran down, almost in tears. He was coming out of his room with Dada. I fell at Maharajji's feet, very shaken to see him there, smiling and loving, almost as if he had been waiting for me. Dada asked me what I wanted, and I said, "A mantra."

Maharajji asked, "Do you believe in Krishna?"

"Yes."

"*Om Krishnaya Nama.*"

I repeated this, my mantra.

"What is your name?"

"Linda."

"From this time on you will be known as Rukmini."

Now this really blew me away even more. I had had trouble with the Maha Mantra [Hare Krishna Hare Ram], because of its association with Krishna Consciousness, a movement I was now working through a lot of negative stuff about. So Maharajji gave me a different Krishna mantra. He also named me Rukmini, Krishna's wife, a name I had thought about as a possible choice if ever he finally did name me, and he pulled it right out of my head.

I started to cry, and Maharajji lovingly wiped my tears. I sat there stoned out of my mind with love and a sense of gratitude. Maharajji also said, "Your goal has been achieved." The whole darshan was such a drama, exactly as if I had created it, and indeed, if the guru is a mirror, then I did.

Teachings on Anger

Maharajji didn't lecture, didn't "teach" in any formal way, but situations were always happening through which we could learn from him.

KABIR DAS: When the occasion demanded, Maharajji became very serious, even to the point of showing what appeared to be anger. One of those blissful autumn days in Kainchi was dramatically changed for us. We, the Westerners, were camped out for the afternoon in the back part of the ashram, when all of a sudden Maharajji's voice was heard shouting extremely loudly. For most of us, this was the first time we had heard Maharajji at this volume. From perches on the second-story veranda we could see over the wall separating the two parts of the ashram. Maharajji was in his "office," and someone was being read the riot act by Baba.

For me it was darshan of an aspect of Maharajji I thought I would not like to see too often. It was an awesome and somewhat frightening experience. Was Maharajji really angry in the same way ordinary people get angry? I was under the impression that a true saint had transcended these base emotions.

Later we came to know that a large amount of potatoes had gone rotten in storage, and apparently the person responsible, a longtime devotee and ashram worker, was reaping his karma. When we were called to Maharajji for our final darshan, it was as if nothing had happened. Maharajji was as he had always been, all love and smiles. He told us that a saint never throws anyone out of his heart. Sometimes a person's time with Baba was over and the big *jao* came. This person was out of there that day and never allowed back in, though he often came to the ashram gate over the next two years and cried. His bus had come!

MOHAN: In Nainital, Radha and I would be fighting. The next day Maharajji would say something like, "You were thinking of me last night."

I would be, "Oh, that's very good." I felt his pat on the back, *pat, pat, pat.* Then I realized that if he knew that . . . then he knew about our fight.

Then he gave us instructions: "Don't be angry." He said he fixed it, that "it is going to be okay between you. You are going to have a child."

He knew everything, and he still loved me. That was the most amazing part—knowing everything about me, he could still love me. I didn't do anything for him. I was a skeptical New York businessman, ex-hustler. He didn't ask me for one *paisa* [cent]. That was important to me, because probably I wouldn't have trusted him.

Maharajji did one particular thing that was very important for me, because since then I have had vastly reduced anger. I've worked very hard, I've made huge progress, and I'm so much happier (as is everyone else, I might add).

Maharajji was with Sharma, that potato guy, screaming at him. That's bad enough. Then he's banishing him forever from the ashram. A fate worse than death. I was shocked. He really looked lost in anger. Then he stopped. He went from full-on anger to a neutral position. He wasn't angry.

For me to manifest that much anger, it would be days before I would calm down. And he said, "Never throw anyone out of your heart. You don't have to hang out with them, but don't throw them out of your heart." It was a huge teaching about anger, and I figured I saw that because I needed it. It wasn't pleasant. My insides were all knotted up. "How could he do that? Is that who our Baba is?" It was just horrifying. And then, just like that, no anger. He wasn't angry—he was using it as a teaching. He winked at us and smiled.

RAM DASS: At the Evelyn Hotel in Nainital I lived with the Westerners. They were all hippies mainly, good people, all wanting to be with Maharajji. They wanted him for themselves. I got really mad at them because they weren't respecting Maharajji's time. I was seeing the Indians being pushed aside for the Westerners, and I knew that that was my fault. The Westerners didn't care; they just wanted to get to Maharajji. It was like corralling cats. I kept feeling responsible.

Then one night I put a note on my door: "I am going to be meditating." Radha and Mohan were having a terrible fight; they came to me and couldn't get in because of the note. The next day Maharajji said to them, "Where was Ram Dass?"

The previous day I had seen Maharajji get mad at that poor guy Sharma. Dada came back to see me, and I was sulking. Dada said, "Did you see Maharajji get mad?"

I said, "Yes, and he told us not to get mad."

We were all supposed to be in the back at the temple, but I went out front to escort Sharma to the bus. It was like *High Noon*. Later, Sharma followed me wherever I went and asked for money.

The next day, with Mohan and Radha, Maharajji said, "Don't you know that the only people you can be mad at are the people you love?" And he looked at me. He must have loved Sharma very much.

I wasn't touching money then; Laxman was holding the purse. We were at the hotel, and I wasn't speaking to any of the Westerners. I was so fed up with them; they were controlling my funds and I wouldn't ask them for money. They all got on the bus to go to the temple, and nobody thought of me because I was in my own world. The bus went away, and I was left at the hotel. I walked to Kainchi the beautiful forest way. When I got to the temple, everybody was with Maharajji, laughing and eating.

I came down from the hill, and Tukaram offered me a plate of food. I was mad as hell. I took the plate of food and threw it in his face, which was very satisfying, very satisfying.

Then from across the way I hear, "Ram Dass, Ram Dass, Ram Dass, what's the matter?"

I was just *oooh* . . . I was so mad.

Maharajji said, "What's the matter?"

"I'm fed up with them. They're mean, they're impure."

He called for a cup of milk, and he fed me milk. I calmed down. I said to him, "I don't like anybody except you."

Then he fed me more milk and turned me around, and I saw how beautiful the Westerners were. Oh, how beautiful they all were! I ended up passing out apple slices to everybody. He said you couldn't feed anybody in anger, so I went around and fed everyone with love. And it was real love. Then there were times when I appreciated the Westerners and the sacrifice they had made to come. I was so happy to be the one to introduce them to Maharajji.

All in all, those seven weeks of almost daily darshans with Maharajji in Kainchi were an immersion into the heart of the bhakti experience. It also forged us as a satsang, with ties that have lasted now for well over forty years. We may not see each other often, but when we do get together, it's as if no time has passed at all.

Fortunately, the *lila* (play, sport) that was life with Maharajji didn't end when Kainchi closed down for the winter; it was on to Vrindavan and dancing with Lord Krishna.

9

Sporting with
Krishna in Vrindavan

Winter 1971

I am reminded of a story of Lord Krishna when he was a cowherd.
Every night he invites the milkmaids to dance with him in the forest.
They come and they dance. The night is dark, the fire in their midst
roars and crackles, the beat of the music gets ever faster—the girls
dance and dance and dance with their sweet lord, who has made
himself so abundant as to be in the arms of each and every girl. But
the moment the girls become possessive, the moment each one imag-
ines that Krishna is her partner alone, he vanishes. So it is that we
should not be jealous with God.

—YANN MARTEL, *LIFE OF PI*

By the end of October, it got mighty cold in the Kainchi valley. The towering foothills allowed only very shortened hours of daylight. When we arrived at the temple one day and found that Maharajji had "disappeared," we soon learned that he had gone to Vrindavan, down on the plains, where it was much warmer.

Vrindavan was an enchanted place for Maharajji's other main ashram. In the early 1970s, Vrindavan was probably the same as it had been for thousands of years. There were more cows on the streets than *tongas* (two-wheeled horse-drawn carts) and cycle rickshaws. The whole town, sitting in the curve of the Yamuna River, is known as the playground of Lord Krishna when he was young, and the Krishna lila echoes everywhere. Here Krishna spent his days grazing the village cows and playing tricks on the other cowherds. The Rasa Lila—Krishna's love play/dance with the *gopis,* the female cowherds, in which he manifests to each one individually—symbolizes the loving interplay between the human soul and God. Krishna is still said to be sporting with Radha and the gopis in an eternal Vrindavan.

Vrindavan is only six miles from Mathura station, a two- to three-hour journey from Delhi on the express train, which usually pulled into Mathura just before dawn. As you'd clip-clop along the road to Vrindavan, you'd see the huge ball of red sun starting its daily journey, awakening the peacocks, who strutted around flashing their colorful tails. Maharajji's ashram and the Hanuman temple were at the end of a paved road that turned to sand just beyond the temple—part of the sacred walkway that goes around all of Vrindavan, called Parikrama Marg. Here the salutation that greeted you was *Radhe Shyam!* (Radhe is Radha, Krishna's beloved. Shyam is another name for Krishna)—a constant reminder of the union of lover and beloved.

Although in the mountains Maharajji had often been seen as Shiva, as vast and imposing as the Himalayas, here in Vrindavan he seemed somehow even sweeter and more loving. Maharajji manifested as Krishna, with all of us as his gopis.

He knew the secrets of our hearts. I had been smoking Indian beedies—low-grade tobacco wrapped in a betel leaf—mostly so I could hang out with Raghu. I'd go around the side of one of the temple buildings to smoke. Now I wanted to quit, but dropping a bad habit has never been my forte. As I entered the ashram one day, Maharajji shouted out, "Parvati, stop smoking beedies! I caught you red-handed. I am the CID [the Indian equivalent of the CIA] of the heart!" He immediately called me to sit in front of him, where he put his feet in my lap and held my hand. I gave away my pack of beedies. After lunch, Maharajji called me up to congratulate me on not smoking beedies anymore. Instant reinforcement!

RUKMINI: In the beginning of November Maharajji, followed by most of us, went to Vrindavan. Maharajji hadn't been paying attention to me at all. I went through all sorts of ego battles—anger, jealousy, wondering what I was doing there.

At this time, Bhaktivedanta Swami [Krishna Consciousness guru] was having a festival in Delhi. I was wondering if I should go, when all at once I heard "Rukmini, Rukmini." I ran up. Maharajji immediately asked if I wanted to go to the festival. He then asked me to chant *Hare Krishna,* but after the first line I burst into tears. It was all just too much. And there he was, with tears in his eyes, holding my hands, wiping my tears, and caressing my fingers. I felt like Radha making love to Krishna.

From that darshan on my devotion grew, and Maharajji became Krishna to me. He had me chant *Hare Krishna* often, and I would dance for him. He would ask me who my husband was, and I would reply "Krishna," much to his delight. When he asked once who named me, I replied "Krishna," as he had become this to me. By his grace he had twitched his finger and made my devotion increase tenfold. Chanting the Maha Mantra for him had cleansed me of any negative associations. Sending me to the Delhi festival worked out a lot of intense negative karma I had toward the Hare Krishna movement and Swami Bhaktivedanta. Maharajji was there through it all . . . and still is.

RADHA (from her journal):

My head was on his knee, and I was lost in love. He held my hand under the blanket, sometimes with both his hands. His leg is so smooth and his foot so incredibly beautiful and his hands as well. He is my lord. It seems he thinks my thoughts. I cannot describe the intimacy of sitting at his feet, looking at him, rubbing his back, holding his hand. All so perfectly natural. He knows me inside and out. Krishna, my lord, the supreme lover, not in the ordinary way one takes that word to be, but the indescribable way the gopis loved Krishna and he them.

BADRINATH DAS: I walked in the gate in Vrindavan, went up to the takhat, and put my head on the blanket that covered the takhat. As a Jew you don't pray to idols, let alone to people. It is against our tradition. But I just opened myself up. "Whatever will be, I surrender to this experience." Then Maharajji came out. He was just like a nice grandpa. I didn't feel any paranoia. I didn't feel like I had to worry he was going to take my mind from me or control or hassle me. He'd pat me on the head. He'd laugh and joke around. He was sweet, kind, and natural as could be.

We'd go back and forth almost daily to see Maharajji. We would walk there, wearing white, carrying flowers, blissful. I was still not comfortable eating Indian food, because I wasn't familiar with it, so I ended up going to Maharajji's ashram but not eating his food. Maharajji called me over and said, "You don't eat my food. Why aren't you eating my food?"

"Maharajji, I'm not hungry."

"I know why you are not eating my food. Last night you had a Coke and cookies for dinner."

I thought, "Gee, is he following me around? Is somebody watching me? What's going on?" Maybe he thought Americans have Coke and cookies for dinner. Then I realized he was revealing himself to me in a very gentle way. At that moment (and to this day), I felt he knew me and loved me, and I loved him and still do, and since then I have been on the path to loving everyone.

I was there with Maharajji for just ten days. That was it. Yet I feel like I got what I needed from being with him. Over the years I have been continually blessed by being part of Maharajji's ever expanding satsang. It is a big part of my life, and we are family.

One day in Kainchi, Maharajji said, "Mother from America is coming." Everybody was trying to guess who that mother was, and they said, "Hilda." "No, not Hilda." Many names were mentioned, but finally Radha said, "Joan," and he said, "Joan." Radha wrote a letter to Joan, which she never received, telling her that Maharajji said she was coming. In the meantime, Anjani (Joan O'Connell) was on her way to India, traveling with two brothers from New York, Paul (Uddhav) and David Anderson, headed to Bombay.

ANJANI: Hilda Charlton, then our teacher, sent us to see Sai Baba (her guru), since we weren't sure of how to get to Maharajji. We flew first to Bombay, where we were to go to American Express for a message from Ed and Chris, who were already in Puttaparthi, so we would know what to do. When we landed in the airport, a stewardess walked up to us and said, "You have reservations on a flight to Delhi this afternoon."

We thought, "Oh wow, we're in India. That's the way things are." So that same day we flew to Delhi. We wondered, "What now?" I said, "I'm supposed to have a message at American Express in Bombay, so let's go to American Express in Delhi." Indeed, there was a message for me from someone I didn't know named Balaram: "Maharajji expected in a few days. Come to Jaipuria Bhavan in Vrindavan."

For the first and only time we took a third-class coach train to Mathura; I won't ever forget that ride. It's like the New York subway, except for the open window, the dust flying in, the heat, and all these people squeezed in all around you.

We got off in Mathura and took the bus to Vrindavan. We're walking through the bazaar in Vrindavan; it's like being back in the fifteenth century, with the cows and the dogs and the carts and the rickshaws. We were saying "Jaipuria Bhavan" to people, and we would be sent this way and then that way. Soon it was starting to get dark, and I was thinking, "Oh no. We're going to be in a doorway tonight with the cows." We're staggering around with packs on our backs, when suddenly coming toward me was somebody I knew, Ram Dev, although I knew him as Dale from California. I shrieked and jumped on him and said, "Where's Jaipuria Bhavan?" Right around the corner it turned out, and he took us there.

Balaram Das

Anjani with Maharajji.

One or two days later Radha took me to see Maharajji after
getting me rigged up in a sari, which was like being put in
swaddling. The door was opened by the chaukidar, and then
you were looking right down the veranda. At the very end
Maharajji was sitting on his takhat, and all the Westerners
were sitting on the porch across the courtyard. We ran up to
him and pranaamed. There was a lot of crying and laughing,
and Maharajji was kind of hopping up and down on the takhat
saying, "Mother from America has come! Mother from America
has come!"

Vishwanath, or Vish (Daniel Miller), had been friends with Rukmini and Murari in Philadelphia. After not having seen them for two years, he ran into Rukmini when he first arrived in India (having no idea that she was there). She brought him to Maharajji in Vrindavan, where he had real darshan of Hanuman before ever seeing Baba.

> VISHWANATH: One time sitting in front of Maharajji I was feeling intensely burdened with all my "stuff," just mired in it. I thought, "If you would just look at me, eye to eye, you could burn all this out. I know you could!" As soon as I had that thought, he snapped around and stared at me. I might have held his stare for a millisecond, but for that millisecond it was like looking into the deep universe. It was overwhelming and I couldn't hold it.

The Gang's All Here

Jai Gopal (Jai Uttal) is an incredible musician who started learning Indian music as a teenager. We frequently refer to him as a *gandharva,* one of the heavenly musicians. Back in the early 1970s in California, he and his friends—Gangadhar (Mark Gerhard), Kathleen Haley, Janaki Rathod, and Govind (Charlie Burnham)—were a little crew, and they wound up going to India together.

> JAI: On the eve of registration for my freshman year at Reed College, Ali Akbar Khan performed a concert of Indian classical music. I had been listening to Ali Akbar Khan for years, taking acid, playing my guitar, trying to follow what he was doing. Gangadhar and I took mescaline that night and, although the musicians left the stage, it seemed to us that not only didn't the concert ever stop, but we also had just heard the true music of

the spheres! I dropped out of Reed a few months later (failing music and religion!) and moved to the Bay Area to study with Khansahib, as Ali Akbar Khan was called by his students, for about a year and a half before going to India. When I returned from India my studies and relationship with Khansahib and his family continued. His death some years ago still is very painful.

During this time in California, I got into a yoga society called Ananda Marga, and we had an ashram in Berkeley. The guru, Ananda Murti, had guaranteed us enlightenment. Perhaps I misunderstood him, but this is what the eighteen-year-old Jai wanted to believe. We were so American: we got a guarantee! We had tasks each day that we had to do in exchange for the guarantee. Now, of course, it's like, "Enlightenment? What does that even mean? Can I somehow remember God and be kind to those around me? Can I feel, for one second, what bhakti really means?" You know, the simple things that are actually not simple at all. But back then "enlightenment" was in the bag!

The message came that if we went to one of the guru's big ceremonies, he would do a mudra, and if we were in the presence of that mudra, enlightenment would be ours. So that was the motivation to go to India. Charlie's aunt had died and left him an inheritance; he bought tickets for me, him, Gangadhar, Kathleen, and Janaki to go to India. Our plan was to go to that ceremony, get enlightened, and come back as new and improved people!

I remember stepping off the plane in New Delhi and feeling, "Wow, I have just come out of a nineteen-year exile." It was so profound. I was finally home. There was an American guy who had gone to India three months before us to become a monk in the Ananda Marga organization. He met us at the airport and said, "Ananda Murti is in jail for mass murder. He allegedly killed thirty or forty of his monks, and the rest of his monks are fleeing for their lives."

Though shocking, this news was kind of liberating; we were now in Delhi with no agenda. We had been planning to perform for the guru, so we all had our instruments. What now? I was wandering around New Delhi, browsing in the Piccadilly Bookstore, when the proprietor said to me, "Ram Dass is in town. He's giving classes at the Palace Heights Hotel." I knew Ram Dass from America, so I immediately went to see him. When I got to the hotel, they said, "Ram Dass left three days ago to go to Vrindavan to see his guru." It seemed as good a direction as any.

We got on a train to Mathura and proceeded to Vrindavan, where we found out that Maharajji had *jaoed* everybody for a week. Gangadhar, Charlie, and I went out on the lawn of Jaipuria Bhavan and started chanting and jamming. Then this guy in a red kurta came down from his room yelling at us, "You can't do that hippie stuff here in India. Go to your rooms!" That was the start of a lifelong relationship with my dear *gurubhai* [brother devotee] Krishna Das.

It was absolutely amazing to be there, December of '71. Every night we would all do aarti and a little kirtan on the roof. There was a big altar with all different gods and goddesses and Maharajji in the middle. I found the aarti ceremony to be incredibly moving and beautiful. And what a heavenly realm Vrindavan was in those days: every other house was a temple, and kirtan was literally everywhere!

When the week was over, I was like, "Okay, I'll go and see Maharajji. No big deal; as far as gurus were concerned, been there done that!" Yet I remember running through the streets and getting there before any of the other Westerners or Indians, without really knowing why. Maharajji hadn't come out yet.

I sat there in the courtyard, enchanted by the kirtan that was being sung. Finally Maharajji burst out of his room. Fruit was flying, *pow, pow!* A dozen conversations were happening at once. Maharajji turned to Janaki and asked who her guru was, and I was kind of surprised when she said, "Ananda Murti." Maharajji said, "Oh, Ananda Baba, the railway clerk. You Americans are so easily deceived." That was intense, right?

Three or so weeks passed in this way, and every day I ran to the temple. I didn't think he was my guru—it wasn't even an issue—but he was a thousand percent magnetic.

One day I got some berries to offer to Maharajji. They looked like mulberries. I washed them, and when I put them into the bag, the bag broke and they fell to the floor. I picked the berries up and washed them again individually. Somehow it became a big job. I had to wash them twice. This time I packaged them carefully. It wasn't because I was trying to do something special; I just didn't want to offer something dirty. Maharajji opened the package, took each berry, and looked at me as he ate it. He was laughing and kept repeating the Hindi word for berries and gazing at me. Then he hit me on the head a couple of times. I was totally turned inside out. I couldn't feel the ground.

After darshan, I was walking to the hotel with my prasad, feeling like I was on acid. The elephant that lived at the neighboring ashram came over to the low fence and looked at me inquisitively, so I gave him my banana. He gobbled it up, then turned his trunk to the side, and squatted on his back legs. He lifted one front leg in front of the other, crossed it like Krishna, tilted his head, and stuck his trunk out like a flute. I felt like the elephant gave me darshan of Lord Krishna for real. Maharajji had opened me up to see between the realities for that moment. I'll never forget it. The elephant became Lord Krishna to me.

Left to right: Ram Dass, Jai, Uddhav, Gangadhar, and Maharajji.

At the end of those weeks, I came to the temple one morning and was told that Maharajji had left in the night. They didn't know where he had gone or when he'd be back. I was heartbroken. I hadn't realized how incredibly attached to him I had become. In some ways this was the beginning of my spiritual life. The super well of anguish that had been hidden within me flooded the gates of my heart—not because Maharajji had left, but because, in leaving, he had forced those doors to open. At that moment I began to sing from my deepest heart, my real emotions. Suddenly this dormant part of me woke up, painfully and miserably. And then this feeling, "Where's Maharajji? I love Maharajji. I need Maharajji. I want Maharajji. Where is he? Does he even know I exist?"

About thirty years ago I was in Vrindavan with Siddhi Ma [one of Maharajji's very close devotees to whom he left the running of his ashrams after he died], and she was showing me Maharajji's books where he wrote his *RamRams* each day. She got to this one page where, instead of the *RamRams* being written vertically, they were written horizontally. I said, "What happened then?" Ma said, "Oh, that's the day you came, Jai Gopal." I started crying. It was like seven centuries of tears poured out of me. Just the fact that she would know the day I got there, that I was even noticed, made me fall apart.

Janaki first heard a sitar concert at the Asian Arts Society in Berkeley when she was fourteen years old and immediately wanted to learn that music. She started with the sarod and then moved on to voice, studying at the Ali Akbar College, where she met Jai and Gangadhar. They were serious music students and serious meditators. They lived in a group house where Ram Dass had come to do some workshops, so they had heard of Maharajji, but never thought they would ever meet him.

JANAKI: We got off the train in Mathura and went to Maharajji's ashram. The pujari comes to the gate and tells the driver to take us over to Jaipuria Bhavan. Krishna Das was the one who met us there. I remember everyone else was wearing white clothing and malas, and they were smacking of the Ananda Marga vibe. I was like, "Oh no, I'm just not into this."

When we went to the temple for darshan, Kathleen and
I dressed up in our saris. We were feeling nervous because
obviously everyone else was really into this. I'm from an
intellectual Berkeley family, and nobody in my family is religious.
To do yoga is one thing, but to be smitten with a personality
was definitely not part of my upbringing; it was pretty much a
struggle to see other people like that.

We sat in the back. Maharajji looked at us and said to Kathleen,
"Sing in Sanskrit."

Kathleen said, "That's not me. That's her."

"Oh, *accha* [good]."

He sits up, then he says to come, the way he did with his hand.
"What's your name?"

"Janaki."

"I love that name." He was being really charming. "Who's
your guru?"

"Ananda Murti was, but we left him."

"No, no. Who really is your guru?"

"No one, Maharajji. No one is my guru."

"*Accha.*"

I sang *Akanda Mandala*—one of the songs that I had learned
in my Indian music courses. *Akanda mandalakaram vyaptam yena
characharam tat padam darshitam yena tasmai shri gurave namaha.*
It's a Sanskrit song that goes to the deepest core of the identity
of everything that exists. It asks, "What is the guru?" and goes
on to say that the guru is not a person in a body; the guru is
that infinite matrix that we are all a part of. I had sung this song
every day, many times a day, and that's what I really knew, and
continue to know. It all comes down to one thing: that the whole
universe is this infinite matrix of divine love.

He was really listening. Then he asked, "Who is your guru?"

Krishna Das (Roy Bonney)

Janaki, Kabir, (unknown), and Carlos Vishwanath with Maharajji.

"No *person* is my guru."

He liked that answer. He told some other people, "Did you hear what she said? Did you hear what she said?" He started to make a big deal about it.

When we came back the next day, Maharajji asked me the same questions again. It evolved into our routine. He would tell Indians, "You should be ashamed when this American woman can speak Sanskrit and you can't." Little did they know that I only knew a handful of Sanskrit songs, or *slokas*.

We were supposed to go for a month to India, and that turned out to be impossible. We all decided to forego the return and stay for whatever our visas were. Jai, Gangadhar, Govind, and Kathleen stayed for four months and then left, but Maharajji had me stay for years. He arranged my visa so I had a residence permit.

Gangadhar was in the Ananda Marga group and thought he "had God's address." He wanted to go to India and meet the guru, who was going to slap him on the head and put him into *samadhi,* the state of enlightenment. When that didn't work out for obvious reasons, he went with his friends to Vrindavan.

GANGADHAR: There are all these people in the hotel that I knew from California—Ram Dev, Vishwambar, Ram Dass, Krishna Das, Anjani, Balaram. The women's underwear salesman who was on the plane with us is in the hotel. The guy who threw me out of the Muktananda retreat is in the hotel. I am thinking, "This is just too weird. Where am I?" It's very dreamlike. I get the last hotel room, which is right on the corner on the street. At four in the morning this guy outside starts loudly singing *Radhe Shyam,* coughing and shaking, fantastic awakening. We get some fruit and flowers and go to the temple early in the morning to see the guru.

I am thinking, "What if he really is God? Maybe this is the guy. We came all the way to India to see the guy; maybe this is the guy." I'm getting in that "give it a chance" mood. I go in, and there's this beautiful statue of Hanuman. I am looking around. Where is the guy? I see a man, so I pranaam to him, and it is the gardener. Then I see another guy, and I go over there, and he's the gatekeeper; he opens this little door, and I go in, and there in the back Maharajji, wrapped up in a blanket, is sitting on a table in the sun. When I first looked at him, I thought, "Oh, the poor old man is blind." Immediately he bugs out his eyes at me, and I feel it in my chest.

He's laughing and bouncing around. He says, "What happened to your guru? What happened?"

I think, "We didn't tell anybody about this." The five of us all

had five different answers. One person says that we don't have
a guru. Another one says the guru is in jail. He says, "Krishna is
born in jail, and Krishna goes back to jail." Then I think, "Oh shit.
Baba Ananda Murti is really Krishna. I better get my butt over to
see him even though he is in jail."

Then somebody says he's a madman who deceived a lot of
Americans. Maharajji says Americans will believe anything
anybody tells them, and then he says, "Who's the guru?"

There is a guy walking along the road with a cow. Maharajji
says, "He's the guru." I look over and I think, "Oh, he's the guru.
I better go over there."

Then he says, "Americans are the guru, because they put milk
in cardboard boxes, and they put a man on the moon."

The translator looks at me, because he can see I am really
confused now. He says, "You see, the saint sees everyone as a
saint."

At that point Maharajji asked us to sing. Govind led a song.
Janaki led a song. Maharajji liked the song she sang, "Akanda
Mandala," and made her sing it at least ten times that day, for
every person who came. Then he sent us away to go have a meal.
We sat in rows on the ground with our leaf plates in front of us.
People ran up and down with buckets of food. I felt like I had
never been full before, but suddenly I was actually full. I was as
happy as can be. I remember thinking, "Who is this guy? And
what's he doing in my head?"

The next day I give Maharajji the fruit I brought and put my
head on his feet, and he makes me sit down. There is a fellow
next to me sitting in full lotus, Gurudatt Sharma. Maharajji
whacks him on the head, and then he tells me to take Gurudatt's
pulse. When we were in Delhi, someone had told me that if you
want to know if someone is really in samadhi, you should take

their pulse because they won't have one—they'll be in a state of suspended animation. So when Maharajji said, "Take his pulse," I thought, "Wait a minute. I was just thinking about that." Then I realized I didn't know how to take someone's pulse!

Maharajji is laughing and laughing. He grabs my fingers like in a Three Stooges movie, pokes the guy in his eyes with my fingers, and says, "Come on. Try to wake him up. Try to wake him up." Gurudatt is sitting there with his eyelids fluttering, and two guys lift him up and carry him off. Throughout the day Maharajji sends me over to check on him to see that he is still in this state.

He said, "Can you do that?"

"No, but I'd like to."

Then he more or less completely ignored me for the rest of the day. The next day we came, and he was gone.

I had figured out that if you go where Balaram goes, he'll find Maharajji. So when Balaram packed his bags and went to the train station, we also bought tickets to Allahabad. First we went to the Taj Mahal to play music there. Then we went to Allahabad and, sure enough, Maharajji was at Dada's house. I was so blessed: I had ten days where I saw Maharajji almost every day at Dada's.

Govind (Charlie) was friends with Jai from high school, where they were both into music and spirituality. He was also part of the Ananda Marga crowd. When he turned twenty-one, he inherited $6,000, a tremendous amount of money in those days. He was able to get tickets for himself and the others. So off they went to India, with Govind carrying his fiddle and a flute.

GOVIND (CHARLIE): My interactions with Maharajji were few, but fairly intense. There was a woman there, I think she

was Australian, whose boyfriend was an Indian. She and I took
a journey together to do a meditation retreat with Goenka,
and during that time we had a little romantic affair. When she
became pregnant, there was some confusion about the parentage,
and there was jealousy and so on. I was called over at one point to
meet with Maharajji about this triangle. We talked back and forth
about what was going on, and he mentioned that the baby wasn't
mine. Since I was pretty forthcoming about what had happened
between the two of us, he said to Dada, who was translating for
us, "See what an honest boy he is. How honest. How lovely."
That stuck with me forever.

The Name Game

MIRABAI: My name was Linda, but Maharajji wouldn't call
me by name. Then one day he was being really loving to me
and said, "Your name is Mirabai." He asked Radha to tell me
about Mirabai. I now know there are many different versions of
Mirabai's story, but they all have to do with her being a queen
who is devoted to Krishna while living in a Shaivite family. She
doesn't want to be a secular kind of queen. She spends all her
time doing her prayers and singing to Krishna, and her husband
is very upset with her. He tries to get her to worship Shiva and to
play her appropriate role in the family. She won't do it. The only
way he can get out of this situation is to get rid of her. He first
sends her a basket, and inside the basket is a poisonous snake, but
because of Mirabai's purity, the snake turns into flower petals.
Then he sends her poison in a glass, and when she drinks it, it
becomes *amrit* [nectar] because of her purity.

Radha told me these stories about Mirabai, how pure she was
and how she loved God, and how they say that Mirabai is the

embodiment of erotic bhakti. She loved God as her lover. I was completely enchanted by the stories, even though her husband kept trying to kill her. Maharajji gave me a name, a beautiful name! I love you Maharajji, I love you. From that moment on, in my mind and heart I became Mirabai. I never thought of myself as Linda again.

However, John was sitting next to me, and when he heard the stories he jumped up and ran to leave the temple grounds, which none of us ever, ever did. Maharajji looked up puzzled. He sent Ram Dass to bring him back. John was crying. Maharajji said to Ram Dass, "Why did he run away? Why is he crying?" Ram Dass said, "He doesn't want to be the husband that keeps his wife from God."

This is one of my favorite Maharajji moments. He kind of cocked his head and said, "Why does he think that way?"

Maharajji said to John, "You are Krishna, and you should be called by that name."

It was stunning for John, and for me. Since then I have asked myself that question so many times: "Mirabai, why do you think that way?"

KRISHNA: *Be Here Now* had come out. We used to have Maharajji all to ourselves, and all of a sudden people were jumping on airplanes and flying over. Didn't have any relationship with India, didn't like India, didn't like Indians, but they liked Maharajji. The scene was getting more and more like high school. We used to call it the "grace race." There was a lot of gossip and backbiting. It seemed to me that the scene had metamorphosed into something much bigger and less cohesive than it used to be. And I missed being with Indians and sadhus and going to holy places.

I had had an argument with Mirabai that morning. Maharajji

was getting ready to leave Vrindavan, and I wanted to leave the satsang and go out into India. She wanted to stay with the satsang; if we went out into India, we might miss when Maharajji came back. We patched up the argument and went for darshan, and he calls her up.

Radha is sitting with them and translator Sharma. About five minutes went by, and Maharajji asked me to come sit down next to Mira. The translator said, "Maharajji's given her the name Mirabai. Do you know who Mirabai is?"

I didn't. Maharajji had Radha tell me the story of Mirabai. I started feeling, "Oh my God, I am being cast in the part of her husband, the jealous king who is keeping her from Krishna," because of that argument we had earlier in the morning. I was horrified. Instead of feeling happy that Mirabai had been given this beautiful name, I was like the bad guy in the story. I became overwhelmed with grief, with sorrow.

I was really going to lose it emotionally, so I got up, bowed to Maharajji, and walked out of the temple as fast as I could. I stood in front of the Hanuman *murti* [consecrated statue] and started crying inconsolably. At that point Ram Dass came out and said, "What's the matter? Why are you acting like this?"

I said, "I don't want to be the king who keeps my wife from being with Krishna."

Ram Dass said tenderly, "I think you've got a mis-take on this." I remember that word. I'd never heard "mistake" as "mis-take." "Come back. Maharajji wants to talk to you."

I came back in, wiped my tears away, and sat back down in front of him. He said, "What's wrong?"

I blurted out to him that I don't want to be that person who is keeping my wife from Krishna.

He looked at me with this look of real kindness and said, "Why do you think that way?" I'll never forget it. It became my mantra from that point on. He said, "Mirabai's true husband was Krishna, and your name is Krishna, and you should be called by that name."

The marriage lasted ten years and created a wonderful son and granddaughter. I continue to ask myself, "Why do you think that way?"

No Doubt

Steven Schwartz always wanted to go to live in Paris, so when he finished law school he planned a trip: he would go to India in November and Paris in March. He landed in Bombay in December 1971, went to Goa, and then traveled all over; he found out about Goenka and took the course in Bodhgaya. He had read *Be Here Now,* so he knew about Maharajji, but during the meditation course he met Krishna Das and Sunanda, who told him to go see Maharajji in Vrindavan.

STEVEN: I only had a week left before I was supposed to leave India and go to Paris. I got on a train to Mathura, and when I got off there was the entire satsang at the station. There must have been thirty people. I yelled across the tracks because I saw Krishna Das, "What are you doing here?"

He said, "Maharajji is sending us to see Sai Baba in Delhi."

I said, "Well, I'm going to see Maharajji. I only have a week, and I've already seen Sai Baba."

Tukaram and Sita were at Jaipuria Bhavan when I arrived. Tuk said, "Did you bring something for Maharajji?" I thought, "You jerk. Can't believe you're going to see a saint and you don't bring him a piece of fruit." So Tukaram went into his *jhola* [a cloth bag] and gave me a bunch of oranges, and we went to see Maharajji. I bent down and handed him an orange, and he threw the orange right back at me.

He said, "You have a question."

My question was whether I should change my ticket and stay, or go on. Before I asked the question he said, "*Jao*, New York."

I looked at Tuk, and he said, "He said 'Go to New York.' Go back to New York."

"Well, when should I go?"

Maharajji said, "Four days. Stay with me for three days, then you should go to New York."

At first, just the physical interaction, his saying, "*Jao*, New York," stopped my mind. Totally stopped my mind. I realized that I had come home in a way.

On each of the next three days, I spent the whole day at the temple. Maharajji was there, but he didn't call anyone over. I was waiting for something to happen. I would go there in the morning and sit for a couple of hours, and I would say once in a while to Tuk, "Hello? What do we do here?"

"Just sit and be quiet. If he wants to talk to you, he'll call you over."

Those couple of days were an inquiry into what this was about. The more I looked, the emptier it got. I realized there was absolutely nothing happening, and the more there was nothing . . . it didn't get edgy, but it got confusing. "Isn't something supposed to happen?" Then there was, "Maybe this is really boring." Then there was, "This is incredibly beautiful," and then it was, "This is just empty. This is whatever I bring to it, whatever I fill the space with." I could fill the space with endless thoughts and ideas and worries and visions and fantasies. As much as I wanted to fill it, he wasn't going to put anything in the space.

I spent three days there. At the end I went to see Maharajji and said, "Do I really have to go?"

He said, "*Jao,* New York."

"When?"

"Now!" That was the only thing he ever said to me.

When I went to leave, I was really sad, but he was so firm the second time when he said, "Now." Tukaram said, "Get out. He's not kidding around."

No Paris. I took the train back to Delhi, stayed there for a night, then flew to Kennedy airport. I called my mother in New Jersey, and she started sobbing and sobbing. "You are supposed to be happy I'm home. What's wrong?"

She said, "Oh, thank God they found you. I've been trying for the last week to find you, because your brother's in the mental hospital. He tried to take his life." I went right to the hospital in New York.

From that time on, in addition to Maharajji being who he is— your teacher, your guru, your spiritual guide—he was also the synchronicity that he knew and created a way for me to take care of my brother. I have found that the whole journey since then is becoming more and more friendly with Maharajji, so that now I think of him as my friend.

I didn't have a lot of time with him. Just those couple of days. But from the end of March '72, when I left, there has never been a moment of doubt. I've never had a single moment. Nor has there been a moment of longing. I wasn't there for months and years and didn't have as intense a falling in love, but there has never been a moment of doubt.

Each place where we spent time with Maharajji was magical in its own way. India is a vast subcontinent, yet every part of it is imbued with the different colors and manifestations of Spirit. It truly is the land of the saints—from the caves of the high Himalayas to its holy rivers and sacred plains. From the lake formed by the "eye" of Sati in Nainital to the banks of the Yamuna River in Vrindavan, where Krishna merged with the gopis in a dance of love, we watched as Maharajji embodied the spiritual essence of each place. We next followed Maharajji to Allahabad, where the sacred rivers meet.

10

Where the Sacred Rivers Meet

January 1972

After I had stopped visiting the ashrams [after Baba left his body], some ardent devotees started saying, "Dada has left Baba." When faced with a statement like this, the only reply I could give was, "When did I catch hold of Baba that I could leave him now? He caught me! I could never catch him, so there is no question of leaving him." That is all of it.

—DADA MUKERJEE, *BY HIS GRACE*

Maharajji stayed in Vrindavan for most of November and December (although he had sent us away during the three-week war between India and Pakistan). In January he went to Allahabad, a city on the plains of northern India. It was originally called Prayag, which means "place of offerings"; it is mentioned in the Vedas as the place where Brahma, the Creator, attended a sacrificial ritual. Allahabad sits at the junction of three holy rivers (called the Sangam)—the Ganges, the Yamuna, and the underground spiritual river Saraswati. The Kumbha Mela is held here every twelve years, a mass pilgrimage of tens of millions of Hindus, who bathe in the confluence of the sacred rivers at an auspicious astrological time to cleanse themselves of karma.

Ram Dass and those who had been "on the bus" had spent a few days at Dada's after their surprise meeting at the mela grounds almost a year earlier, but by now the satsang had grown considerably. We were put up nearby in a large house owned by one of Maharajji's Indian devotees.

Maharajji and Dada Mukerjee.

Watching Dada's daily interaction with Maharajji was a great teaching for us. He was incredibly in tune with Baba. Dada would be serving food, telling stories to the Westerners, or talking with his wife (Didi), mother, or auntie (who all lived together in the house), when he would suddenly turn and leave to go to Maharajji. It was only *after* he was headed in Maharajji's direction that we would hear Maharajji calling for him! He spent over forty years as one of Maharajji's closest devotees and had an endless storehouse of wonderful stories that he gladly shared with us Westerners.[1]

LAMA SURYA DAS: February '72, I heard people were going to Allahabad to see Maharajji. All the Westerners who got off at the train station were going to Dada's house.

I walked in, and there's kirtan going on in the living room. This is my first kirtan except for a tiny bit of Hare Krishna in college in Buffalo, along with their free sweets and veggie dinner. Goenka courses weren't a kirtan scene, not at all. My buddy Krishna Bush was leading the kirtan in Dada's living room, and I just fell into it. I knew I belonged. There were twenty or thirty Westerners. Half the people I recognized from Bodhgaya Vipassana meditation retreats with Goenkaji. I saw my people and sat down next to Mohan and Radha, or maybe it was Tukaram and Sita. Everybody's chanting and grooving. There was the takhat, the bed/bench with the red plaid blanket, and many flowers. There was a nice picture of Maharajji. I'm looking at the picture, I'm chanting along, and my heart's opening like never before. It was home. And I really had darshan of Maharajji in that space.

Then I noticed a few people coming in and out of some entrance to the living room. What was going on? They said they were going in to see Maharajji. I was already having darshan, heart open, as if he was there himself, so I didn't jump right up, but eventually I got in that room with Maharajji by myself.

Dadaji was twirling a towel to keep the bugs off Maharajji. Here was our gray-haired Indian Brahmin professor host with a white shirt and a black vest with beedies stuck in the pocket and a dhoti wrapped around him so he looked like a kindly pasha or sultan. He was a nice old gentleman, and I thought that must be Dada with this ancient baba, who's sitting there in a funny posture on the takhat, smiling and welcoming me. Baba doesn't speak English. I bow down. Dada said something like, "Oh, you have come," as if they were expecting me. Dada said, "Maharajji says take this prasad," and he gives me a banana.

This is what it was like. This is what we studied at that ashram: *have a banana.* So what does Jeff Miller from Long Island think to himself? "I hate bananas!" It's practically the only food in the world I don't eat, haven't eaten since I was a baby. I didn't think, "Banana, monkey, Hanuman, Maharajji, blessed prasad." I didn't even know enough to form such associations and concepts. He gave me something I didn't like and called it prasad. I knew prasad meant "blessed food or substance." He must have given me a blessing. I went back into the kirtan. I gave this banana to somebody, and they divided it up, laughed, and said, "Oh, Jeff gave away his prasad. He didn't even have a piece." People weren't judgmental, but it was funny. We were all laughing together. What a dufus! It was so innocent.

I don't have a lot of Maharajji stories, because I was only with him for a few weeks here and there. The first story is that I had my darshan of Maharajji first doing kirtan with the satsang in Dada's living room. That for me is my first Maharajji darshan, like I met the *big* Maharajji right then. Then I went in that room and met the old man in the blanket, his human form. The

Maharajji in that room left a week later, but the big Maharajji didn't seem to leave. The one in the room died like a year or two later, but that big Maharajji never left. So that's my Maharajji—always right here with me, with us.

Lama Surya Das's experience of the "big Maharajji" before meeting the "Baba in the blanket" who gave him a banana contains the essence of our relationship to Maharajji now. Thousands of people have met the "big Maharajji" without ever meeting him in the body and have the same connection and devotion to him as those of us who were in India with him. Maharajji himself said that the guru does not have to be in a physical body. A great siddha transcends time and space to connect with people and speed them on their path.

The next story shows the power of Maharajji's name. Over and over again, saying "my guru, Neem Karoli Baba" to a complete stranger could bring unexpected acknowledgment. It also shows Maharajji's ever present hand behind the events in our lives.

KRISHNA PRIYA: I am on the train. The conductor gets to me and asks for my ticket, and I don't have one. He says to me, "Young lady, this may be India, and this may be third class, but you still need a ticket. Where are you going?"

I hear myself saying I am going to Allahabad to see my guru. I don't even know what a guru is.

He goes, "Really, and who is that?"

"Just a minute." I take out my Om butterfly book, which didn't have anything in it except little anecdotes, addresses, recipes, the location of a cool bookstore, or the name of a cute guy. I flip it till I get to the address, and say, "Ah, his name is Neem Karoli Baba."

The guy just stopped. He comes back after a few minutes and gives me a ticket. This is a local train, and at every stop he buys me chai, he buys me sweets, he buys me *namkeen* [peanuts]. By the time I get to Allahabad, I've eaten more than I have in ten months. I don't understand what's going on at all.

I get a rickshaw and go to Dada's house. I, who weighed about ninety pounds, in my tie-dyed crushed-velvet fringed cape, with my guitar and frizzy hair, had no idea what I had walked into. Maharajji was not there, but Dada was there and the Mas [Dada's wife, mother, and aunt]. Some time later all these Westerners arrived. A fellow called Ram Dass seemed to have some influence, maybe because he was older.

A few days before Maharajji appeared, six or seven of us went to the Sangam. We took a boat to the reef in the middle where the rivers join, dipped around in the water, got back into the boat, and were getting ready to leave. All of a sudden by the side of the boat is a man standing in the water holding two malas in his hand.

I see the malas, and I go, *"Kitna paisa?* How much?"

He goes, *"Nahin, nahin, nahin, Ram bhakta* [No, no, no, devotee of Ram]," and he points to a Hanuman necklace around his neck. He drops the malas in Govind's hand. Sunanda and I are the only two in the boat who don't have malas. I grab the quarter mala, and she grabs the 108-bead mala.

My mala is made of tulsi beads. Each bead has been hand carved and is shiny with use. One bead has *Ram* burned into it, and the next one has *Sita. Ram Sita Ram Sita.* Engrossed in the malas, we look up and the man is gone. Disappeared. We're all blown away.

A year later I was in Vrindavan, and Maharajji took the mala off my wrist and started playing with it. He looked at me and said, "Where did you get this mala?"

Before I could answer, he said, "You got this mala in Allahabad."

"Yeah."

"Where did you get this mala?"

Before I can answer, "You got this mala at the Sangam in Allahabad. Who gave you this mala?"

"A sadhu gave me this mala."

He looked at me, "Your guru gave you this mala." Finally he acknowledged that he had given me the mala.

JAI: We got to Allahabad, and Maharajji wasn't there. We were hanging out, every day going to Dada's and doing a little kirtan, praying that Maharajji would arrive soon. The Westerners were a larger group then, maybe fifty or sixty people. My girlfriend, Janaki, met Carlos and immediately fell in love with him. He was an extremely handsome dancer, charismatic, with hair down to his knees, and dressed like a god from ancient times. On top of that, I got my first really bad bout of dysentery. I was sick. I was depressed. It was one of those "why did I ever come to India" moments.

I went to sleep one night and had an incredible dream. I was at the train station in Allahabad by myself in the middle of the night, toward early, early morning. The train rolled in, and Maharajji stepped off onto the platform, alone, wearing a grayish blanket rather than his usual plaid one. He wrapped his arms and the blanket around me, and I began to cry. Maharajji was crying and crying as well. Not tears of sadness. These were tears of homecoming—this feeling of finally, finally having come back. I don't know if he was saying that to me or I was saying that to him. It was incredibly deep. From that moment on I knew he was my guru. I had an awareness of our ancient connection, that he had been protecting me life after life, and the miracle that in this life we were together again.

I woke up in an altered state of consciousness. I looked at the clock and saw it was about one twenty. I went back to sleep feeling like something huge had happened. As usual, I woke up in the morning and went to Dada's. Everything was quite different. There was a hush in the air. Someone told me that Maharajji had arrived at one twenty in the morning, alone, at the Allahabad station. A chill ran through my whole body. I hadn't felt that I needed that confirmation, but when I got it, it was sealed. It was a big change in my little, tiny understanding of what was happening.

Mahavir Das, the women's undergarment salesman and Ram Dass's East Coast mala maker, finally made it to India to see Maharajji.

MAHAVIR DAS: Pauline and I and the two kids decided to go to India. She and the kids stopped in Bangalore to stay with Sai Baba, and I went up north to see Maharajji. I found the temple in Vrindavan, walked in the door, and sitting on a table was this battleship, this big powerful shiny creature. He was really enormous, covered with three or four blankets in the boiling Indian sun. He motioned for me to come. I was afraid because I had heard stories of him kicking people out. First of all, I was cheating on my wife, plus I was lying to everyone, and I was a lousy father. I was a hideous creature, and I knew he was going to kick me out. As I walked up, he called me a name, which Dada told me later was not a compliment.

Maharajji looked at the bag I was carrying and said, "What do you have in there?" I immediately knew that he knew what was in there. I gave him the oranges, and I thought he was going to thank me very much, but he just threw them to others. "What the . . . ? Now what do I do?" Then he went through pictures of my kids and wife, telling me that all children are my children and all women are my mother. At least he didn't throw me out.

Then we were in Allahabad. The last day I was there I thought I would go to the Sangam, where the mela is held, so I woke up really early. I figured I would sneak out before anybody saw me, but there they were, Dada and Maharajji. Narcissist that I am, I knew they were waiting for me.

Maharajji said, "Where are you going?"

"To the mela."

He said, "Take this and fill it with water and bring it back."

This filthy old Coca-Cola bottle. "Okay, he wants me to do something. Finally I'll do something for the guru."

I went to the Sangam, and I knew that I had to get a pujari to dunk me in the water and say a prayer. This had to be like eight or nine in the morning. I saw this skinny little Indian guy, gave him a rupee, and he dunked me in the water. I came up . . . *and it was night!*

I went back to Dada's place, and there are Maharajji and Dada waiting for me. Maharajji looked at me and said, "Very good, very good." I gave him the Coke bottle, which I had cleaned out and filled with Ganga [Ganges] water. He said, "Come here, come here," poured the water over my head, and started to laugh uproariously.

I said, "I have to go home tomorrow. Come home with me."

He said, "You will never be any place where I won't be. We won't be separate. Now go. Go home. Go."

There were those who had inexplicable experiences that involved loss of time. To this day, Mahavir Das doesn't know what happened between getting dunked in the river in the early morning and coming up many hours later when it was night. But clearly the immersion in the holy waters cleared a lot of his negative past, which Maharajji reinforced by pouring the Ganga water from the Coke bottle over his head—yet another cleansing of karma. (In the years that followed, he got divorced, became a therapist, and married the true love of his life.)

Marriage

Marriages were one of the ways in which Maharajji changed the direction of our lives or set us on a particular path. Some of the devotees came to Maharajji as a couple already, like Mirabai and Krishna, but most were single. Although celibacy was considered the spiritual ideal, the reality was that we were a group of young horny hippies. There were inevitable pairings—some of which were definitely fostered by a push from Maharajji—and eventually there were quite a few "arranged" marriages.

MIRABAI: We were all being celibate, more or less, partly because we were usually sleeping in a room with five other people. Maharajji had sent us to Puri, and a whole group of us were living in a house there. When we first got there, it was just John and me and Kabir. Kabir went down to the beach and got sunstroke and didn't come back that night. It was our one night alone.

Some weeks later, Ram Dass came to visit. He and I were both feeling awful and thought we had worms, so we took the dreaded black-worm medicine. We would fast for a day, then take the medicine, and then fast again. It was horrible. Some weeks later we met up in Delhi. By that time I had gone to the doctor, because I continued to have symptoms. I said, "Ram Dass, I'm pregnant. What about you?" He had hepatitis.

I went to Maharajji and said, "Maharajji, I'm pregnant. What should I do?" Of course, I thought he was going to give me the

Krishna and Mirabai at their wedding.

secret teachings about mothering and that I would have a whole
special sadhana.

He looked right at me and said, "You should get married."
All of a sudden he was a concerned uncle. "You should have
a wedding, and you should have rings." A different kind of
sadhana.

The wedding was at Dada's house in the garden. Someone
built a fire. The hems of our clothes were tied together, and we
walked around the fire, while Krishna Das chanted. Maharajji
was sitting there and after we walked, he said, *"Shaadi ho gaya.*

[You're married.] It's done." There were many sweets. All the guests were given a garland of jasmine and roses as they arrived. After the ceremony everyone put their garlands on the bride and groom. Laden with flowers and tied together, we looked like murtis. It was a wonderful day.

Ram Dev experienced a different type of marriage—that of Buddhist meditation practice and the path of bhakti, devotion.

RAM DEV: I came to Maharajji and said, "Maharajji, my mind is so busy all of the time. Can I go and study with these Buddhist meditation teachers?"

He said, "If you wish."

He didn't seem too enthusiastic about the idea, but I decided that I would go anyway. I had some deep experiences at the courses, where my mind went into slow motion. I was thinking, "Wow, this is going to be great to go back to Maharajji, because not only do I have all of this love that I had before, but now I've got this quiet mind, so I could really drink in the nectar that is his being."

Back in Allahabad, I came into the room, people were singing, and everybody was happy. I could see him. I could see form, shape, and movement, but I didn't *feel* a thing. I might have been in such an expanded and empty place that that was love, but I was missing the emotional piece that all of these other people were feeling. This happened for three days in a row.

Finally I decided I would go to the Sangam. I prayed there, "Please open my heart, please open my heart, Baba." I immersed myself at least partway in the Sangam. I came out of the water, and it worked! I had this really still mind and something had sprung open in my heart; every leaf of every tree was glowing with consciousness. It was an incredible feeling.

I'm really excited to go back and see Maharajji. I hop in the rickshaw, and I realize, "Wait, there's no place between here and Dada's house to get prasad. What am I going to do?" Just as I had that thought, right by the side of the road was a guy selling Indian spiritual calendar pictures. They were all so tacky. Then I saw this one picture that was a very sweet rendition of that scene in the *Ramayana* where Ram is embracing Hanuman. I bought it, jumped back into the rickshaw, and said, "4 Church Lane. Let's go."

In those days if you came late, it was so crowded that there was virtually no chance of getting up front. You would have to sit in the back and pass your prasad forward. But for some reason this day there was a pathway right up to the front.

In the past when I had offered him prasad, it was usually with the thought, "I'm poor and unworthy and need your help immensely, so please accept this, please be kind to me." Now I was in a state of consciousness where there's no me, there's no him, it's just the act of putting the picture on the takhat. He picked it up and looked at it, and he started crying. Maybe it was my imagination, but it felt like he was remembering that event. Pretty soon everyone in the front of the room was weeping. The feeling of love was so thick you could cut it. All of a sudden Maharajji jumped off the takhat, gave the picture to Dada, and said something in Hindi. He left the room, slammed the door, and didn't come back out for an hour.

We went to Vrindavan some weeks later, and in the back of the main Hanuman temple in Vrindavan was that picture. It had been framed. It was in that temple for many years, till long after he died.

Give Your Father the Medicine

Most of us were quite young when we were with Maharajji, in our late teens and twenties. Now, as a mother and grandmother, I have an inkling of what our parents must have gone through when we were literally halfway around the world in the days before cell phones, e-mail, and instant texts. Placing a call (in the few places that had a phone) could take hours or days. Some of our parents tried to entice us "home"—my mother sent me a Polaroid of a bagel to try to woo me back to the world she knew and understood. Occasionally, some parents' curiosity got the better of them, and they came to India to see what their kids were up to. You could say that they got "the call" through their children, and Maharajji used the opportunity to clear up a lot of family history and dynamics.

RAGHU: When my father arrived in India in December 1971, Laxman, Parvati, and I went with him to Vrindavan. There was a big wall around the inner compound. On the outer side of the wall was the statue of Hanuman and a place to take your shoes off. My father was there for a while because he was wearing shoes with laces instead of the flip-flops we all wore.

I ran in first, and Maharajji said, "Your father's here!" As my father came in, Maharajji said, "He's very good. He came all the way from Canada to see you. He loves you very much. You don't love him as much as he loves you. *Tora tora.* [Little bit.]"

Some of the backstory to this is that my father and I did not get along. When he said he was coming to India, I was horrified. I had a lot of anger toward him. He was a real tyrant when I was a kid. So this was all new territory for me—to be sitting in front of Maharajji with my father.

"Did he give you money? You only love him because he gives you money." At this point I'm going white in front of him. Maharajji asks, "What does he do?"

"He's in advertising."

"How much does he make?"

"I don't know, around $30,000," which was a lot at that time.

Then he says to my father, "Will you give me money? I'm your son too. Can you show me some American money?"

My father gave him a $5 bill, which Maharajji gave to Parvati, and then took it back. "I won't give it to her. If you want, you can give it to her. Did Raghvindra Das tell you they are going to get married?" Which I had no idea about at that moment. At all.

"Ed, give Parvati $100 and a sari." He had Parvati touch my father's feet. Then he had my brother and I touch my father's feet. "You have to love and honor your father to love God."

Then he said to me, "Did you give your father the medicine?"

"The medicine? Yes, he had a cold, and I gave him some aspirin."

"Nay! The little pills that Ram Dass gave me."

"LSD?"

My father went, "LSD?"

Maharajji said, "He hasn't taken them? Why not? Take care of your father while he's in India."

He said to my father, "You came here not only to see your sons, but also to find your own truth. How did you find your sons?"

My father said, "Well, they seem happy."

Maharajji said, "Happiness is everything. Go to Benares and meet me in Allahabad in a week."

I did find some acid, and my father did take it in Benares on a houseboat about a hundred yards from the burning *ghats* [steps], where they've been cremating bodies every day around the clock for thousands of years. He thought he wasn't afraid to die. He had been a bomber pilot in World War II. He took the acid. We walked through the streets of Benares—dead animals, a dead person. We walked to the burning ghats and watched a cremation.

A week later we met Maharajji in Allahabad. The only thing he said about the trip was, "The Ganga is very pure." Then he told my father the whole story about how my father had saved a horse that was going to be shot, euthanized, because it had a bad leg, and he stayed up all night, put healing clay on it, and saved the horse. My father fell apart, sobbing.

We became friends after that; for the first time we had the start of a real family. It wound up that my brother and sister and their

Raghu, Laxman, Dasaratha, and Parvati sitting in front of Maharajji.

spouses were all devotees. Even my mother eventually went to India and had darshan with Siddhi Ma. What Maharajji gave me was so miraculous as it related to a really broken-up family that he mended.[2]

PARVATI (from her journal):

January 5, 1972
Today Raghvindra Das fulfilled Maharajji's order to take care of his father in Benares. Ed took acid. We waited for instant enlightenment. After all, Maharajji said to give him acid. He sat there looking at a book. Finally we left the houseboat to take a walk. Up the river, past the burning ghats, washing ghats, bathing ghats. Up to Ganga Ma temple. Through alleyways of brass shops. Passed a dead cow. Saw a dead man, people throwing coins/rupees to cover the cost of wood for the funeral pyre, and dead bodies wrapped in white sheets, awaiting their turn to burn. Ed was just stoned enough to have it all be a confrontation with death. And for us, a lesson in expectation.

Part Three

The Second
Wave

March 1972–September 1973

11

Comings and Goings

Spring / Summer 1972

What would live on for a lifetime are your memories
of it [experiences had during travel], your processing
of it, and how that experience elevated you to
actually live in your own current life.

—OPRAH WINFREY[1]

In February and March of 1972, the visa melodrama was in full swing for many of the original group of Westerners. Danny and Anasuya had left. Ram Dev and others had been *jaoed* back to America. Canadians didn't need visas, but Americans certainly did. Maharajji sometimes drew out the visa game, sending people to high-level government officials so they could be permitted to stay, while he sent others to local offices where applications for renewal were usually rejected. Some he would send to Nepal, so they could reapply for a new visa. In February, he had Ram Dass, Radha and Mohan, and Rameshwar Das go to Delhi to appeal their visas.

Despite all attempts to get extensions, it was time for some of us to go. Maharajji had told me early in my stay that I would leave when Ram Dass did, and sure enough, Raghu and I (Maharajji had married us in Allahabad), Mirabai and Krishna, Radha and Mohan, and Ram Dass all left together in early March 1972. We had a stopover in Rome, where we raced to the nearest airport restaurant to eat some pasta. From there we flew to London, stayed a short while, and then went on to our different destinations.

Balaram Das

Kausalya, Sunanda, Laxman, and Vishwambar with Maharajji.

With the departure of Ram Dass, the scene in India changed. There was no longer a "commander in chief," as Maharajji had called Ram Dass. Many of the Westerners who came to Maharajji after this time had never heard of or met Ram Dass, although some had read *Be Here Now.* So there were no Western "elders." Any type of hierarchy was gone, and things started to loosen up.

Some who were in both the first and second "waves" have said that there was now less "teaching," meaning no one was asking the type of questions that Ram Dass and the others had asked of Maharajji about meditation and various spiritual concerns. And by this point, a number of Westerners had learned enough Hindi that it wasn't always necessary to have one of the Indians acting as translator. The Westerners understood more about what Maharajji was saying as he interacted with his Indian devotees about their everyday concerns—about home, work, school, health, children—as well as about politics and current events.

Spring 1972

SUNANDA: Laxman and I were getting involved. One night we decided we were going to get married. We got into a cab with Vishu and Kausalya, who also decided they were going to get married, and the four of us went to Vrindavan. There were only a few people there, and Maharajji let us spend a lot of time with him. As we walked in he said, "They're married, they're married." And then he kept mixing us all up, like who was married to whom. Afterward I heard that he had said, "What difference does it make?"

It was very hot in Vrindavan and he was wearing a white sheet, so he looked extremely elegant. As I watched him stand up and wrap the sheet around himself, he seemed to take up vast amounts of space. When he was walking, with each step it felt like the earth was shaking.

Keshori was doing Vipassana meditation, and Maharajji said, "Buddha meditation." Then he said, "I am the Buddha." I was rubbing his hands, and all of a sudden he closed his eyes, and I felt his hand going down into that Buddha mudra—touching the earth. He went into this really powerful state, and I knew this was not a time to be touching him.

We left because my visa was up, and Laxman was ready to go home. We went to Delhi, and I got pregnant on our way leaving India. My daughter and I were both "made in India."

Krishna Das (Roy Bonney)

Maharajji's hands.

SARASWATI: Once I was reading his palm for fun. He asked me what I saw, and I laughed and said, "It says you will have God's darshan," to which he humorously responded, "They found out!"

We all had our moments of feeling unworthy of the extraordinary love that Maharajji showered upon us. Our desires, our moral defects, our personal issues would come up and block the light that was always shining on us from Baba. Maharajji would reflect our feelings back in ways that made them visible to us, like ignoring us, or not giving us a name, or pulling back a banana—whatever worked to get through our particular attachments.

KRISHNA DOBRER: The first time I saw Maharajji in Vrindavan he said, "You have a flute with you. Play it." There was kirtan going on in the background. I wondered whether I should play the kirtan or do my own little Jethro Tull.

I could barely squeak out some notes. He said, "Very good," and then he asked me, "Who played the first flute?"

"Krishna."

He looked at me and said, "Krishna."

At the end of the darshan I went to pranaam, and he hit me in the head and said, "Krishna." That was the moment when my whole life flashed before me. It was like beads that were in a strand, and they all kind of lined up.

I knew why I got out of the draft, I knew all of the grace; all of the things that had supported me in life came in the culmination of that moment. And then, of course, I couldn't do Vipassana. Maharajji would come into my attention, and I was just head over heels in love. I gave up the whole idea of taking myself and my liberation so seriously. I felt this is what it must have been like for the disciples around Jesus.

Of course there was a period when he didn't pay any attention to me, and I thought, "Well, he finally sees that I am worthless and I don't belong here. I knew all along I wasn't pure enough for this." Then it was like this needy thing. "Give me some prasad. Look at me, give me some inkling that I belong here." Nothing, nothing. At the same time I felt so guilty. How could you possibly want anything from the person who gave you the most precious thing in your life?

When I was at the peak of feeling worthless, Maharajji looks at me, and *gasp,* he picks up a banana from the takhat and hands it toward me. As I reach for it, he pulls it away and hands it to the person behind me. And I got it. In that moment I got that I was still lovable and I didn't need a freakin' banana. Of course, after I got it, then every day there were piles of prasad, ripe peaches on my lungi.

One of the deep lessons we learned from Maharajji concerned service. In his injunction to "love everyone, feed everyone, and remember God" was the kernel not only of bhakti yoga, but also of karma yoga. How does one live in the world? By "feeding" everyone, whether that takes the form of food or caring for the elderly or starting meditation centers or writing books or making movies with a spiritual message—whatever helps those who are "poor and suffering." Maharajji's temple at Kainchi was built in a very poor valley, and the prasad that was given to everyone who came—those ubiquitous potatoes and puris—often was the main meal of the day for the villagers. Of course, they were also being "fed" the love and peace of the ashram's atmosphere. Although most of us just soaked up as much as we could and didn't get into "feeding" everyone until we were back in the West, some Westerners became immersed in service while still in India with Maharajji.

In April, Maharajji left Vrindavan and returned to Kainchi. And by late spring there were some Westerners living in the ashram, although most were still staying at the Evelyn Hotel in Nainital.

DWARKANATH: In Nainital in April and May of '72 we were going to Kainchi daily. I was frustrated at going back to the hotel in Nainital. One day I just couldn't stand the idea of going away, so I didn't get on the bus when everyone was supposed to leave. Instead, I walked up the path above the ashram until I got to the top. I lay down in the grass with the shawl I had on and slept for the night; in the morning I woke up to a loud animal noise, a buffalo grazing nearby. I was afraid that I was going to get into trouble because we were always warned about tigers and leopards in the hills. I went back down to Kainchi with some trepidation, but I was never called out on the fact that I hadn't gone back to the hotel that night.

There was an Indian family staying in Kainchi at the time. The Sahis were there with their lovely teenage daughter and her younger brother, who was bored at Kainchi, so I was his entertainment. That day when I came back down to the ashram, Mr. Sahi had conversations with Gurudatt and with Maharajji that I wasn't a party to. Suddenly I was asked if I would like to live in the ashram. I got moved into the room that I stayed in all that summer.

That sort of broke the ice, because very soon other Westerners also got to come stay in the ashram. Balaram was one of the first of them, and he was sent to share the room with me. Saraswati got to move into the ashram. Draupadi did. When the Westerners were sent back on the bus to Nainital, I and the others living in the ashram would have the chance to have darshan.

The Sahis at the time were privileged among ashram guests, and Mrs. Sahi had a kitchen that was given to her to use in the back of Indra kutir. When we were sent away after darshan, I hung out with her as she was preparing all of this food, like rice and dal and vegetables. Number one, she did it in order to be able to offer Maharajji something she herself had cooked, but also she was cooking enough that all of us Westerners were being served. We really welcomed having a little more variety than just potatoes and puris. I was helping her do that.

The day came when the Sahis left. The next morning, the doors to her kitchen weren't locked, and the supplies were still in there. I went in and cooked food for the Westerners on my own initiative. Then Maharajji said to move the kitchen into the adjoining room of the shed that was the puri kitchen. It was quite wonderful how we would be provided with more staples as they were needed. I went on cooking without actually having been told or asked to do so, and without asking for staples.

At one point we also started making chai. At its peak we made chai before darshan, we had chai and *dalia* [cracked wheat] for breakfast, and then chai during morning darshan and lunch, and then chai in the afternoon. And those of us staying in the ashram had our meal in the back kitchen. That's a full day's work.

Dr. Larry Brilliant (Subramaniam) and his wife, Elaine (Girija), went on their first trip to India with the Hog Farm, traveling overland from London to Nepal. They had first seen Ram Dass when he gave a series of three lectures at the Unitarian Center in San Francisco, fortuitously held on the only night of the week that Larry had open during his internship. After the first talk, Girija went to work and told her colleagues in the Ju-

Maharajji and Dwarkanath.

venile Probation Office in Alameda County, "I went to this talk. I don't remember anything that he said, but it was great!"

GIRIJA: When we were in India, Ram Dass got the first edition of *Be Here Now* in the mail and gave it to Wavy Gravy; we took it with us on the Hog Farm bus. I read the introduction and was very touched by it, but then we went on to Nepal and trekked from Pokhara up to Mustang. When we came back, Wavy was very sick. Larry left to take Wavy to the States, and I went back to India with a friend. We wanted to purify ourselves and decided to study meditation. After the Goenka retreat I did a second retreat on my own. I was in Delhi thinking about taking a third retreat, but Krishna Das was staying with us at a friend's house. He said,

"I am going to get my bus ticket for Nainital. Do you want to come?" That was it.

DR. LARRY: What called me to Maharajji was Girija. She phoned and said, "Come here," and I said, "No, you come here." She said, "This is Ram Dass's guru. This is wonderful. I've got a new name." We reached an agreement: she would come home for Christmas to San Francisco, we would stay married, we would sell everything, and we'd go back to India, which we did.

I hated it. Well, I mean if Maharajji had said, "Oh, Dr. America," which is what he called me later, "I have been waiting for you, you're wonderful," I would have loved it. But that's not what he did, of course. I genuinely thought that Girija had been captured by a cult. I didn't like the idols. You can see how much I dislike them now [his house is filled with idols!]. I hated the idea of touching his feet. I think it probably took me about a week to feel completely, totally rejected.

I told Girija that I was going to leave, which meant ending our relationship, because if that was her place and it wasn't mine . . . I cried, and I was really sad. I told her that I wasn't going to see Maharajji that day. She went to Kainchi, and I went and walked around the lake in Nainital. I got a boat, went out on the lake, and found myself doing something I had never done as an adult, which was praying, asking for a sign, trying to figure out who this fat man in a blanket was and if I belonged there. But no sign. I was begging God for a tiny little insignificant sign that only I knew.

I told Girija I was going to leave and packed my bags. She said, "Well, are you at least going to go say good-bye to him?"

"Of course," I said. "Look, this might not be the right place for me, but I am polite."

We took an early taxi out of Nainital and were the first ones there. We told the taxi to wait with all of the luggage in it and went into the ashram. Girija and I sat before Maharajji's takhat waiting for him to come out.

On the takhat, folks had created a mandala made of apples and flowers that spelled out *Ram* in Hindi/Sanskrit. While we were waiting, one of the apples fell off and rolled onto the straw mat. In my mind at that moment it seemed that God's name was incomplete, so I reached down to pick up that apple and complete the mandala. The moment I had my hand down, Maharajji pushed out of the doors and stepped on my hand. Now I was doing exactly what I never wanted to do, which was to touch his feet, but he had me pinned down. I was incredulously wondering how such a small person could apply the force of hundreds of pounds. I couldn't get my hand out, and he started laughing.

Maharajji said, "You weren't here yesterday." I was kind of pleased he at least noticed, because he had never noticed before. He said, "Where were you?"

I didn't answer.

He said a couple of things that were joking around. "Were you horseback riding?" He was laughing. Then he got serious for a second, and he looked at me and said, "Were you at the lake?"

I recoiled. Then he diffused it the way that he did when he said something that made you realize he was better than the NSA at tapping your internal phone system. He said, "Were you swimming?" That lake was so polluted. There hasn't been any swimming in that lake since the British left.

I didn't answer, and he said, "Oooh, yes, were you talking to God? Did you ask for something? Did you ask for a *nishan*? Did you ask for a sign?" That's when I started to cry.

He had sat down, but his foot was still on top of my hand.

That's when he started slapping me and hugging me and pulling my beard. "Did you ask for a sign? Did you ask God for a sign?"

By then all the others—Tukaram, Sita, Krishna Das, Ravi Das—had shown up. Girija grabbed me and hugged me, and then they all kind of just came around me.

None of us have really talked about it, but we all had an experience like that, which was the real initiation. You read in all these Sri Krishna Prem books and *The Yoga of the Bhagavad Gita* about what the initiation of the chela by the guru is supposed to be like. They've always got some Sanskrit mantra that gets exchanged and maybe some ghee burned and some incense. But that was my initiation. More important than opening my heart, it is what broke my head. Because it was only my head that was keeping my heart from being open.

The car was still waiting. It hadn't taken the luggage away. It was a very expensive taxi ride.

Shivaya (Alan Cain) was living in Greenwich Village when he read *Autobiography of a Yogi,* which said that when the time was right, a teacher would appear. A few days later he read in the *Village Voice* that Yogi Ramaya had just arrived from India to teach Mahavatar Babaji's kriya yoga. Every day Alan sat in front of a picture of Babaji and meditated on him. One day he felt like someone was in the room with him, and sure enough, when he opened his eyes, Babaji was sitting there. Telepathically, Alan said to him, "I want to go to India, but I'm really terrified." Babaji raised his hand in blessing and said, "You will go to India, and you will have no fear."

SHIVAYA: I spent years studying with Goenka and Munindra and doing Buddhist practice. I was in Bodhgaya in '71 when that bus to Allahabad happened. Ram Dass suggested that I not go on the bus trip, and I accepted that. Then one day I was walking down the street in Delhi, and this friend I knew from Buddhist meditation courses, Marty Worth, who was a very reserved type of character, was now dancing down the street and acting sort of weird. When he saw me he did a spin.

"Whoa, Marty," I said. "What's going on?"

He said, "I've just come from Neem Karoli Baba." He pulled out a color photo of Maharajji. "Neem Karoli Baba, the greatest saint in India. There is a bus at eleven tonight. Take it to Nainital, you'll see him tomorrow."

You know how you look at disciples or devotees of various gurus and think, "Do I want to be like that?" I looked at him and I said, "No, I don't want to be like that," so I went on my way.

I went to a money changer in Connaught Place. At that time money changers were out in the open. This guy had a room, a desk and two chairs, and a picture of Maharajji on his desk.

I asked, "Who's that?"

"Neem Karoli Baba, the greatest saint in India."

"Why do you have his picture?"

"All of his devotees come here. This man is such a great saint that you get blessings just by having his picture."

I changed my money and went on my way.

I had a friend named Mahendra, and I would usually spend the night with him when I was in Delhi. We would wax philosophical into the night about God, and his wife was a great cook. After the money changer I go to Mahendra's, and while we are waiting for dinner, he says, "I have a book of other friends who have stopped here along the way. Do you know Wavy Gravy? Do you know Dr. Larry?" He brings out this book, and I open up to an 8-by-10 glossy of Neem Karoli Baba. "That's Neem Karoli Baba. He's the greatest saint in India."

It is about nine thirty when his wife comes in and says dinner is ready. I said, "Mahendra, I'm going to have to skip dinner. I have to catch an eleven o'clock bus. Three times today this face has come into my face. One time I can forget about it. Two times I can think about it, but three times and I have to get to Nainital tonight."

It was now morning. From Nainital, I got on the bus to Kainchi. My head was shaved, and this Indian man on the bus had a Gandhi hat. I was used to putting a *gamsha* [piece of cloth] around my head. He took his Gandhi-style hat and gave it to me. When I walked into the ashram Maharajji was up on the takhat. There were fifteen or twenty devotees sitting around, and Maharajji jumped up and started screaming, "Gandhiji, Gandhiji, Gandhiji has come. Come, come, Gandhiji!" He's laughing and everyone gets hysterical, and of course I am laughing, and it was just this huge laughfest going on. "Come, Gandhi, sit. It is so good, Gandhiji is here." That was a cool entry. I was blown away.

There were other new people who had come that day, and everybody was asking him where to stay. He told everyone to go to Nainital. But I wasn't going to Nainital. Robert Friedlander says, "You can come and stay with me. I've got a room in Bhowali." He not only had a room; he also had a bag full of dynamite acid. That night I dropped a hit and sat in front of the photo of Maharajji with the finger. Needless to say, tripping while looking at that photo, every conceivable thing that I had ever done in my whole life ran through me. Now it was about three o'clock in the morning, and I got up and walked to Kainchi, singing kirtan all the way. When I got to Kainchi, I was exhausted and fell asleep at the gate. When I woke up, people were stepping over me going to darshan.

Balaram Das

The famous finger mudra.

I went in and Maharajji again greeted me with a big Gandhiji hello. I was still tripping. I was having these flashes, and I didn't want to sit too close to him. I had been through so much through the night with that finger. I was really feeling this incredible connection to this being, but I didn't want there to be any doubts in my head. I thought, "Maharajji, if you and I have any connection at all, I would like to see that mudra that I spent the night looking at." He was talking to somebody, but he turned and lifted that finger, then went right back. That sent this electric

Shivaya (with shaved head, behind Maharajji).

current racing through me. It was just an instant, but it was direct.

Now I felt we had a connection, but I wanted something more. After being there a few days, I said to Dada, "I think it would really be interesting if I could have a personal audience with Maharajji." Sometime later in the afternoon Dada comes over to me and says, "Maharajji will see you now."

Dada and I go in, and Maharajji is sitting in the office. Here I had been getting all that happy Gandhiji laughing, and now in a really gruff voice it was, "*Kya hai*? What do you want?"

I said, "I don't know what to do."

He said, "You keep silent. *Jao*."

Dada said to me, "We call it *maun,* and he says now you're maun. You don't speak." I was maun the whole time. I spoke only when I went in and saw Maharajji personally.

Summer 1972

When we talk about Maharajji's "miracles," it's because they make good stories. But we weren't really interested in the miracles per se. After the initial shock of realizing that he knew absolutely everything about us, we expected that omniscience of him. We were far more impressed by his presence, by the awesome combination of power, love, and wisdom of the heart. Of course, the Indian devotees told us tales of Maharajji turning into Hanuman before their eyes, of bringing the sick back to health (and even of the dead being brought back to life), of his giving an apple to sterile women who then became pregnant, and of his being in two different places at the same time. When confronted about doing something miraculous, Maharajji would say only that God did it.

One of the Westerners experienced a rather miraculous start with Maharajji. The initial meeting of "English" Sita (Heather Thompson) with Maharajji took place in London . . . *while he was in India.* She was a student at the University of London and very interested in Buddhism. She went to hear a Zen teacher talk at Gandalf's Garden and met Iain, who had just come back from India and told her about Maharajji. She thought, "Well, he sounds like a nice old man, but I'm not interested in Hinduism. I like Zen, the direct approach."

"ENGLISH" SITA: I heard about Maharajji again, probably about five months later, and I had the same reaction. Sounds like a nice old man in a blanket, but nah, not really interested.

The next day I was on a bus in London going to the university. It was a bus route that I knew very well, because I traveled it every day. Also, the part where I saw this old tramp was one of the few straight and wide streets in London. There was only one other man on the bus, and he was sitting opposite me. The bus conductor was upstairs; it was a double-decker. The bus stopped, and this old tramp got on, dressed like a hobo, wearing layers and layers of tattered clothing, needing a shave, with grayish hair. He was carrying a plaid blanket under his arm. For some reason he stood in front of me, even though the bus was practically empty, and gave me this beautiful, beautiful smile, as if to say, "Move over. I want to sit beside you." I moved over, he sat down, and I could feel the seat depress because he had some girth to him.

I was very shy in those days, so I didn't look at him again. I was fascinated, but it wasn't polite to stare. I turned around, looked out of the window, and I thought to myself, "What a beautiful smile, what a nice old man." As I said "old man" to myself, I thought "old man in a blanket," at which point I kind of took note. I turned to look at him again . . . but he wasn't there!

I knew the bus route so well. There was no bus stop. Even if for some reason the bus had stopped and he had gotten off, which would have been very difficult to have happened because this was in the space of a couple of minutes, he would have stuck out like a sore thumb, because there was hardly anybody out on the street.

The next day some friends came around saying that the previous morning they had very strong feelings that I should go to India to see Maharajji, this old man in a blanket. They wanted to give me the money to buy the ticket to India—with the proviso that if I didn't use the money to buy a ticket to fly to India, I should give them the money back. I still needed to finish my studies at the university, so it was about a month before that would happen. I finished my exams and bought the ticket.

In those days in England students didn't work while they were going to university, only during the summer holidays. I had the ticket, but I didn't have any money to be in India, and my parents didn't want me to go, so they weren't a source of money, not that they had any anyway. This was the last time that I could apply for excess traveling expenses from the university to my home. I thought I might ask for a little bit more money. I had everything itemized, and I think maybe I asked for about 5 pounds too much. The check eventually came, and it was for about 25 pounds too much; in other words, it was excessively large compared to what I had asked for.

I thought, "They're going to catch up with me; I better phone them." We didn't have a phone in the house back in those days. Every time I go back home to Norfolk I always go into town, and they still have that public phone there. I step into the phone booth and remember all of this. I phoned the Norfolk County Council, and they checked their records. Lo and behold, they came back and said, "Oh no, we can see you itemized everything. Everything is taken care of." I didn't argue with them. That gave me the money to go to India.

I flew into Delhi, and Iain, who had returned to India, came to the airport to meet me. Then it was cloak and dagger, going around to the money changers—at least that's how it seemed to me at the time. We spent a day in Delhi and then went up to Nainital and straight to Kainchi.

I walked into the ashram with the express intention of asking, "Were you that old man on the bus in London?" When I got there in front of him, he was wearing the same blanket, and he gave me the same smile. I didn't need to ask if he was the same old man. For the first time in my life my heart really opened, and it was like, "Yes, yes, Baba."

There's that wonderful Rumi poem, and one line of it is, "From the beginning to the end of time, there is love between thee and me; and how shall such love be extinguished?" That's what it felt like.

Gopal (Paul Singer) earned a postgraduate degree at law school in New York City. Then he heard a tape recording of Ram Dass, which started him on the path. In 1972, at the end of a Sufi camp in Mendocino, California, Pir Vilayat Khan gave individual darshan to some attendees. He told Paul, "You should go to India and seek initiation in a Hindu sect."

GOPAL: A week later my girlfriend and I drove to the Lama Foundation, and Ram Dass happened to be there. I told him my story about Pir Vilayat's darshan and asked his advice. He paused and in great wisdom said, "I think you are exactly where you need to be for the next step on your journey." Then after a minute or so he looked at me and added, "However, if you should find yourself in India this summer, go to the Evelyn Hotel, look for S. L. Sah, and tell him I sent you." I drove directly across the country, sold my VW van, bought a ticket on Air India, flew to Delhi, and went up to Nainital, where I found S. L. Sah at the Evelyn Hotel.

Early the next morning six or seven Westerners staying at the Evelyn took me along with them in an old Ambassador taxi. We stopped in Bhowali to buy fruit to offer to Maharajji as prasad. After descending narrow winding roads, with magnificent green mountain vistas, waterfalls, and steep drops to the valley below, we got to Kainchi. I remember walking across the bridge. There was a chaukidar who looked like a Gurkha warrior with a curved knife in his belt. He seemed formidable, and I was worried because I didn't know if there was a password. I said, *"Namasté."* It seemed to work.

There were maybe eight or ten people seated in front of the takhat meditating when we arrived. I placed the fruit on the takhat and sat down. After five minutes or so, *bam,* the door opens and out comes Maharajji, blanket flying, and he settles himself on the takhat. He's tossing fruit to people here and there, he's talking to this one and that one in Hindi, and Dada's busy with the towel, keeping the flies away from him.

Then he's still. After a long pause he looks over at me and says through a translator, "You came from America?"

"Yes, I did."

"Do you like it here in India?"

"I love it here in India."

"Is that your girlfriend over there?"

I turned to look. A woman from Australia bore a striking resemblance to the girlfriend I had left behind. I could see a bit of consternation on her face. I didn't know at that point that Maharajji had previously married people to one another; I now understand why she might have been somewhat concerned. I turned back to look at Maharajji. But in that moment of confusion, before I could answer, Maharajji looked at me and waves of light radiated from his eyes, like concentric heat waves, only closer together and quicker.

The base of my spine began to buzz, and suddenly I felt this intense rush of energy, like being on a rapidly accelerating elevator going up, and it reached my heart. This all happened in forty-five seconds or so, although it seemed much longer, as I held Maharajji's gaze. Then I just felt love for everybody. Someone said we all had to go eat breakfast. I said I wasn't hungry. I didn't want to leave. Someone said, "You don't understand. You have to eat breakfast." And they guided me to the back of the ashram.

After that initial moment, Maharajji paid absolutely no attention to me. How could that be? This was the most profound moment in my life, and I didn't exist? It was obvious I had no control over this situation, so after a few days I decided I might as well do something useful. I went to Dwarkanath and got a job in the western kitchen, picking stones out of a large tray of rice. It was a contemplative practice, and I enjoyed doing that and scrubbing the brass cooking woks with rope and ashes. I did this for a week or two and eventually got out of the emotional roller-coaster head space of "Why isn't he paying attention to me?"

Then one day at afternoon darshan I was standing behind the Westerners seated in front of the takhat, and I could see that this person had just broken up with his girlfriend, that one was ecstatic, and that one . . . It was as if they all had cartoon bubbles with their thoughts in them above their heads. Simultaneously I felt this upwelling rush of compassion that rose to my heart, and I felt such love for these people whom I didn't even know.

At that moment Maharajji suddenly looked up at me, radiating love again, and tossed bananas to me over the heads of the people.

It was a continuation of our first meeting, but with a deep and lasting lesson, one of many to follow over the next four months.

Sometimes Maharajji directed certain Westerners in a very specific way. After his "psychedelic period" and then meeting Ram Dass in 1968, Ralph Abraham (Vyed Vas) wanted to go to India to make contact with the philosophy and the practice of yoga. This was well into his tenured professorship in mathematics, so he was older than most of the Westerners who were called to India.

RALPH: When school was out in 1972, my idea was to make a tour of different ashrams in India. I ran into Ram Dass in Amsterdam, and he gave me instructions for finding the Evelyn Hotel. I arrived at the Evelyn, and the next day I went to Kainchi on the bus. I was really put off by the amplified *bhajan* [songs] and the atmosphere of the place; I thought it was sort of a Himalayan Howard Johnson's. I went two or three days in a row and decided to move on to a cave near Dinapani. After two weeks, I began having nightmares in which it was demanded that I leave the cave immediately and go back. I followed a wild-looking jungle sadhu for some miles, who pointed out the path to Kainchi. I walked into the ashram as they were calling out, "Where is that professor from California?"

I stayed for six months. Maharajji gave me a program to do. I was assigned to study certain Sanskrit classics in English translation along with an Indian devotee who read Sanskrit fluently to help me out. Maharajji had people bring me books from Delhi. A book would arrive and it would be handed to me inscribed by Maharajji with *Ram Ram Ram Ram Ram* inside the covers, front and back. I kind of intuited what I was supposed to do.

There was one book in particular called *Yoga Vasistha,* a later mystical tome in the yogic tradition, all about the theory of vibrations—*spanda,* in Sanskrit. It was about a kind of model of consciousness that I later found out is in the Kashmiri Shaivite tradition: what a thought is, how thoughts are communicated from one mind to another, and how things are connected up at a higher level.

I never saw Maharajji again, but he had given my work in mathematics and chaos theory a new direction.

The Westerners were clearly "foreigners" in India, but Ravi Khanna was a young Indian who was as skeptical as any American. He had left home and hitchhiked to Kathmandu to start his hippie life. While working at a crepes place in town, he and a friend met Chaitanya, one of the Western devotees, who told them about Maharajji.

RAVI KHANNA: In early September, it was getting cold. Usually the scene was that you came to Kathmandu in the summer and moved to Goa in the winter. Jim, the guy I was hitchhiking with, wanted to stop on our way to Goa to see who Maharajji was. I was very cynical in those days. I had no interest in all these gurus; they were all cheats, and dumb Americans were getting ripped off, but since we were traveling together, I said, "Fine." It wasn't going to cost us any more money, just more time. I was going to stay in Nainital while he went on to Kainchi, but when we got to Nainital there was a bus leaving right then, so I ended up going with him.

In the ashram, the Indians who ran the scene looked at me with immediate suspicion, wondering who this Indian hippie was and whether he was going to rip the Americans off. They were kind of protective of the Westerners, and they kept shooing me away. "Go, go, go. Go outside." Then Maharajji came out, and I wandered back to where he was. I saw him and that was it.

That was it. Something happened to me. This was what I'd been looking for all my life. I'd run away from home several times, the first time at twelve. I was searching for something and not really happy, and I saw him and it was instantaneous. This is where I needed to be, and I was not going to leave. He said, "Come over here. Who are you? Where are you from?"

"Kathmandu."

"You're lying. *Jao.*"

Naima, Suil, and Ravi Khanna at Naima's house in Kainchi valley.

I went. A bunch of folks were staying in Bhowali, and they offered us space. Jim soon left, but I stayed. The next day I came back, and he threw me out again. That went on for four or five days. Every day I would come, and he would throw me out. I got quite discouraged, but I wasn't going to give up. Then he told Draupadi, "Give him some money so he can go to Kausani." He also told her to give me some money for pot as well. *"Ganja piita hai."*

In those days it was a bumpy ten-hour bus ride to Kausani. I got there in the evening and stayed at the guesthouse. I took the first bus back in the morning. He said, "I told you to go to Kausani."

"Yes, Maharajji, but you didn't say how long I needed to stay there." So he started tolerating me.

Most of the Indian devotees did not like me at all. Here's this guy, he's kind of this hippie, he smokes pot. How does he get access to Maharajji? The Indians living in the ashram and the ones who worked there didn't particularly like me either, because they didn't trust me. Mostly I hung out with Kabir and Dwarkanath and Ravi Das, helping prepare the meals in the western kitchen that Dwarkanath and Ravi Das were cooking. He wasn't throwing me out anymore.

RAVI KHANNA: I started translating for people. Dada and others would selectively translate. There was a lot of screening going on, a lot of editing. With me it would be just straight whatever he said. Sometimes he would yell at me, "Hey, don't . . ." Other times he was amused that I was translating and people were understanding more, like the gossiping that was going on, or his commenting on the news or politicians, or the salty language.

IRA ROSE: One day we were all in front of Maharajji having darshan outside on the takhat, and Ravi Khanna with a real serious face said, "Maharajji says you all look tired. You should take rest. Go to your respective homes." So we all got up and left.

About an hour later Ravi came up to the white house where I was, with a big smile on his face. I said, "What's so funny?"

"Nothing."

"Ravi, don't bullshit me. Something's funny."

"Well, that's not exactly what Maharajji said."

"What did he say?"

"What Maharajji really said was, 'These people are all a bunch of sister fuckers. They are not thinking about God. All they want to do is fuck, spend money, and eat ice cream. Get them the fuck out of my sight.' I didn't know what to say, so I said, 'You all look tired. Maharajji says you should take rest.'"

Maharajji was not the image of "holiness," as some might have expected him to be. He had devotees who were *dacoits*, thieves, whom he had met during his years of wandering, when he often stayed under a bridge for the night or in other locations where those on the other side of the law might hide. His language was "salty," to say the least. And in his earlier days, he had eaten huge amounts of food—going from house to house, where devotees would prepare entire meals for him— sometimes as many as thirty in a day. He also didn't follow any of the Hindu "rules," such as separating the women and men.

He loved to shake up his Indian devotees by having us Westerners do things they would never do. For example, we were once sitting in front of him, and he was also sitting on the ground. Instead of looking as vast as the Himalayas to me, he suddenly looked like a small child. I walked over and kissed him on the top of his head. The Indian women around him gasped! The next time he had Indian women sitting with him, he called me over and pointed to the top of his head, clearly wanting me to do it again!

12

The Music of the Spheres

Fall 1972

You are the sky and the ground.
You alone the day, the night air.
You are all things born into being.
Also, these flower offerings
that someone brought.

—LALLA *NAKED SONG* (TRANS. COLEMAN BARKS)

By this time, enough people had returned to the West from India that word was spreading, and *Be Here Now* had found its way into the hands of many seekers. The Westerners who had left India departed mainly because of visa issues, and some returned after being away the requisite amount of time to get a new visa. The rest of us felt that we had plenty of time—time to have our babies, start or resume college or careers, renew our documents, and get back to India to be with Maharajji again. Little did we know.

A group of us were living together at the Markus "farm" in the eastern townships of Quebec, holding tightly to our concept of what it meant to live a holy life. We tried really hard to incorporate the Indian way of life into the Western world, but it wasn't easy. I remember being upset when my new mother-in-law gave me a beautiful pair of leather gloves as a gift. Leather! From a not-so-sacred cow.

Mirabai, Anasuya, and Sunanda gave birth to their babies in the farmhouse. We had a large tepee on the land and sang with Bhagavan Das around the fire. Many of the satsang came to the farm on their return from India—sort of a halfway house for getting their Western land legs back. Other gatherings of the satsang were happening in the San Francisco Bay Area and in New York and Boston. Coast to coast, the word was getting out about Maharajji.

As we all agreed, the true culture shock was coming back to the greedy materialistic West after being immersed in Maharajji's spiritual family in India. As we slowly came to realize, we had to find a middle path—finding work that wouldn't offend our spiritual sensitivities while trying to keep up with our meditative and devotional practices in the midst of "the world." Fortunately, there were still people heading to India and others returning with a renewed "bhakti hit" for those of us who were back in the West.

Devaki (Louise Markus) was seventeen when she got letters from her brothers, Raghu and Laxman, still in India, in which they reported that Maharajji said she would be coming to India. She was scared to go to India, because of all the horror stories about lepers, scorpions, and spiders that Raghu had fed her. She didn't feel it was necessary to go to India, since she already felt connected to Maharajji through photographs, but her boyfriend, Bruce, really wanted to go. Her father,

From Dasaratha's journal.

who had been named Dasaratha (or Das), decided to hook up with their entourage—Louise, Bruce, and their friend Harold Harris—for a second round with Maharajji.

DEVAKI: Parvati had baked an eggless chocolate cake to bring with me, which was a really good idea, because it was my ticket

to push up right in front when I got there and give it to Maharajji.
I was very excited. I remember rushing across that bridge like a
bride going to meet her lover. He patted me on my head. I had
a very physical relationship with him. We were always holding
hands, or I was always sitting up front at his feet. I was eighteen.
Quite frankly, I didn't know anyone else existed.

I knew that other people had been given names—my brother
was Raghvindra Das. It's a big name. My other brother was
Laxman. I was sitting there one day and Maharajji asked me my
name. I said "Louise," and he went "Loosh?" Dada said, "Louise."
He went, "Loosh?" Then there was a discussion. Maharajji and
Dada were throwing names back and forth. This name, that
name. They finally landed on Devaki. So that's how I got my
name. I would say everybody has their own Maharajji, and my
Maharajji couldn't pronounce my name, so he gave me a Hindu
name. What is a name, you know? It means everything, and

Maharajji and Devaki.

nothing. But here is the irony: that name is part of my connection to him.

Bruce Granofsky saw the picture of Maharajji in *Be Here Now* and knew immediately that he and Louise would be going to India. They worked for five months putting together the $400 to stay there and for the tickets. Bruce was terrified of planes, but after that torturous flight they landed in Delhi and took a cab through monsoon floods to Nainital. The smell of the mountains reminded him of home, and he loved everything about it.

BRUCE: The next morning we went to see Maharajji. It was fun. There were a lot of questions like, *"Kya naam?* What is your name?"* and passing oranges to everybody and fruits. He asked what my relationship with Louise was, and Louise said, "Friends." I was hurt by that, going, "No, we're lovers. She is my woman."

Probably the third or fourth night we were in Nainital, we were hanging around in Krishna Das's room at the Evelyn Hotel. Chillums were going around the room. I don't smoke dope. Basically I can't handle that stuff. I had bad acid trips. I had bad pot experiences—paranoia plus hallucinating. The chillums were going around, and I just wanted a taste. I took a little puff and blew it out real fast to make sure nothing stayed in my system and I didn't get stoned.

The next morning Maharajji turns to me and says, "You smoked *charas* [hash] last night." That set off a whole bomb in my head. My first reaction was, "Bad guess, old man. I don't smoke dope." I completely denied it in my head. Everyone else was smoking. I didn't. I had a certain amount of pride about not being a dope-smoking hippie.

Balaram came down on me so fast, with his finger in my face.

Cartoon from Bruce's journal. Left to right:
Dasaratha, Harold, Bruce, Maharajji, and Devaki.

"You can't lie to Maharajji. You can't lie to him. He knows."
Which made me deny it even more. Basically what I was saying
was I didn't get high, but I did take a puff, which I only admitted
to myself four months after coming back from India. That is
something I have been savoring over the years.

Then right after that he looked at me and said, "You can't
smoke charas. It is not good for you." He knew. I got that part.
The other lessons were, what's the truth, lying, not lying, pride,
all that stuff. And that's the way he worked.

More Parents

KRISHNA DAS: I was recovering from hepatitis, living in the
temple with Maharajji. One day I didn't feel good, so I stayed in

my room all day. The next day I came out and Maharajji said,
"You were sick?"

"Yes, I didn't feel good."

"When's your mother coming to India?"

Excuse me? The next day I got a letter from M. L. at the hotel
in Nainital saying that my mother had called and she wanted me
to call her. I went to Nainital to make the phone call. She said, "I
want to come see you!"

"Oh, really? Okay, I have to ask Maharajji." Can you imagine
how my mother must have felt? I had to ask my guru if she could
come see me! I said, "I'll call you tomorrow."

I went back to the temple, and Maharajji said, "Tell her to
come."

I picked her up at the airport. I was walking around with long
hair, a long red dress, barefoot, and that's how I appeared at the
airport. The whole time she was in India she looked slack-jawed,
mouth open in amazement and fear. I had to lead her around by
the hand, but she was a trooper.

We went to see Maharajji whenever he would let us come.
He was very kind to her, very kind. I had told her to bring the
nicest sweater she could find for him. He immediately put on this
beautiful cashmere sweater and looked at his Indian devotees,
"You miserable people. You live right here, and you don't bring
me anything. This woman brought this sweater from so far
away." This was his way of dispensing love, and they knew
it. If you got abused by him, it meant you were really close.
I remember the first time he called me "cunning"—I almost
melted down. Now I'm in!

Maharajji said to her, "Will you give him money?"

"Well," she said, "he should work."

Maharajji said, "Don't worry. He will work." At the time I'm sitting there in a red dress, and I don't know what he's talking about. Work?

Maharajji said that I was his son, meaning he wasn't taking me away from her, but he wanted her to know how he felt about me. It was very beautiful.

On the last day we're about to get in the car and drive off to Delhi. He was sitting on the takhat; wherever he sat, it felt like the center of the universe. She turned, looked back into the temple, and broke down, sobbing uncontrollably. I had to lift her into the car because she couldn't move; she was crying and crying. That's the moment that most of us had, where all the pretense of your life, who you think you are, crumbles and you feel that love in your heart for the first time.

She was going from India to Jerusalem, and Maharajji had given her some flowers to put on Jesus's tomb. My little Jewish mother. My instructions were that when she left, I was to get down on my knees and do aarti to her, to worship her in the airport. The look in her eyes at that moment, when she was looking at me, was quite amazing. One of the most beautiful moments we ever had together.

She spent her whole life kvetching and complaining and worrying and trying to do good for others—she helped a lot of people in her way. But the minute someone would ask her about her trip to India, she'd do a 180-degree turn, get soft, and go into a whole other space. All the rest of the time, she didn't seem to have any contact with it, but she felt what it was about. She understood why I was there.[1]

Not all encounters with parents went as smoothly. Girija's mother came to India, and she and Larry took her to see Maharajji in Vrindavan.

Maharajji with Sylvia, Krishna Das's mother (seated).

When they arrived at the ashram, her mother refused to get out of the car! Then there was Krishna Priya's dad . . .

KRISHNA PRIYA: Michael and Rukmini went to Nainital and came back saying that the police were looking for me. Pictures of me were posted in every police station in India. They had been questioned. Did they know if there was a Florence Klein staying at the ashram? The police had received a letter from my father saying I had been brainwashed by my guru. A spell had been put on me, and my mind had been stolen. Michael and Rukmini said they didn't know any Florence Klein.

Maharajji took that story and ran with it. All day long for a couple of days he kept saying, "Her mind has been stolen by her guru. Her mind has been stolen by her guru." He loved it. My father never owned up to it, even to his dying day.

The Power of the Name

Getting a name from Maharajji was a big deal; some would call it an initiation, especially if he also gave you a mantra. It was certainly an initiation into thinking about yourself in a new way and served as a reminder that God, guru, and self are indeed one. We were intimately connected to an aspect of the divine by a name we could grow into.

Vidura (Francis X. Charet) was raised Catholic and even went into a Benedictine monastery for a while. He had been involved with Tukaram and others in setting up an organization in downtown Montreal where they processed draft dodgers from the States. When Tukaram came back from India for a brief time, he prompted Francis to go back with him. The last thing Vidura expected was the intensity with which Maharajji named him.

> VIDURA: Entering Kainchi in early September 1972, I looked to
> see if Tukaram was among the small cluster of people gathered
> around Maharajji. The next thing I knew, a high-pitched shriek
> came from that direction, and I could see Maharajji signaling
> to me to come. A few people rushed over and ushered me up to
> him. Smiling, he looked at me and said, "You have come from
> Canada."
>
> "Yes," I replied and kept looking around for Tukaram.
>
> Maharajji bent over, stared straight into my eyes, and pointed
> to himself. He said, "You have come here to see me." Then
> he pushed my long hair aside and added, "Where are your
> earrings?"
>
> "I don't wear earrings."
>
> "All Shaivites wear earrings," he said, and gently slapped me
> across the top of the head. "You are very clever, very intelligent,"

he said, slapping me again, pulling my hair, and laughing. Was this the routine? What was going on?

The next day at the ashram the doors flew open, and he came out. He immediately pointed his finger at me and told me that my name was Vidura. I had no idea who Vidura was. He signaled for me to come near him and asked, *"Apka naam kya hai?* What is your name?"

Everyone around me shouted, "Tell him your name is Vidura."

"My name is Francis," I replied.

"Nahin," he shrieked, "your name is Vidura." This routine happened a number of times. Some days later he came out of a room where potatoes were stored and unexpectedly grabbed hold of me, spun me around, looked at me straight in the face, and asked, *"Apka naam kya hai?"*

Completely taken off guard, I nervously looked at him, gulped, and said, "Vidura."

"Accha," he said.

The intensity of that encounter has stayed with me ever since.

I heard the story about Vidura from a pastiche of different sources. He was a prominent character in the *Mahabharata* and, according to another source, the incarnation of Dharmakaya Yama, the god of death. Yama had been cursed by a yogi who had suffered unjustly to be born on earth as Vidura in order to restore the balance of things. His father was Vyasa, the author of the Vedas, and his mother was a *shudra* [low-caste] woman. So Vidura was born as a mixture of these two castes and therefore never assumed official royal status. But he became a great counselor, the adviser of King Dhritharashtra, and is considered to be the embodiment of wisdom. Vidura comes from the root *vid,* "to see," and implies seeing deeply into things.

When I heard the story, I have to say it really struck a deep chord. It's as though Maharajji identified an archetypal core in each one by naming us after a mythological or historical figure or attribute in the Hindu tradition. It took me a while to unpack it all, but it really did resonate.

Let me jump ahead. In 2008, I went to Delhi for a conference on spirituality and psychology; Goddard College was one of the sponsors. After the conference, I traveled to Rishikesh and stopped at the Baba Neem Karoli Ashram and Sri Hanuman Mandir nearby, where I met a number of older devotees. When I mentioned the name Maharajji had given me, one fellow told me, "Vidura Kutir is on the way to Delhi, near Bijnor, in the old section of ancient India that had been uncovered by archaeological excavations. You must go there. A devotee who lives near there is visiting at the ashram and can give you directions."

I took a different route on the way back to Delhi and found my way to Vidura Kutir at the end of a long dusty road, with a view of the Ganges in the distance. The door of the temple was locked, but some locals who had gathered around ran to get the pujari. When he arrived, he was a little flabbergasted to see me, and I attempted to explain my reasons for visiting. At first he misunderstood and said, "Yes, yes, this is the Vidura Kutir. What is it that you want?"

"I have been given the name Vidura by Neem Karoli Baba."

Suddenly his face lit up and he said, "Oh, well, so you must come in."

Leading me to an altar, he lit an oil lamp and conducted aarti, circling the lamp around my head and shoulders. Then he took me on a guided tour through the temple, which consisted of panels along the walls, and small altars with figurines depicting the different stages of the life of Vidura. The tour ended before a great murti of Mahatma Vidura. "Here, look," he said, pointing to the white-haired, bearded statue.

"Oh my God," I said. "Except for the beard, *we actually look alike!*"

"Yes," he said, "when I saw you, I wondered. Vidura spent his last years here, you know."

Afterward, we sat in the open having chai, overlooking the Ganges. I thought about being named Vidura and how I had issues with it in the beginning. Now I had come full circle with the whole scenario of Vidura's life laid out in front of me. I could almost hear Maharajji's saying, *"Apka naam kya hai?"*

So often we didn't have a clue about what was going on. Maharajji might give us a name we didn't immediately take to or the scene around him might not be to our liking, but there was something about him that was nevertheless irresistible.

MEENAKSHI: I walked across that bridge at Kainchi, and Maharajji was sitting on the takhat with Westerners all around him. I realized that I didn't ever have to say anything to this person or ask him anything—instant inter-communication. He asked me what I did in America before I came. I told him that I had driven a taxi, and he thought that was so hysterical. I really liked him. But I was looking around at all the Westerners and thinking, "This isn't what I came to India for, to be around a lot of Americans. What am I doing here?"

He said, "You go and stay with Keshori." I stayed in her room in Bhowali, and all she talked about was how Maharajji married people. I was like, "Okay, I am so outta here. I did not come to

India to be with Westerners and talk about getting married. I'm eighteen years old."

I went the next day, and the first thing Maharajji did was to change my name. Then he said, "I want you to go to the kitchen, and I want you to clean dalia." Everyone is calling me that new name. "What am I doing around this place where he marries people, he changes your name, he's bossing me around telling me I need to clean this thing in the kitchen? I really like this man sitting here, and I feel really at home, and a very heartfelt thing is happening, but this scene is so whacked."

So I left and went to Sattal, a beautiful Christian ashram that's up in the hills. I was there for maybe three or four days, but I couldn't stay away. I just could not stay away from Maharajji.

It's said that the words spoken by a real master must come true. Maharajji told many of us that he would come stay with us in America. He told Radha he'd stay at her house, and she would cook chapatis for him in America. I was to prepare "double rotis"—his name for toast! He told Anasuya he would come to live with her and Danny in America, and she would cook for him. When Ram Dass said we would all take him to America "in our hearts," Maharajji said no, he would come physically, on an airplane. He would wear a kurta and pants. Of course, that meant that whoever came to our homes would have to be honored and fed as if they were Maharajji, as we never knew what form he would take.

The power of his words could not be denied. Even those who were not his devotees recognized their potency.

SITA: Janaki had two fine-quality tambouras made so we could sing for Maharajji. One afternoon while I was singing, Maharajji said, "Sita will go to Benares to study singing."

Krishna Das (Roy Bonney)

Maharajji writes Ram on Sita's forehead.

Once I arrived in Benares, I was directed to the best vocal music teacher in town, Amiya Bhattacharya. I explained I wanted to learn singing, and he readily agreed; I intended to take daily lessons, nearly doubling his monthly income. Amiya Babu told me to come the following day for a "test." He sang the scale, and I had to imitate his singing, "Aahh" for each note.

Then I went to Kainchi for Durga Puja to be with Maharajji, who said, "The Bengali teacher is very good. He will teach you good music." He said, "His home has narrow stairs." I was astonished that somehow Maharajji knew about the narrow stairwell leading to Amiya Babu's room.

I was eager to begin singing lessons, but when I returned to Benares and arrived at my music teacher's home, he said, "I cannot teach you singing." He had realized from the "test" that

I was so bereft of any natural talent, my voice was so utterly out of tune, that it was not worth his effort.

I was in shock as I left his room. I stumbled down the narrow stairwell, sat on a step, and began to cry. He found me moments later. "What's wrong, what's happened?"

Through my tears I told him, "Neem Karoli Baba said you would teach me good music."

He said, "If Neem Karoli Baba says I am going to teach you good music, I will teach you good music."

Perfect Masters

Premananda (Tom Forray) was in high school in the Bronx, taking acid, and reading *The Tibetan Book of the Dead;* he got very curious about God and spirituality. Then he got *Autobiography of a Yogi* and joined Self-Realization Fellowship. Here he was, a seventeen-year-old kid doing kriya yoga. When Meher Baba came to America, he visited the Bronx Zoo on one of his trips, right near where Tom lived. Even years later, everyone was walking around with Meher Baba lockets, reading his books, the discourses, which is what made Tom want to go to India, to go to Meher Baba's ashram.

PREMANANDA: As soon as I graduated from Hunter College in 1970, I went to Europe with a friend, Bobby. We split up in Greece. I took a house on an island in Greece during the off-season to prepare myself for India. The specter of India was kind of scary. When I was ready to go, I went from Greece to Iraq and from there through the Persian Gulf in the hold of a freighter. Their whole gig was to take pilgrims who were on their way to Mecca; we're talking about goat herders from the

mountains, primitive tribes. Within two days you could not use
the bathrooms.

We ended up in Bombay, and it still blew my mind when I got
off that boat. First thing—beggars, the smell, the whole scene.
This guy says, "Oh, you have landed on a very auspicious day.
It's Shivaratri, and here's a special drink. It's called a *bong lassi* [a
yogurt drink made with hash]. You'll see God, you'll see God."
So we drink this stuff, and we were tripping. We couldn't read a
sign, we didn't know what we were doing, where we were, and it
made it a scary trip.

We went straight down to Meher Baba's ashram and had the
most phenomenal time there. In those days a lot of his original
disciples were still alive, as were the *masts* [the God intoxicated]. I
stayed there for four or five months. Then my friend Bobby wrote
me a letter saying, "Hey, I'm up north in the Himalayas in a place
called Almora. This is a different scene from southern India. You
gotta come up here."

I went to Almora. We're looking at these high mountain peaks.
There's English people left over from the days of the Raj, Evans-
Wentz's stupa. There's a lot of black magic going on. There's
Nepalis, Tibetans, sadhus running around. I love this, but my visa
is running out, and the only district office is in Nainital.

I go to Nainital and find the local police place. I'm dressed all
in white, I have a shaved head, no beard on my face. The chief of
police or captain looks up and goes, "Yes, can I help you?"

"I would like a visa extension, because I am a spiritual
seeker."

Now politically that was a time when Indians were very
upset with Americans, because Nixon had come out in favor
of Pakistan, and they felt so hurt that we, a fellow democracy,
would betray them that way. He starts yelling at me.

"You Americans. You think you can come here to my country, and you can do this and that." He looks at my passport. "You only have three or four days left. You better get to Delhi now and go home. Get out of my office, I never want to see your face again. Get out. *Jao!*"

I'm blown away. I'm standing outside the police station and suddenly I see a bunch of Westerners all dressed in the ashram whites. I explain to them what's going on. They suggest that I would feel a lot better if I went to see their baba. But Meher Baba's thing was, "Don't go to other masters; they confuse you with different directives." I'm like, "Nah, nah, I don't want to see any other babas." But there was something about these folks, so I go, "Okay."

They lead me through hills and dales, and suddenly we're at this river, with a bridge going over it, and there's this gorgeous ashram. I go into the courtyard, and I see a little old man sitting on his takhat with a bunch of Westerners sitting around his feet. They're all laughing and giggling, and he's hitting them with flowers, throwing fruit, and my heart is going *boom, boom.* What's going on here?

That day he does something he didn't do very often in the time I was there. He let people come into the office one by one and ask a question. Here I am, I had just arrived. When it's my turn to go in, I touch Baba's feet, and Dada says, "What is your question?"

I could have asked any question in the universe, but I go, "What should I do about my visa?" Of all things. He looks at me, and I have the strangest sensation; he's kind of in my head; I actually feel something going on inside of me. He says through Dada, "Tell him to go back tomorrow morning." I touch his feet, thank him, and leave.

I go back to Nainital and take a room, and I'm in major conflict. Like an idiot I didn't say, "Go back to America and go home? Or do you mean, you can't mean, I should go back to that guy's office?" I wrestled with it all night. The police station wasn't far from the bus station in Nainital. I said, "What the hell. I'm being kicked out of India. Let me go in there."

I walk in to the police station, and I look exactly the same. The same guy looks up from his paperwork and goes, "Yes?"

I cringe and say, "I want to ask about a visa extension."

He goes, "Oh sure. Come in and sit down." He calls a boy to go get chai and offers me a beedie. We're smoking beedies and drinking chai, and he's telling me how much he loves Americans. I tell him how I want to stay, I'm a spiritual seeker. He goes, "Sure, no problem." He takes my passport and stamps it . . . *for a year!*

I start crying because I know what's going on now. What Baba did was make the officer the loving person he was supposed to be, the real self that he is beyond all of the ego stuff. I go running back to the ashram. Same scene, he's there on the takhat, playing with everybody, and then my mind snaps, "Now wait a minute. Yes, he did a miracle for me, *but why?* Maybe he wants to possess me and capture me. See, Meher Baba said you shouldn't go to these people."

Then my mind goes, "But Meher Baba also said that on the planet there are many gurus and saints of different levels, but at all times there are five perfect ones, five perfect masters." I'm thinking that maybe he's one of the five. From a far distance, maybe a couple of hundred feet away, Maharajji stops what he's doing and looks up at me. He holds up his closed hand and opens one finger after another, counting to five. My mind exploded!

Courtesy of Premananda

Premananda (with shaved head) in a group singing kirtan.

Then he waves me to come over. He says, *"Beto."* I didn't know what *beto* means, but it means "sit down."

And I didn't leave. Every day was love, crying, joy, laughter, bliss, amazement. I had no doubt over time that he was truly a *satguru,* a perfect one, and that we have something to do together.

What it always came down to in the end was simply love.

BALARAM DAS: I have a beautiful memory of Diwali [the Festival of Lights, held in the fall] in '72. We were setting up the lamps. We had spent all day rolling these cotton wicks to put in the little clay dishes; then we had to fill them all with oil. When we were making those lamps, Maharajji goes, "How do you do this in America? Do you make these by hand?" We said, "No,

Baba." He said, "You do it by machines!" Of course nowadays the ashram's all decked out with flourescent tubes.

At sunset we started lighting the oil lamps and setting them all along the tops of the walls, along the windows, along the ledges. Everyone was running around, frantically setting up the lights. Maharajji was walking by himself up and down through the garden while everyone else was scurrying around. The sky was all golden, and it was beautiful.

As all of the lights were coming on, he walked over to me, and I pranaamed. He put his foot on my shoulder or my neck and said, "Balaram is my very great devotee." That's something I don't talk about very often. All those little touches that were so affectionate. It was the experience of being loved in a way that there was nothing else to compare it with. When you felt that love, it changed you.

13

Following the Path

Winter 1972–1973

Kabir says: Listen, my friend,
There is one thing in the world that satisfies,
And that is a meeting with the Guest.

—KABIR, SONGS OF KABIR

There was no "winter camp" at Dada's in Allahabad in 1973. Instead, Maharajji disappeared in January and February before returning to Vrindavan in March. Only two people managed to find him during this time—Krishna Das and Draupadi—while the rest of the satsang went here and there exploring other parts of India, other ashrams, or meditation courses.

KRISHNA DAS: Maharajji disappeared, as he always did. I went to Delhi with Draupadi, and we asked some of the old Indian devotees where they thought he was, and either nobody knew or nobody would tell us. Then we kind of bribed the driver of one of the devotees to tell us where his boss had gone. We somehow figured that Mr. Barman was with Maharajji. The driver told us that Barman had gone to Bombay and was staying at a particular hotel, so we flew to Bombay, went to this hotel, and sat in the lobby all day long, waiting to see who would show up.

Finally that evening Mr. Barman shows up and says, "Krishna Das, you're here! What are you doing here?"

We told him we heard Maharajji was in Bombay.

"Really, in Bombay?! Well, I have some work to do. Come up to my room and order food, relax. When I come back, we'll try to find him."

Well, if he didn't know where Maharajji was, nobody knew. I'm looking out the window in despair, when all of a sudden the door to the room opens, I turn around, and it's Maharajji! So we got rooms in the hotel, and every day he'd come and hang out with us.

A lot of incredible things happened, mostly in silence. One day he called us to come be with him. He was sitting on the bed, and Mr. Barman was there. I was sitting on the floor with my eyes closed for a long time. All of a sudden Maharajji sits up, looks at me, and says, "Courage is a really big thing."

All I could think was, "What's gonna happen? I don't think I'll be able to deal with it!"

Barman says, "Oh, but Baba, God takes care of his devotees."

Maharajji shot him a look, then looked back at me, and said, "Courage is a really big thing." And he closed his eyes again.

I had no idea what it meant. Not a clue. But there have been a few times in my life when all I had to hold on to was the memory of his saying that. There was no possibility of courage, no possibility of action, I was completely lost, completely drowning, but I had the barest memory of his saying that . . . and it was enough.

After his Bombay excursion, Maharajji returned to Vrindavan.

BRUCE: Now I am an eighteen- or nineteen-year-old at this point, full of hormones going through the body, very much in love with my girlfriend and not getting laid. I am basically sitting there for four months very sexually frustrated, and that was creating a lot of anger inside me, and a lot of tension between me and Louise. So when I heard that Maharajji's hand brushed across her breast in some kind of way, it was like, "Game over. He's a fake. We're out of here." I'm packing my bags. I was frickin' peeved. Also the jealousy—he touched her and I can't even touch her?

I was in the *dharmasala* [a simple building where spiritual seekers can stay] next to the main temple. I was the only one in the compound. Everyone else was on the other side in the ashram. I could hear a bunch of people singing *Gopala Gopala*. I never liked that song. It usually meant Maharajji went somewhere else and they were just sitting there. It was like an intermission.

I was really pissed off. I took a shower and released myself after all those months in India. I was doing it next to the temple; it was like, "Fuck you, Maharajji." That's exactly what it was. "If you can do that, I can do this." I just couldn't wait to tell everyone we were out of there.

After taking that shower, I sit down at this little table in front of my window that overlooks the yard and the entrance coming into it, and I'm drawing the dirtiest pictures of Maharajji having sex with women and men. I went total Cromwell. Pure blackness. All-out anger. The evil press working underground.

Anyhow, I was sitting there with all this anger and self-righteousness, and who do I see walking right toward me? *Maharajji!* Dada's holding his arm. I'm looking at him going, "What? What's he doing here? He's not supposed to be here." All these people are singing *Gopala* next door. There is not a Westerner here. He's walking right toward my window! I am sitting there going, "Whoa, whoa, whoa." I'm looking at these dirty cartoons and thinking I have to show him these cartoons. Then a part of me went, "No, don't. This is not for an Indian person to see."

He went right by my window, and I heard him talking in the next room right behind the shower, where only about half an hour ago I had pleasured myself. Then something clicked. "Bruce, this is an opportunity to get Maharajji alone." I figured he could always *jao* me.

The door's open, he's sitting on the takhat, and the two people standing beside him are waving rags to keep the flies away. I'm kneeling before him. I put my head in his lap, and I gave him all my anger. I even pictured pleasuring myself in the shower. I didn't hide anything from him. I said, "Here, here, here is my anger. Here, you touched her, my anger about that." I gave it all to him. He patted me on the head, went, "*Bohut accha* [Very good]," and then got up and left. That was the end of my anger. It was very powerful.

It was a gift. Of course he came for me. That's the way I take it, narcissist that I am. He definitely came for me, waited for me, did the thing, and then left. That was the last time I saw him.

Shaping Our Destiny

There were many ways in which Maharajji molded our lives, sometimes gently taking away our anger or despair, as he did for Bruce, and at other times intensely pushing us in a certain direction. I remember one *jao* when Maharajji told me to go to Puri—ah, the beach! I was excited about that. But Raghu was going to take the Vipassana course in Bodhgaya, and Maharajji told me to stay with him rather than go off on my own. That's a simple example. What he did with Dr. Larry was to push him along a path he would follow for most of his life, despite the many attempts it took to get him there.

DR. LARRY: In March of '73, we were sitting in front of Maharajji. He was talking to each person about their own path. He got to me and said, "Dr. America, how much money do you have?"

I thought about it for a while. "I've got $500."

"No, I don't mean here. I mean back in America. How much have you got in America?"

All that I had in America was $500.

He laughed and laughed and said, "$500 here, $500 there. You are no doctor. *Tum to doctor nahin.*" He is laughing and chanting, "You are no doctor." I am thinking that's what my mother would have said about me. You have no money—you are not a real doctor.

Then he changed this chant from *"Tum to doctor nahin"* to "UNO doctor, UNO doctor." I didn't get it. We call the United Nations the U.N.; Indians call the United Nations the United Nations Organization, its proper name. UNO. He was saying, "UNO doctor, UNO doctor. You will become a United Nations doctor. You will go to villages, and you will give shots. *Katara mahamari khatam ho jayega.* Smallpox will be eradicated. It's God's gift to humanity."

Then after all this giggling and laughing, this great effervescent pixie dust–like moment, he said, *"Tum jao.* You go. You go to WHO [World Health Organization]. You go to the U.N. You go to get your job."

What job? I had never seen a case of smallpox. It had been eradicated in the United States by 1949, twenty years before I went to medical school. India was one of only four countries in the world that still had smallpox. But India was exporting smallpox, so the rest of the world could never eradicate smallpox until India did.

Right after Maharajji said that, I met someone who worked for WHO. I said, "Oh, that's really funny. My guru says I am supposed to work for WHO."

"Oh, are you a doctor? Well, there is no smallpox program, but there is this amazing woman, Nicole Grasse, who was sent here to try to start a smallpox program. While smallpox might be a priority for the rest of the globe, it is just not a priority in India. Kids are dying of diarrhea and respiratory diseases."

I went to WHO with him, and he took me to the personnel office. I was still wearing my ashram whites, I had a beard down to here and hair down to the middle of my back; "scruffy" would have been a bit of an upgrade. They kicked me out.

Girija and I went back to the ashram. Maharajji said, "Did you get your job?"

I said, "No."

He said, "Go back. Go get your job. Now."

I went in again to the Human Resources office, and they kicked me out again. This kept going on. We kept going back to the ashram, and Maharajji would kick us out to go to Delhi to get my job.

After ten, twelve, fifteen times I was growing pretty skeptical, and it was certainly not fun anymore. I still had never seen a case of smallpox. I still had no training. I still had no job. Although I had finished my internship, I didn't do a residency, never had a medical job unless you count running a small clinic in the back of Kainchi. Where is your resume? It's very short.

Somewhere along the line I trimmed my hair, and Mr. Barman gave me a shirt, tie, and one of his jackets to wear. I never quite got the pants part right, but each time I went back, I got a little bit more cleaned up.

I did meet Nicole, and she was extraordinarily nice. She said, "I am sorry. Let's leave aside the obvious about how you look, and the fact that you've never worked anyplace, and that we only recruit Americans from the CDC [Centers for Disease Control] or a university. WHO has never hired anybody as young as you. Never hired anybody as inexperienced as you. And certainly never hired Americans while they were living in India. There is no job for you."

I went back and told Maharajji what she had said. He said to go back and get my job. I went back another time. There was a receptionist there who was like the heart of WHO, Mrs. Boyer, an Anglo-Indian. She was intrigued by my story of this guru in the Himalayas who told me that I was going to get a job. I went to sit down in the waiting room in the chair that she always had me sit in. There was already an American sitting there, so I sat next to him.

He said, "Oh, are you an American?" There was obviously some doubt.

I said, "Yes."

"Why are you here?" he asked.

"I am here because I am going to work for the smallpox eradication program. Smallpox is going to be eradicated. This is God's gift to humanity."

"Who told you that?"

"My guru, who lives in the Himalayas. He sent me to come work for the World Health Organization smallpox eradication program. What do you do?"

"I am D. A. Henderson, the head of the smallpox eradication program. I work in Geneva, and India is one of our problems, because we don't have a program here yet. I am waiting for Dr. Grasse to arrive, so we can go visit Mrs. Gandhi. Let's go have a cup of tea. I'll interview you, and we'll put it in the record."

I think we are now at seventeen visits to WHO. Back at Kainchi, we got a telegram from Nicole saying, "Come immediately to Delhi. Something interesting."

Girija and I went, as always, on the bus.

Nicole said, "I had this feeling yesterday that I should hire you. Maybe it was your guru coming and talking to me." She said it half sarcastically, but half very sincerely. "We can't hire you as a doctor. Can you type?" Yes. "Would you be interested if I could get you a P2 position?" P2 is the lowest starting level for an Indian national who is literally going to take notes.

I said, "Of course I will take it." Maharajji didn't say I was going to come in as a P4; he just said I was going to go to work.

She called D. A. and said, "Look, I need a secretary. I don't speak English that well. The Indians don't speak French. I am going to hire this American guy who speaks Hindi and is at a low enough level that I don't need government of India approval."

I went back to Maharajji and told him there was something cooking. He said, "You'll get your job."

Then Nicole said, "I am having trouble getting your security clearance." Security clearance? Americans may not know that there is a loyalty board, and you've got to be adjudicated loyal to work for the U.N. I am thinking of all those marches I did with Martin Luther King. Getting arrested with Martin Luther King. All those marches against the war in Vietnam. "That's it. The gig is up," I thought.

We went up to Kainchi and told Maharajji there was a problem with the security clearance. I told him about marching against the war in Vietnam, about Martin Luther King. There were about twenty of us medical students who used to put on white coats and conspicuously dangle our stethoscopes as we made a phalanx around Martin Luther King to protect him. He said, "Who gives you this security clearance?" I had no idea. The only name I could think of that was high enough was D. A. Henderson, the head of the program. He said, "Henderson, how do you spell it?"

At that moment in Geneva, D. A. was at a reception at the American Embassy, and the Surgeon General was visiting from the United States. He asked D. A. if all the countries were helping in the smallpox eradication. D. A. replied that the Russians were giving vaccine, the Canadians were giving money, and the Czechs were giving epidemiologists. He said, "Oh, good. What are the Americans giving?"

D. A. said, "Not much." Then he said, "I don't know why I would ever bring this up, but there is a kid we are trying to hire at the lowest possible grade, and he can't get a security clearance because he was an antiwar activist."

The Surgeon General said, "Who gives that security clearance?"

"I think you do, or I think you can."

The Surgeon General took a cocktail napkin and asked, "What's the kid's name?" He wrote on the napkin, "Brilliant, okay to start work." He gave it to D. A., who sent it to Geneva.

We were with Maharajji when the telegram came: "Okay to start work. Report immediately."

Dr. Larry, left, behind Maharajji.

In the beginning I was taking notes and editing papers. That lasted about three weeks. Then WHO was beginning what they called an intensified campaign, because India was the last place on earth that had a massive amount of smallpox. There were 150,000 people searching for smallpox and 500 doctors from 25 countries. They came in waves, never more than 30 or 40 at a time. During the first wave for the first search, one of the Russian doctors couldn't come, so they had a hole in this nice map that showed all of the epidemiologists' assignments. I was at a meeting and they were asking who could fill the hole. Nicole said, "Larry?"

The reaction was kind of mixed, everything from laughter to one of the doctors saying, "Well, let me take him into the field." That was it. We wound up searching every house in India for twenty months. We made over a billion house calls. And smallpox was eradicated.

And who knows what Maharajji activated back then that was set to manifest many decades later?

KABIR DAS: Construction was going on in the ashram and each morning the laborers would pass Baba en route to their work site. Indians for the most part are very caste conscious, but Maharajji was beyond the duality and prejudice of the caste system. These days he was in the habit of calling the workers over one by one as they came by and asking for a *roti* [chapati, round flatbread] from their lunch tins. Of course they were only too happy to comply. Maharajji might retain one or two morsels for himself, but the majority of the collected breads he pulled apart and distributed as prasad to all of those gathered around.

One morning a rich elderly devotee was pleading with Baba that he be given the blessing to become a multimillionaire. Maharajji was quite amused by this request and enjoyed playing with the man, telling him that since he was already a rich man, he had no need for this blessing. At the same time Baba was carrying on half a dozen other conversations, playing with the foreigners and asking for his favorite songs, and issuing instructions to ashram staff. The old man continued to pester Maharajji.

Meanwhile the laborers had come and gone. The rotis had been collected and passed around. I received my piece, took a bit out of it to eat, and kept the remainder in my hand. After persistent pestering, Maharajji finally relented, saying that although he wouldn't bless the old man with riches in the millions, he would bless his grandchildren. The old man indicated that he was willing to accept that compromise. Maharajji wanted to give him something to symbolize the blessing. He asked if anyone had any prasad. Without hesitation, I offered the piece of roti in my hand, and Baba accepted it. He then handed it to the old man, who was delighted.

Just then I felt a tap on my shoulder. Another Indian devotee who had been closely observing the whole play and who no doubt was concerned with Hindu proprieties whispered to me, "Did you not eat from that piece of roti?" I replied that I had. He then whispered something to the old man. As if he suddenly became aware of a hot ember in his hand, the old man thrust the roti back to me. A foreigner had eaten a piece of it! I took it from him and chewed it up. Only later did the realization dawn upon me of the "significance" of that twice-blessed roti. [Kabir has not yet become a multimillionaire, but perhaps his grandchildren . . .]

Sadhus

The word *sadhu* is translated as "good man" or "holy man" and usually denotes a yogi who is aiming for liberation in this lifetime. The root of the word, *sadh*, means "to reach one's goal"; *sadhana* means "spiritual practice." Although Maharajji had been a sadhu in his early years, he had long since reached the goal. As Westerners and as his devotees, our sadhana had to do more with following the path of *bhakti*, or devotion, than with any form of rigid discipline and austerities. But there were those who did take the path of the renunciate, at least for a while.

Sadhu Uma (Marcelle Hanselaar) dropped out of art school in the Netherlands and hitchhiked to India in 1967 with her lover, Shambhu, in search of the truth that would set them free. In 1970 they returned to Amsterdam. Shambhu stayed there with his new girlfriend, while Uma hitchhiked back to India in 1971 on her own to continue her search.

SADHU UMA: I became a Giri sadhu, a devotee of Shiva, and practiced meditation and lived off what people would give me. I had great faith that I was protected by the gods, although life was often very hard for a girl who came originally from a protected background. More seriously, I had become disillusioned by the teachers I'd met over the years, the hierarchy of the monastic system, and I also began to doubt my own motivations. Therefore I decided to take a bath in the Ganges in Haridwar before leaving India.

On the bus to Delhi I met a Frenchman who showed me a small picture of a sadhu he called Neem Karoli Baba. There was something in the way that Baba held himself in that photo that touched me, so I decided to make a detour and go first to Bhimtal to pay him my respects before my farewell to India.

It was a long journey by bus and on foot, and I arrived at the temple in the late afternoon. I had not seen so many Westerners for a long time; they felt quite foreign and I was a bit intimidated by them, but they kindly welcomed me. They fed me and invited me to join the crowd for darshan with Babaji. I sat and watched, and at some point Maharajji gestured and shouted at me to come closer. He asked my name and lineage and patted me so vigorously on my *jetas* [dreadlocks that are "washed" with the ash from sacred fires] that ash clouds flew out. He was giggling and welcoming me. He said I could stay a while, and I made my *dhuni* [fire] outside the temple gates, going in for food and darshan every day.

One day he asked all his devotees what they needed. Some needed money, and he asked another devotee to give them some; another needed a blanket, and he provided that as well. At some point he asked me what I wanted or needed. My heart became very still. I bent forward till my head was against his feet and said, "I want your blessing, Babaji." He again patted my head with vigor, ashes flying about, and then everything went still. When I opened my eyes it was evening, and I was sitting on the empty veranda in full lotus. I felt cleansed, cool, and calm.

All those years I had walked about India and asked people to show me the truth; many people helped me, but I did not find what I was looking for—the reassurance it is possible to find it, to live it, to actually experience it. Maharajji gave me that experience.

Because I did not have a visa or passport, Maharajji told me to go south; they would all go to the Vrindavan vihara soon as well, and I could join them there. In Vrindavan Maharajji ordered wood for my dhunni. Wood is scarce in Vrindavan, but he respected my rules as a Girija Shaivite; my practice was not to live inside a building and to maintain a fire. Some of Maharajji's devotees would come to my dhunni, and we talked till late in the night about our questions and quests and how each of us came to be there.

Maharajji was talking to me about Chitrakut, how he had been there. I felt that after my samadhi experience I wanted to deepen my meditation practice, so I took my leave to go to Chitrakut. On my arrival I did my *parikrama* [circumambulation] of that holy mountain, which is the body of Vishnu, and spent the night in the only Shiva temple there. There I met someone who told me there was a cave a few miles away where I could practice. For quite a while I had been suffering from malaria attacks and this, coupled with my being illegally in India, meant that this cave was an ideal solution for me. The cave had clean water nearby. The brother of the man in the Shiva temple was a headmaster of a nearby village school, and he generously promised to send me one meal a day, five times a week, with the woodcutters who worked on top of the mountain.

I sat in that cool airy cave tending my fire, with a photo of Maharajji in a small niche near the entrance. I had few human visitors. Then one day a very old woman came down the mountain, came into the cave without greeting me, and went straight to Maharajji's photo. She looked at it and cackled, "He has tubes up his nose." I was annoyed, partly by her lack of greeting and even more by her criticism of my teacher! I told her that was just a trick of the photo and that she should go. She stubbornly repeated this "tubes up his nose" line a few more times before going away.

Many months later I came down from the mountain, because I wanted to pay Babaji a visit and ask him for guidance. My solitariness, sickness, and little food had given me overwhelming visions and hallucinations, and I did not know what to make of

Courtesy of Sadhu Uma

Sadhu Uma.

them. But when I came at last to the plains, I was met by others
who told me Maharajji had died some months ago. He had been,
they told me, at some point in the hospital with tubes going up
his nose.

I felt he had deserted me, and I was so angry that I kicked
the Hanuman murti in the temple. Sometime later I went back
to Chitrakut and, following some dreams I had, went to a
monastery in the jungle to ask them for advice on my meditation
practice. I also went partly to follow Maharajji's footsteps to
somewhere in the jungle in the direction of Bilaspur, where
Maharajji had stayed as a young sadhu for a while.

I stayed in India as a sadhu till 1974, and then I returned to Europe, where I tried to incorporate all these things into my everyday life as an artist. Sometimes I am still falling down and getting up. And knowing it's all right.

Saraswati (Rosalie Ransom) went to India as a follower of Ananda Murti and was there when he was arrested, but she had had an extraordinary samadhi experience with him, so she never criticized him. While traveling around India after Ananda Murti's arrest, Saraswati ran into Govind, whom she knew from America. He was radiant, beaming. He told her he had just come from Neem Karoli Baba. Twenty-four hours later she walked into Maharajji's ashram in Vrindavan and went into an exalted state before ever seeing Maharajji. She realized that all of creation is the ashram and everyone she meets is the guru.

SARASWATI: At one point Maharajji *jaoed* us from Vrindavan. "Go away. Go to Allahabad. Go to Benares, go to Chitrakut." He was naming places. I had of course read *Autobiography of a Yogi*. I recalled that when Yogananda's guru sent him away, he didn't know what to do, so he sat under a tree and waited. I didn't know what to do either. I had no money whatsoever, so, like Yogananda, I went and sat under a tree and waited. Not long afterward, one of the women said, "Hey, we've got an extra ticket. You want to come with us to Benares?" That was the opening for getting to Benares, Allahabad, Chitrakut—those places he had mentioned.

Chitrakut is where I took personal vows as a renunciate, a sadhu. I was at a little temple by the river, doing my puja, when an Indian man rushed up to me and said I had a sister there. Uma was staying on top of a hill by a little temple, just a little place, no murti, and she was really sick. That was the beginning of my

close connection with her. I modeled my own renunciation on
hers. What her vows were I would take as well. She gave me the
daring to give up everything, start walking, and not to ask for
food or lodging or money . . . to focus on being in the Presence.
Ask for nothing; it must all be offered. The strength comes from
within.

My feet cracked open, so they bled. I got infections on the tops
of both toes, so I packed them with sandalwood to keep them
from getting worse. I accepted only one meal a day because that's
what Uma did. She had lice in her dreadlocks; I didn't do dreads,
and I covered my hair at all times. I used neem branches for a
toothbrush. I didn't ask where to go but accepted suggestions.
I stayed no more than three days in a place and didn't keep any
possessions.

Maharajji and Saraswati.

Krishna Das (Roy Bonney)

At one point I was in a remote Hanuman temple outside of Khajaraho with all those carved erotic statues. I was getting ready to move on, as I'd been there my allowed three days. As I was sitting on the steps of the Hanuman temple, Ravi Das walked up out of the blue and for some reason he had all my mail. I read the letters in order: "Your grandfather is sick. Your grandfather is very sick. Your grandfather has died. You have inherited a thousand dollars." A sadhu had inherited money? Well, that had to be dealt with. Now I had to go to Delhi. In Delhi I ran into satsang who told me Maharajji was back and giving darshan. Even though I was a renunciate and had given up gurus, I at least had to pay my respects. And that brings us to that picture, because that is me at the first moment of coming back. That was the end of my wandering sadhu days.

Naima Shea had seen pictures of Maharajji in *Be Here Now,* but wasn't particularly attracted to him. She had met Swami Satchidananda, who was more her image of a spiritual teacher—tall, handsome, slim, with long flowing hair and robes, while Maharajji was a dumpy old guy. After finishing college at UC–Berkeley and getting tear-gassed during peaceful protests, she was disillusioned with American culture. She went to the Lama Foundation, but it turned out not to be the utopian community life she was seeking. Then she met someone who asked if she wanted to go to India. She arrived mid-March of 1972. Within moments of getting off the bus from the airport in New Delhi, she spotted a Westerner dressed all in white and asked where Ram Dass was. He told her Ram Dass had just left, but Maharajji was in Kainchi, so she headed up there.

NAIMA: In the beginning, I couldn't relate to the bowing and foot touching and all that, but I was intrigued enough to hang around.

One day Maharajji and I made eye contact, and we both started laughing out of pure joy. It wasn't long before I started telling him I wanted to be a sadhu, a full-time renunciate. I took off my sari and started wearing a shawl wrapped around me and left my hair loose. He started saying, "Oh, you want to be a sadhu. You want to take sadhu vows. You want the orange robes." He was really teasing me about it all. I kept saying, "Yes, Maharajji." Every so often he would say, "I am going to get you the robes. This guy is dyeing them for you now." I was getting excited about the idea that I was going to be this wandering sadhu in India for the rest of my life.

One day he gave me a piercing look and said, "Are you ready for your robes?" I said yes. He clearly let me know that it is not about what you are wearing or anything external. It is about what is inside you, what's in your heart. At that point the idea of changing what I wore and adopting the life of a sadhu became irrelevant. He was saying it's an inside job. I let go of that illusion, that spiritual ego of wanting to become a sadhu because it was romantic and cool and conceptually I would be "more spiritual" if I was a sadhu. This was a wonderful teaching for me.

14

Over the Wall

Spring 1973

Out beyond ideas of wrongdoing
and rightdoing, there is a field.
I'll meet you there.

When the soul lies down in that grass,
the world is too full to talk about.

—RUMI (TRANS. COLEMAN BARKS)

There was a period of time when Maharajji was not seeing Westerners in Vrindavan. They were staying at Jaipuria Bhavan, down the road from the ashram, and coming daily to knock on the gate to see if they would be let in. Part of the reason—if we can be so bold as to assume we know Maharajji's reasons behind anything—had to do with the fact that Indian officials were searching for some Westerners who had overstayed their visas or thrown away their passports.

One of Maharajji's favorite words for us was *badmash,* which means "wicked" or "naughty." In India, it is a term of endearment for small children when misbehaving; it also can be applied to criminals and other lowlifes. Maharajji loved his badmashes, even those who overstayed their visas. When Balaram Das, for example, repeatedly ignored Maharajji's *jao* and found various ways to get around it, his badmash behavior was more times than not rewarded with more darshan. But sometimes breaking the "rules" could lead to an encounter with Maharajji's fierce side.

One note: You will read here and in other places that Maharajji slapped or hit someone, sometimes repeatedly. Please understand that he was not beating up or physically abusing anyone. His touch conveyed a huge amount of spiritual energy. I remember the first time he touched me with just a fingertip on the top of my head; I could feel all the cells in my body rearranging themselves. In the following story, when he hits Krishna Priya, she goes deeper and deeper into a state of God intoxication.

KRISHNA PRIYA: We were coming daily to the Vrindavan ashram, but we were not being allowed in. For many days I had been desperately needing to talk to Maharajji about a personal matter, and I needed a private darshan to do so.

In those days, if you stood behind the Hanuman murti you could look over the wall and see into the courtyard; if Maharajji was on his takhat outside, then you could see him. One day, Trilok, who was the chaukidar at the time, was moving furniture and thus had the door open that led to the inner courtyard. Tukaram was fooling around with Trilok, playfully teasing him. He was stepping over the doorsill and then back. They were joking and laughing. At one point I said to Tuk, "Why don't you just go in? Go ahead, go." Before I knew it, Tukaram had taken me by the shoulders and switched places with me. He said, "Okay, you go."

None of this was premeditated. I found myself inside the ashram. I closed the door behind me and locked it. I locked everyone out, including Trilok, and made a beeline to Maharajji's office. There was nobody in the room except Maharajji. He starts moving from one end of the takhat to the other in a state of utter agitation. I go mast and completely forget what I was going to ask him about. I know that there is no way I could be there if Maharajji didn't want me to be and that this is all show. I was not being a badmash.

Maharajji is yelling for Bhaiyu and Bapu, those guys who were supposed to be security. Nobody's coming. At this point I've given up trying to calm him down. He's hitting me and hitting me. "Badmash. Badmash. Bhaiyu, Bapu, help." The more he's hitting me, the more I'm going into a state of intoxication. This was completely Maharajji's lila.

When I was finally escorted out of the room, a number of Baba's close Indian devotees ran up to me, elated. They had been trying, without success, to get Baba to grant me a private darshan. There was no question in their minds that Baba had created this lila. And many years later Trilok told me that that day was the greatest of his life. "Hanuman himself boxed my ears!" he said. Baba had roared at him, "What kind of a chaukidar are you?" Later, Trilok became the Hanuman pujari in Kainchi.

The next day I somehow found myself sitting right by his takhat, which rarely happened, and Maharajji was caressing and praising me. Everyone in the satsang noted that I was not getting into massive trouble for what had taken place the day before.

A couple of days go by, and we are again not being allowed in. Tukaram, who is six foot five, leaps over the wall, and nobody notices him because he just vaults over. Unbeknownst to me at the time, Chaitanya had already done the same thing, and they were hiding there behind the pillar. They had just gotten away with going over the wall, and now it could possibly turn into a free-for-all.

I was not tall enough to get over by myself, so I asked Gita to give me a hand up. She's hoisting me up over the wall. The Hanuman pujari was maun at the time, so he couldn't say anything. He sees me start going over the edge of the wall. He's going, *"Om Om Om Om,"* trying to get attention. I go flying over. Apparently the moment Chaitanya and Tukaram saw me, they knew the game was over. I don't remember having even two minutes on the other side before we were all caught and summarily thrown out.

The next day the wall around the ashram had been doubled in height; this was called Krishna Priya's wall. The sorrow of it was that when you stood behind Hanuman, no longer could you look over the wall and see Maharajji. The wall became my fault, but what nobody knows is that I was simply following in my older brothers' footsteps.

RAVI KHANNA: We were in Vrindavan; then he closed the place down for a while to the Westerners. Indian families would come. They would get announced, they'd be let in, and then the doors would close again. We would come every day, hang out there for three or four hours, and then go back to Jaipuria Bhavan.

When Krishna Priya jumped over the wall, we got thrown out even farther from the ashram. Then one day this Indian family came, the chaukidar opened the door to let them in, and I stuck my foot in the door. I said, "I am not going to let you close the door until you at least tell him we're here." After a while he had

stopped announcing us. I said, "You have to tell him we are here."
He wouldn't, and I kept insisting. Then he opened the door and
pushed me. I fell back. He closed the door and told Maharajji that
I was causing trouble.

Maharajji called for me. He said, "Wasn't it your fault?"

"Yes, Maharajji."

Maharajji and Ravi Khanna walking together.

Then he called the chaukidar over and said, "This is my son. Don't ever stop him from coming."

That was it. This changed our relationship. From then on I was like his personal assistant. I had access. Everyone was sent away, and I would be there with him. I got to travel with him. It was incredible. A few weeks later he invited me to come stay in the ashram. After Maharajji went back inside for the evening, everyone would fall into gossip about who was doing what, and I was really not interested in that kind of stuff. It was just Maharajji. That was all I was interested in.

ANJANI: I had been in India for almost a year and a half, when I heard that I had a Quit India notice in the winter of '72–'73. So I was in hiding. Maharajji had sent me into the mountains right before the officials came looking for people in Vrindavan. My sister Revati had come, and we went to Nainital and Kausani, because we would be safe up there with Maharajji devotees.

When we returned to Vrindavan, we learned that Maharajji was heading south for the winter. I said, "Well, let's go to Benares and do a Goenka retreat." When we got to Benares, however, I got very sick with hepatitis and spent a while in the hospital there. In the ward, all they did was come in once a day to see if you were still alive. There was no medicine, and the families were cooking in between the beds. If you needed medicine or food, the family had to provide it.

My poor sister would come and see me, and I was completely out of it. She would go out in the evening, and there would be all the bodies wrapped up waiting for the burning ghats. She kept thinking, "Oh, if I have to go home and tell mom that she died and they burned her body in Benares . . ."

After hepatitis, we went to Vrindavan. There had been a lot of bad behavior, like Krishna Priya climbing over the wall, and Maharajji had *jaoed* everyone to Jaipuria Bhavan; they weren't allowed to come to the ashram. We thought, "Well, we're innocent. We weren't involved in any of that." So we went to the ashram. Dada came out and told us that Maharajji wouldn't see anybody, but we could walk around to the back of the mandir. We get on the back side, and we can see Maharajji in there; he's walking up and down in the courtyard; then he goes to the building in the back and walks on the roof. So we actually had darshan, though not the kind we wanted. That was the last time I saw him.

I realize now that we usually didn't understand what was happening until some time later (if then). Even now I'll remember a certain incident in a whole different way, and the significance of it. The things he did were very personal, very secret. He would be talking to other people about something that for some reason you were having an emotional reaction to; he would take your hand under his blanket and hold it while that was going on, totally acknowledging that he knew just where you were at; not looking at you, but there was this hidden contact. Even when you were "bad."

There was one incident when I was really bad. We were in his office in Kainchi. I got very upset about some interaction between Maharajji and another Western devotee, and I hopped up and walked out. I was very angry. I stamped up to the back of the ashram and was marching around and marching around and crying, of course, because I'm thinking, "Bad, bad move, leaving like that." Finally I thought, "I have to go back. I can't stay out in the back for the rest of my life or drown myself in the river."

Those were the only obvious choices. So I went back in, and he *jaoed* everyone else. I was crying with my head in his lap, and he was patting me on the head saying, "Oh, you're so good, you're so good." No matter what you did, the worst, it was okay. He was one person who was not going to judge you. He might pretend to be mad sometimes, or ignore you, or pretend that he liked someone better, but he was always right there, and there was always love. There was just so much love all the time.

Old Friends

Mira (Karen Goetsch) and Gita (Marci Gendloff) were friends from San Diego who had planned to meet up in Delhi and then travel south to see Sai Baba, whom Gita had met on a previous short trip to India. Mira arrived in India first and did a series of courses in Bodhgaya before her old boyfriend showed up and said, "I'm coming from Vrindavan, where I met this boy named Ravi Khanna, and he showed me where Maharajji's ashram is." She had heard of Maharajji through reading *Be Here Now*.

> MIRA: When Franz and I got off the train in Vrindavan, Ravi Khanna was there to meet us. He took us straight to the ashram and educated us: this is Hanuman, this is who Hanuman is, this is how you bow to him and walk around clockwise. When I got to the back of the Hanuman mandir, I looked over the wall and I could see this man who looked like the man from *Be Here Now* sitting in this big courtyard with a blanket on him.
> "Is that Maharajji?"
> "Yeah, that's Maharajji." Then Ravi Khanna says, "We should go to Jaipuria Bhavan."

We're walking down the road looking for a rickshaw when all of a sudden I feel this tug from the back. Krishna Priya says, "Girl, wait. Wait, wait, wait. Maharajji said, 'Where's that girl? Bring that girl back.' He's calling for you."

I knocked on the gate. The chaukidar came back in a minute and said, "Maharajji says that you should go to Jaipuria Bhavan, get yourself settled, and come for darshan in the morning." Great, perfect.

The next morning Ravi Khanna took me to the fruit stand to buy some apples and flowers, and we took a rickshaw to the ashram. We knocked on the gate, and the chaukidar left to announce us. While he was gone, Franz and Ravi Khanna left to pay the rickshaw *wallah* [driver]. In the half a second that they were gone, the chaukidar opened the gate, and I got swept into the ashram with a *whoosh,* the gate slamming behind me. I was left alone without my guide to show me how to conduct myself in the presence of this obviously very different, very elevated man.

There's Maharajji sitting on the takhat with a group of Indians focused on him. What should I do with the armful of apples I had? I just stood in the back, not wanting to intrude. He looked up and motioned for me to come closer. He had me sit down right in front of him, and all of the fruit and flowers fell into his lap.

Mr. Barman translated, "Where did you come from? Were you comfortable last night?"—just very practical and very loving. Then he said, "What's your plan now?"

"My friend is arriving in Delhi in a few days. I plan to go meet her."

"Go to Delhi, get her, and come back here."

Gita and I got to Vrindavan about ten at night. Of course, the ashram was closed up, but he had told me the two of us should

come, so I knocked on the gate and the chaukidar let us in.
Maharajji was in one of his little rooms by himself. I don't even
know how we communicated, because there was nobody to
translate, but somehow we understood him. He arranged for us
to stay next door at the Goenka Dharmasala. The chaukidar had
the keys, and we were taken, as if by magic, to a very large, newly
built, immaculately clean private room. We were blown away
and barely slept all night.

The next morning, word got out about the Goenka
Dharmasala, and all of the Westerners sent notes and messages to
Maharajji asking to stay. Over the next week, everybody shifted
over from Jaipuria Bhavan to the Goenka Dharmasala. Soon after
that he gave Gita her name. I had to ask for one later.

After the Goenka opened up, Maharajji started seeing
Westerners again, and then there were darshans every day. Gita

Maharajji and Mira (far right).

and I slept on the roof of the Goenka. It was beautiful. You'd wake up with the bells, *Radha Krishna* kirtan going through the air, the peacocks calling, and Maharajji every day—it was the most amazing time of my life.

GITA: Mira met me in Delhi, and we went to Vrindavan, where Maharajji quickly captured my heart and soul. After some days, I didn't understand why I lost the desire to continue on to Sai Baba's, so I prayed to him. That night Sai Baba came in a dream, kissed me on the forehead, and said that I was where I belonged. He was letting go of me.

Several weeks later, when Maharajji went to Kainchi after Holi, he was much more accessible; being in his presence for hours a day was an experience unlike any other. From the first time with Maharajji, he was lover, father, best friend, child, and so much more to me, all in one.

Eventually he let me move into the ashram and that was really nice, sitting with him when the Indians came in. I didn't speak Hindi, so it didn't matter that I was there. In the early mornings I would meditate on the side of one of the temples, facing Maharajji's room. One morning a friend told me that I was gaining weight and that I should walk with her instead of meditating. I did so. When Maharajji came out that morning, the first thing he said was, "You weren't there. How come?" That set my priorities straight. In the night I would sometimes get up and go look at his window just in case I could get a glimpse of him. The yearning to be with him was so intense.

At night after the gate was closed was the best time, because it was just the people who were in the ashram, and he was very relaxed. I had a little mala that was on elastic thread. I would sit behind him, he would put his hands behind, and we would play

GITA: One day somebody who'd just come from the States brought me some vitamin C powder. Maharajji had a cold. I made him vitamin C powder and water and said, "Maharajji, I want you to drink this. It's good for you."

He was very fussy about what he would put in his system. He said, "I will not drink that, but I will drink whiskey with you in America."

Years later I was in Berkeley with a friend, and we went into a bar. I had a glass of wine, and my friend was drinking an Irish coffee. I asked for a taste, took a sip, and asked what was in it. Whiskey. This incredible wave came over me. "Yes, I'm with you all the time. Don't forget that. I told you I was going to be with you."

Maharajji with Gita (center) and Draupadi (right).

handsies with the mala. He could be so childlike. Those simple little things are so precious.

While at Kainchi, I got a telegram from my parents: "Grandfather died, is being buried in Israel." I got it late in the afternoon. In the evening when everything was quiet, there were just a few of us sitting around. My mind was on my grandfather. Suddenly Maharajji stopped what he was talking about, looked at me, and *jaoed* me; then he looked at Ravi Khanna and *jaoed* him.

Ravi said, "I don't understand why he *jaoed* us. All Maharajji was talking about is when somebody dies, we can't worry. It's just their body, and we have to know that it is all okay. He kept saying it over and over."

I said, "I think I know why, and I think we can go back now." When we returned Maharajji asked me if I was okay. I told him about my grandfather, and again he repeated how it is just the body and the importance of knowing this.

Maharajji had me buy 100 kilos of *laddoos* [Indian sweets] every Tuesday in honor of Hanuman, to be passed out at the temples. When my money was for the most part gone, I told him. He seemed concerned and said, "Oh no. What will you do?" I said I wasn't worried, as I would be staying with him. After that he started giving me money. When he left his body, I felt I needed to stay in India and learn from other teachers, and I had the money he had given me, which allowed me to stay there for a while.

Busted!

Everyone's story of coming to Maharajji follows its own special twists and turns, but Vishnu's (Frank Hutton's) is unique in that in order to have Maharajji's darshan, he had to get busted!

VISHNU: I was living in Humboldt County [California] with my first wife and going to college on the GI Bill. I had no money. I knew some friends who were hash smugglers. They had made six trips back and forth between America and the tribal area above Peshawar by the Khyber Pass. One day they said, "We're going to India again in two weeks. Would you like to come? We'll pay your way. All you have to do is carry one of the suitcases. We'll be in India for a month, so you'll be able to go find this master you're looking for."

We flew to New Delhi. On the flight there was a beautiful young Western woman sitting in the seat beside me, every young man's dream. She had been in India a year before for two weeks and was so moved by it she worked as a legal secretary for a year and literally saved every penny she earned, so she could return for a long stay. At the time I was playing my cards very close to the vest, because there I was—a smuggler. She thought I was working with the CIA.

She went her way in Delhi, and my friends and I went overland across the border into Pakistan and up to a village in the tribal area just below the Khyber Pass. The locals don't recognize any borders there. We stayed for a couple of weeks and went up into the hills to the hash factories, made our false panels in the suitcases, and put the hash in.

We were coming back to India as planned, when my friends suddenly told me, "We can't stay now. We're going to have to go back to America right away. Don't worry, we will be coming back again in a few months."

But this wasn't our deal! I didn't come to India to smuggle hash. I came here because my heart drew me there. Now I was feeling obligated to them because of the money they spent; I needed to be on their agenda whether I liked it or not.

We went over to the other side of Old Delhi to this little travel agency to confirm our tickets. At that time all planes departed for America at three o'clock in the morning. We were in the airport a little before three, and my friends said, "We're going to go through customs first. You sit here for about ten minutes, and then you come through and don't sit by us on the plane."

I waited ten minutes, took my suitcase, and went through customs, no problem. I went up the ramp into the airplane. As I walked up the aisle, I was looking for my friends, but they were not on the plane. An announcement comes over the PA, "Will Mr. Hutton please come to the back of the airplane?" Suddenly I felt like a heavy weight had been lifted from my shoulders and that everything was going to be all right. I went down the ramp, and there was my suitcase. The attendant said, "Please pick it up and come with us." We went into the customs area, and there were my two friends, man and wife, with their heads hanging down. A worker was pulling the false pieces out of the suitcases, exposing the hashish.

It turned out that the agent in that little travel agency happened to be at the airport at three in the morning and happened to be in the customs area when my friends got busted. He remembered that there were three passengers who confirmed their tickets. He asked, "Where's the third man?" That's when they came to get me.

After getting out of jail, which is another story in itself, we had a month till our court date. When they'd been here before, my friends had stayed in a woman's house, Mrs. Banerjee, who had a home near the Coca-Cola factory behind Connaught Circus. Her family had been well off during the Raj, but when the British left, she fell on hard times and would rent out rooms. One day I am sitting on the patio and looking at Maharajji's picture in my copy of *Be Here Now,* thinking, "How will I ever find you?"

Mrs. Banerjee walks by, looks over my shoulder, and goes, "Oh, that is a very good baba. His devotees stay here all the time. As a matter of fact, three of them left the day before you got here. They came from Vrindavan. Maharajji is in Vrindavan right now. You should go see him."

The next morning I was on the Taj Express, all alone in India for the first time. I got off in Mathura and hired a tonga to go to Vrindavan. We clip-clopped all the way there. Mrs. Banerjee had told me the devotees stayed in a place called Jaipuria Bhavan. I asked the tonga driver to drive by the Hanuman temple on the way to the guesthouse, so that I could have a quick look. He stopped in front of the little gate, and I was peeking around the corner. Suddenly, about eight or ten children came running out of the gate and surrounded the tonga. I felt like a peeping Tom who had been caught looking in the window at lovers. I was so embarrassed. I said to the driver, "We've got to get out of here. Drive."

But the children said, "Your friends are waiting for you inside."

I figured they had the wrong tonga. I said, "That can't be. I don't know anyone here."

"No, no! Your friends are waiting for *you*." They grabbed my hands and my suitcase, literally pulled me off the tonga, and led me into the ashram. There were a few Westerners there at the time, and, much to my surprise, there was that American woman who had sat on the plane next to me. Her new name was Gita.

I said, "You were going to be a Buddhist meditator. It's kind of funny finding you here."

She said, "What's really funny is finding you here. For two weeks now Maharajji has been sending everyone away. Any new people come, *jao, jao*. No one can stay. When Maharajji came out for darshan this morning, he said, 'The Westerner who comes today can stay.'"

Now I was sure I managed to get my tonga in front of the one that was supposed to be there, but then they never even sent me to Jaipuria Bhavan. Magically it was the opening of the Goenka Dharmasala, so they kept me right there at the temple during my stay.

My whole life I'd been looking for my piece in the puzzle, but I never found anything that rang true in my heart. When I saw Maharajji I felt, "This is it! This is what I've been looking for." There was a recognition. I didn't know what "this" was, but I knew that the essence I was looking at over there on the takhat was *the* essence. It was the validation of what I had intuitively held in my heart since I was a small child. He never really said anything in words directly to me; all of the transmission was inside. But when I first looked at Maharajji and he glanced at me, the universe changed for all time.

I could only stay for four days, because I had to go back to Delhi to appear in court. The judge said, "Oh, you Westerners, you are so foolish. Why do you smuggle things out of our country that we feed to our cows? It doesn't make any difference to us, but we are part of the United Nations, so we have to do what America wants, which is the drug war thing." We were found guilty. There was a minimal $200 fine, a smack on the hand—naughty, naughty—and a Quit India notice. Off I went back home.

If we hadn't been caught at the airport, by the time my friends came back again, Maharajji would have already dropped his body. I would have missed my only chance of having his darshan. In fact, it seemed to be the general consensus among the people in the ashram that obviously Maharajji had had me busted so that I would have the chance to be with him.

All the Money in the World

Maharajji once said, "All the money in the world is mine." But most of us didn't have much money while we were in India. Maharajji was always concerned about the financial well-being of his foreign devotees, who couldn't earn money while in India. He would call upon someone with a surplus of cash to give a specific amount to somebody who had none. At one point "the fund" was started with money donated from the wealthier Westerners, which helped to support those who were flat broke. Maharajji enjoyed the redistribution game, which inevitably caused some people to reconsider their attachment to money. RamRani's story illustrates another aspect of Maharajji's fun and games in relation to money.

RamRani (Yvette Rosser) went to Europe after she graduated from high school to visit her mother's family in Belgium. She hitchhiked around Europe and found her way to Afghanistan. After spending a couple of months around Kabul, she arrived in India in December 1970, where everything looked so familiar.

RAMRANI: In February '72 I was in Kathmandu living at Swyambunath. I had a dream about this little triangle-shaped man in plaid, sitting in the distance and moving his palm up and down in Indian style, indicating "Come here." I woke up and wondered who that triangular man was. I rarely had such vivid dreams.

I went down to the Tewari tea shop, and somebody had a copy of *Be Here Now*. I opened it up to the place where Maharajji is sitting in the field, a plaid triangle with his arm sticking out of his blanket. Krishna Dobrer told me all about Maharajji, but then I took refuge with Satya Tulku Rinpoche, stayed with the Tibetans, and loved it.

I finally went down to India on Durga Puja in 1972 and did a Goenka course in Varanasi [Benares], where I met Saraswati and other Neem Karoli Baba devotees. After a quick trip to Goa to check on an Afghani puppy I had left with a family two years earlier, I finally went to Vrindavan to meet this Baba I had dreamed about.

Maharajji was sitting on his takhat. As soon as I arrived, he motioned for me to sit close, then closer. He asked me where I was from many times, and what my name was. He was really sweet to me and very attentive. It kind of embarrassed me, because everybody was staring at me. I recognized some of the people from Goenka courses. Then he *jaoed* everybody and told them to take me over to the dharmasala.

There was a thick bright blue wooden gate that separated the temple area from the back dharmasala area. It was locked from the inside. In the wooden gate, there was a little eyehole. I was staring through the eyehole, and Maharajji kept looking at the door and waving at me to come, just like in my dream. Baba laughed and laughed. He was showing me that he had visited me in my dream state and told me to come meet him.

The next morning there was mayhem. Dwarkanath said, "Baba left during the night. We have to go to Kainchi."

One of my favorite Maharajji stories happened soon after. I hadn't had much money in India; then my sister sent $400 to me in Delhi. I cashed $100 on my way to Vrindavan. I still had $300 worth of $20 traveler's checks (fifteen checks) that I put in a plastic envelope and stuck down in the bottom of my embroidered sadhu bag.

When I got to Kainchi, I rented a kutir down by the farm. Now and then I went to Nainital to cash another check or two. Never looked in that envelope, never counted, just took a few checks out and cashed them when needed. Finally I figured there must be only two or three checks left. I went to the State Bank of India in Nainital to cash all of the remaining checks, so I could be done with going to Nainital to change money. I pulled out that plastic envelope that I hadn't actually looked inside of for all those months. I counted the traveler's checks on the polished wooden counter, and there were fifteen checks—$300 worth! I knew I had started with $400. I changed $100 in Delhi and then I had been cashing checks for all those months. How could this be? I must have looked shocked.

The gentleman at the bank said, "What's the matter? Did you lose some money?"

I felt the earth shake in that old Colonial-era wooden building. I said, "Could you count these for me, please?"

"It's $300. How much would you like to cash?"

"All of it."

I had a big wad of rupees in my bag when I returned to Kainchi on the bus. Maharajji didn't always give afternoon darshan, but he was out on his takhat. As I walked across the courtyard he shouted, *"Kya, RamRani, paisa mil gaya?"* Which means, "What, RamRani, did you get your money?" I didn't tell many people about it. I was a little paranoid that American Express might investigate Baba!

It's now been over forty years since I met Maharajji. All in all, it's been a really wonderful trip on his magic blanket, and Baba is everywhere—the whole world is plaid!

KABIR DAS: From the moment I first met him, Maharajji treated me as his son. Almost a year and a half later, after he had emptied my pockets and put me on the receiving side of the fund, he asked me to contact my father in Canada and request that he send me money. There was no reply after more than a month. Maharajji kept asking if I had received any word from my father. One day, after I informed him again that no reply had come to my request (which I had sent very reluctantly), Babaji looked at me and said, "I am your true father." He bent over from his sitting position on the takhat and kissed me on the top of my head.

15

The Summer of Delight

Summer 1973

I seem to have loved you in numberless forms, numberless times,
in life after life, in age after age, forever.

—RABINDRANATH TAGORE, "UNENDING LOVE"

The spring and summer of 1973 were a sweet time for the Westerners, all of whom were now living either at the ashram or in the Kainchi valley rather than commuting from Nainital. Every little kutir, or hut, in the valley was occupied. Maharajji also opened up the "white house" and the *"kutcha* (unfinished) house" for the Westerners. Some who had gone the sadhu route found caves along the banks of the river.

Everyone who was there describes this time as ineffably sweet and loving.

Krishna Das (Roy Bonney)

Westerners singing kirtan outside Maharajji's "office."

KABIR DAS: That summer even the *jaos* were blissful. Just being in the valley with Baba was a great blessing even on those days when we were banned from the ashram itself. By now even the periodic *jaos* were less effective in diminishing the crowd. People kept coming to see Baba, and many stayed. Most of the time all the houses were occupied, and some, like mine, had continuous guests.

Maharajji for the most part was the embodiment of bliss, and it was contagious. The hours spent with him were passed in merriment, with singing and laughter. By now a good number of us knew a few of his favorites—the Hanuman Chalisa, the Sankata Mochan, Hanuman Aarti, Guru Aarti—as well as lots of kirtan. More and more time was passed daily fulfilling his wish to hear us sing. There was no more discipline in the earlier sense of being put into the back of the ashram for the afternoon. We spent much of the time with him, but were occasionally sent back

when he wished to meet some devotees without thirty or sixty
Westerners around. But usually he let us sit with him, listening
to him storytelling, abusing, discussing current events or people's
situations, and often sharing with him those profound moments
of his awesome silence.

There were ways to get both to serve him and to spend
more time closer to him. My favorite seva was puri-bag duty.
At Kainchi there was a continuous puri and potato bandhara.
Everyone who entered the ashram was given a bag with four
puris and some potatoes to carry away with them. This required
a separate kitchen devoted to these two items as well as packers
and distributors at the other end. Baba was very particular that
the puris were well cooked and the potatoes properly spiced.
The packing took place in a room just to the side of his veranda
takhat. I found hanging out in and near that room allowed me to
serve Baba and also avoid those regular small *jaos* of the whole
crowd when he needed space from the foreigners. I'd remain
out of sight packing puris and would be there when he called for
prasad for the next visitors. Chai was also served to most visitors,
and by this time the western kitchen in Kainchi had assumed
responsibility for all ashram chai. Assistance was often required
for this work also, and it helped to keep me near the king
whenever I was permitted to serve chai.

Ravi Das (Michael Jeffery) was a young attorney at Boston Legal Assistance Project when he heard about Maharajji from Ram Dass. He
started studying yoga and then had a serious car accident—six weeks in
the hospital and more learning to walk again. He went to his parents'
in LA to recuperate and met the boy guru of the Divine Light Mission,
who had just come to the United States. He became involved with that
scene, helping to organize the first jumbo jet that was ever chartered

to take three hundred Westerners to India in 1971. That's how he flew to India. During a short break in his duties, he saw Ram Dass in Delhi. Much later he was able to make it to Allahabad, where he had darshan with Maharajji at Dada's. He was home.

RAVI DAS: When we went up to Kainchi, Dwarkanath was running the western kitchen. I was helping him and, when he stopped suddenly, I took it over. The diet changed to a much simpler menu. We were having cracked whole wheat for breakfast. I would need to roast it and then add milk and sugar. There were days when Maharajji would call me at the exact worst moment—just as I was starting to roast the grains. I'd have to take the grains off the wood fire, go down, and then resume when I got back. I knew he was keeping track of everything.

It came to pass that Maharajji closed the western kitchen. He said people weren't helping enough. He shut it down and had me issue supplies so people could cook for themselves. There were also the puris and all that prasad that the ashram handed out to people.

One time there was a landslide near the ashram, and for three days all these truckers and motorists were held up. Maharajji was telling the Westerners how Christ said to serve the poor and the sick. "It's all in Christ's name." He reopened the western kitchen and told me to cook a special menu for two of the guys: *dal, sabji, aloo*—lentils, veggies, potatoes—that's it. I found out later on that one of the guys had a medical condition, and the doctor told him he had to eat potatoes every day.

SHIVAYA: One day I was helping Ravi Das wash the pots for the four o'clock chai. I had to convince him that I really wanted to do it. Ravi Das was a worker. He didn't ask for help from anybody. One day the pots were all black, and it took a long time to make them shine like new. We couldn't have a spot on them. I was there really late. I was coming down the path to leave the ashram, and there was Maharajji walking up the path. I was terrified; I don't know why. I thought, "I am just not clean enough."

He wasn't looking happy. He had an intense look on his face, and I'm going, "Oh, this doesn't look good at all." I stepped off the path to get out of his way; he stopped right in front of me. This was sort of funny because I had no idea of his size up until then. He looked like this little man. He stood there looking at me, just staring. Then he took a really deep breath and *JAO!* came out with a roar! If anyone had seen it, they would have said, "Boy, was he pissed at this guy. You should have heard the way he roared." But all I felt was this wave of love pouring around me and wrapping me in his blanket.

The appearance was so different from the reality.

SARASWATI: Rather than hang out at night with the other Westerners, I felt a need for solitude, so I chose to sleep out in the jungle up above Kainchi. I found a place under an overhanging rock down by the creek. At darshan, Maharajji questioned me, "Where are you sleeping?"

"Maharajji, I am sleeping outside under a rock."

"Lions will eat you. Tigers will attack you. Snakes will bite you."

"Oh, you are teasing me," I said, and I whacked him playfully on his knee. I was kidding around and having fun.

He laughed at me some more. Then he said, "Dada, get her a room right now." From then on I always lived in the ashram. At night maybe two or three of us would go down and sing to him outside his room. Sometimes he would open those little doors that cover the windows with tears streaming down his face. All was night-blooming jasmine. It was a heaven realm.

One time in Kainchi during Maharajji's darshan, I got up and went over to the Hanuman murti, closed my eyes and sang. I was doing scat, just free-form singing in joy. I was letting the music flow through me. I got tapped on the shoulder by Gita and turned around, and directly behind me was Maharajji. He'd been standing there listening for a long time. Then, like I am doing now at the memory, I burst into tears. Just a beautiful moment.

Each of us after darshan would go our own way and do whatever we did. I think some people got together in groups. I kept to myself. We didn't hash it out; it was totally an internal personal kind of thing. And we didn't all necessarily know each other.

MIRA: In Kainchi, I was really glad for Gita; it was great that she got to have a room in the ashram, which meant more accessibility to Maharajji. Once in a while I would somehow be the one to grab his arm to walk with him down the steps to his office or be close enough to rub his feet, which felt like an inner journey. Then sometime in the middle of the summer, my ego got caught in wanting more of his attention, especially compared to how much attention those close to me, Balaram and Gita, were getting.

"Okay," I thought, "maybe I should go home." I found a little thatched kutir down the road, a hayshed, where nobody ever stayed. I was determined to meditate to get a handle on my unbalanced mind, even though I'd never been a focused meditator. That night, my mind let go, and I found the place of stillness. I sat in the quiet, undisturbed, throughout the night.

The next morning I went up to the white house, took my

shower, and went to darshan. I sat down in the back like I always did. I didn't even see the apple that came at me as soon as he came out. Not one apple, like seven apples. I couldn't catch them all. Then he said, "Mira meditates really well. She meditates." He said it over and over again. So he does know everything. I had my message directly from him, and there was no leaving after that, and no more yearning for that kind of attention. I knew he was in the deepest part of me.

One day I went over to the Hanuman murti, sat down with my eyes closed, and started singing the Hanuman Chalisa. I was wrapped up in it when I felt all of this energy coming in my direction. Maharajji brushed right up against my knee, like the wind coming up like a force. *Swoosh!* I opened my eyes and

Maharajji and a group on the bridge. Left to right: Sita, Saraswati, Janaki, Maharajji, Vishnu Digambar (holding the umbrella), Durga (behind Vishnu), Dada, Mira (behind Dada), Krishna Priya (behind Mira), and Ramgiri (behind young girl).

thought, "Oh my God. I can't be sitting when he's standing right next to me." His energy lifted my body right up to a standing position.

That was the day he walked over to the bridge, and we all followed him walking around the ashram. He went back to sit on the takhat.

I sat back down and started singing again, and when I opened my eyes the next time, everybody was gone. Maharajji was sitting on the takhat by himself. I never had been in the ashram with him by myself, not when the entire ashram was quiet and nobody was there. I gingerly went up to him. He seemed to be in samadhi or just a very quiet state. I quietly pranaamed, put my head down in his lap. He put his hand on my head, patted me, and said in such an incredibly soft, sweet way, "*Mere beti*. My daughter." He's my true father. He's my true everything. That was my last darshan.

The Big Jao

It wasn't easy for Maharajji to tell his Western devotees to leave. As he said, attachment happened both ways. But as his time to pass on approached—unknown, of course, to us—Maharajji started sending away those who would have had the most trouble being there when he left his body. He tried for a long time to get Balaram to leave, but Balaram was sticking like glue. At one point, Maharajji gave him very precise instructions to go back to America. He got on an airplane, flew to New York, didn't leave the airport, and took the next flight back. Eventually, Maharajji got him to leave. A little earlier on, Krishna Priya had been another tough case.

KRISHNA PRIYA: We're in Kainchi, and Maharajji's in his office. I was standing there demurely in my white sari. Somebody comes and says, "Maharajji wants you to move. You are in his line of vision." In other words, Maharajji doesn't even want to see me from his office. Well, that quickly escalates to Maharajji's not letting me sit with him when he gives darshan. He tells me consistently that I have to go sit in front of the Durga mandir. For weeks I sang in front of Durga for hours. I became aware of the little side window to his office, and sometimes it would be half open. I started directing my singing toward there, and all of a sudden it would slam shut.

A few years ago, when I saw Siddhi Ma, she said, "You know Maharajji would sit there and listen to you singing. He'd say, how sweetly she sings. *Mere pagli beti.*" My crazy daughter. That was his nickname for me: *pagli,* crazy. Here I was a young girl from a good Jewish family. Two PhD parents. No history of madness.

Here's how *pagli* started. We were in Vrindavan, and Maharajji had this havan going. We were sitting around his takhat, and he sent us over to the havan to get involved in the puja. Jews don't throw rice in the fire saying it is our impurities. We do Hanukkah and Passover. But he sent everyone there, and everyone went obediently. I was not interested, so I stuck around. He said, "Krishna Priya, you go." I didn't want to defy his orders, so I trotted over there and trotted right back. He told me to go again. This time I figured, "Okay, that didn't work," so I trot to the halfway mark, and I'm standing there so I can see Maharajji. I'm not within distance of his telling me to go back to the havan, and I'm not involved with that *mishegas* [craziness] over there. I hear him say to these Indians, motioning to me, *pagli.*

At Kainchi, it got to where he would not let me be anywhere

around. He would walk out of his office and turn to wherever I was standing and say, "*Jao!*" I tried hiding behind a pillar. He turned to where the pillar was and said, "*Jao.*" Talk about negative attention. This escalated to the point where I was having lunch one day, and Maharajji sent for Balaram and Ravi Khanna and said, "Tell Krishna Priya she has to leave."

They came to me like two henchmen, arms folded, and said, "We are to escort you out of the ashram, and if you give us any trouble, we are to carry you out." I was absolutely mortified.

Mustering all the dignity I could, I said, "I can walk out on my own two feet, thank you very much." After that, every time I came to the ashram, just before I got to the bridge, Trilok would stand there and hold his spear to my chest. I was a twenty-year-old in a white sari, waiting to see my guru, but he meant business. I would sit by the roadside while Maharajji would be giving darshan and sing to him from the road. He would literally get up and move the whole retinue to the back, where he figured I couldn't see him. Finally I gave up.

One day little Scottish Annie came to my hut, weeping. "I got to the ashram," she said, "but they thought I was you, and they wouldn't let me in." I started laughing. "One day you're me, and look at the mess you're in."

June '73, and I hadn't been allowed into the ashram for weeks. Annie comes and says, "Maharajji has sent word that you must leave the country. If you don't leave, you are going to jail." Unlike everybody else who gets help getting a visa, I'm going to jail.

I was allowed to come for darshan for two days. The first day I was sitting by the end of his takhat; he turned to me and said, "Sing. You know the one, *Guru Bina Kaun Kare.*" I'd never sung that at the ashram, but I sang it to him all the time at my kutir. A

sadhu had taught me the song, which is all about the relationship
to the guru. Who without the guru can cross the ocean of
creation? The guru is the one who shows you the way moment
by moment; he is full of compassion and takes away your bad
karma; he's the one that can bring you to the height of heights.
He asked me to sing that song, acknowledging to me once again
that he knew everything.

Later on in the day I'm called to his window, and I ask him,
"Can I do any seva for you while I'm gone?"

"No." Then he said, "I won't see you again."

I said, "I'm going to get a new passport and a visa, and then
I'll come back."

"How? You never have any money." Famous last words.

"Well, then, I'm not going."

Then he said, "Okay, you'll get a passport, but you won't get
a visa."

I figured as long as I have a passport I can get back (I did get a
passport, but no visa).

I didn't have any money. He asked Saraswati to give me $50
to get back to America from India. I went overland by myself,
twenty years old, hitchhiking. I almost died from a violent
encounter and near rape in the process.

Anyway, the next day I come for darshan; it's raining.
Maharajji has come out, and everybody's singing the Hanuman
Chalisa. I sit down, but he won't even let me do one chalisa.
"Abhi jao. Leave now." Sweetly, but firmly. I know that it's the end
of this round, so I go and do the longest procrastination in the
history of my departure from the ashram. I ring every bell I can
find. I turn around and look at Maharajji as I'm departing. Every
time I turn around, Maharajji is turned away from me talking

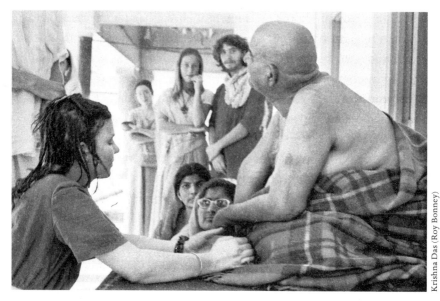

Krishna Priya and Maharajji.

to someone, and people are singing. I can look at his side or his back. Finally there are no more deities to pranaam to or bells to ring, and I leave.

A year or two after Maharajji left his body, Naima told me, "You know that day that you were leaving, it was raining, and you were doing the bells? I was watching that whole departure scene. You kept turning around to see Maharajji, and he had his back turned to you each time. What you don't know is that every time you turned away, he would turn and look at you with so much love; the minute that you turned around to look at him, he would whip away and start talking to somebody else, so you wouldn't see that he was looking at you."

I started weeping when she told me that he was looking at me with so much love. And for him to have Naima watch it, so that she could be a messenger of his love later on. If I had turned around and seen him looking at me, I would have gone mast again. But that he would tell me through her was just so sweet.

Ramgiri (Andreas Braun) was born in Germany six years after World War II and inhaled the heavy collective consciousness there. He became a spiritual seeker, read *Be Here Now,* and was sitting in a health-food restaurant in London when Ram Dass and those of us on our flight back from India walked in. Ten minutes later, Ramgiri had the name of the Evelyn Hotel. Ram Dass said, "These are some friends of mine; you should go see them when you are there." He got to India almost a year later.[1]

RAMGIRI: Kainchi was like stepping into a heaven world. We would sit around the takhat and wait for Maharajji. When he came out, we would sit enthralled in his presence. Then he would walk into the office and see people privately there, while we sat in front of the office and sang to him. When he went in for lunch, we would go to our respective places and cook our lunch. Then we'd do the whole thing all over again in the afternoon.

It was such a timeless space. One time I sat in the room with the kirtan *wallahs* [singers] and listened to them for what I thought was about ten minutes; when I left, four hours had passed! I felt no need to learn Hindi; the communion was so deep that language would have been in the way of steeping myself in his love.

Traditionally, when it was Krishna's birthday, you got to be with the guru at midnight. We were sent to the upper part of the ashram, and it started to rain. Finally at midnight we went up to Maharajji's office window and stood there. I remember Sita and Janaki standing there, both in pink saris, like two goddesses singing to him in the rain.

In the month before he died, Maharajji stopped any semblance of teaching. All he did was hang out, and the love was so brilliantly powerful. I sat in front of him singing *Gopala,* and he completely turned into baby Krishna; then, in an instant, he could be back to being the timeless ancient sage. The love just flowed through him.

Once I was sitting in front of Maharajji when I suddenly saw his huge cosmic form, beyond imagination; it was both completely impersonal and yet the most intimate moment I had ever experienced. When I came "back," he tenderly *jaoed* me. I got up, barely making it down the three steps of the porch, and turned the corner between his rooms and the Devi temple. My knees were shaking so hard from that experience that I had to sit down—and there was a three-legged stool right there, just waiting for me (although I had never before seen any sort of chair in the ashram)! I realized that this absolute vastness of God I had just seen is of equally limitless caring, proving to me that it pays attention to every tiny detail of our lives with unfailing compassion.

He *jaoed* many of us two weeks before he died. We picked up our belongings, and on the way out Maharajji was in his room shouting at us, "Get out of here!" He was fierce, but it did not touch us. We bowed at the window, feeling nothing but absolute love in front of this wrathful deity. That evening Maharajji walked out of the ashram and sat on the far end of the bridge on a little wall. From up the road, I could see this little figure against the vast backdrop of the Himalayan foothills. That was my last darshan.

Vivekananda (Michael Attie) became interested in Eastern spirituality in the 1960s and read Ramakrishna. He had already gone to Japan and stayed in Zen monasteries. Living in Berkeley, he connected with people who were into spirituality and had a mystical theater called the Floating Lotus Magic Opera Company. When he was going to the Ali Akbar College of Music in '73, he heard a talk by Ram Dass, in which he made it seem that finding Maharajji was impossible.

VIVEKANANDA: I met Jai Gopal at the Ali Akbar College of Music. He had come back from India and said I could go meet Maharajji. My cousin Gita also said that, but I was very happily living in a little shack in a backyard in Marin County. Then one evening I had a calling, this deep, deep meditation, where first I thought I was going to die. All of a sudden it hit me like lightning—I'm going to India! I have to go right away. The next day I moved down to LA, worked for my dad for two months to make some money, got my passport and visa, and flew to India. I was there for the last three weeks with Maharajji before he *jaoed* everyone. I count that as one of the miracles of my life.

Maharajji's first words to me were, "Will you give me 500 rupees?"

I said, "Yes, Maharajji, yes."

Other people have told me that is the greatest blessing, because you never have to worry about money for the rest of your life, and I have never had to worry about money. Later I inherited my father's lingerie store, Playmates of Hollywood. I called it a Hanuman temple disguised as a clothing store.

After I was there [in India] maybe a week or so, my friend said to Maharajji, "Maharajji, what should I do?"

He hesitated for a second and said, "Go on pilgrimage. Go to Ramanashram, go to Sivananda Ashram, go to Anandashram. See Anandamayi Ma. Go to Dakshineswar." Then he said, "And bring Gita's cousin with you."

So basically I was *jaoed*. The next day I said, "Maharajji, please. I don't want to go."

He laughed and laughed and said, "Then don't go." He looked at me very seriously and said, "You'll go soon enough."

A week or two after that the big *jao* came, and I went to exactly all the places he had said.

Ira Rose was a construction worker, living in a section of Chicago called Rogers Park. One night he had a vivid dream of being in India, and for the next three months he was on fire with shakti. He moved to Toledo and was working on the cooling tower for a power plant when he started to have palpitations in his heart, not so much physical palpitations as a cry for Maharajji, this saint he had never met. He eventually had to quit and go to India. He knew where to go because Kausalya had come back, and he had gone to school with Kausalya's brother. She said, "You and Rick were close, so I'll tell you where to find Maharajji."

IRA ROSE: I told my mom, "I am going to India."

She said, "You're Jewish; you're not Hindu. What are you going to India for?"

Delhi was 110 degrees, and I couldn't believe what was going on at the bus station. Goats and chickens and people dying and people being born—it was off the charts. In the middle of all that turmoil, I saw what looked like two Westerners wearing white.

I said, "Do you know which bus I take to get to Kainchi or Nainital?"

"Are you going to see Neem Karoli Baba?" That was Dwarkanath and Girija.

On the bus ride up to the temple, I started doing probably the greatest guilt trip any Jew has ever done in his life. "I, who am an inappropriate, oversexed, gross slob, anything but spiritual, why am I being given this chance?" At the height of putting myself down, I walked into the temple and was told he wasn't there.

I had three days to decompress from myself. When Maharajji finally showed up, I was so scared. When I first saw him, that was it. I knew just by looking that he was drunk with God. I knew he was on a million other planes of consciousness, and he was giving us amrit. At the first darshan I was dizzy. I knew I was with someone who knew God personally.

The second darshan I had with him was interesting, because Vivekananda was sitting in front of me, Maharajji asked Vivekananda for all his money, and Vivekananda started stuttering like Jackie Gleason in *The Honeymooners*. I started to laugh.

Maharajji immediately said, "Who's laughing?"

Everyone pointed at me.

Maharajji says, "Kick him out of the temple. Get him out of my sight."

My second day, and I am already wearing the dunce cap.

Dwarkanath, with whom I had become close on the bus ride to Nainital, said in that soft buttery voice, "Maharajji, Ira has come all the way from Chicago to see you, from the United States. Please give him another chance. Don't ask him to leave the temple."

Maharajji says, "All right. Have him go sit by the Hanuman temple."

I was the bad boy. He wouldn't even give me a name. I asked him for a name and he said you're *mistri;* someone who is in the trades, in construction, in India is called a mistri.

One day I was sitting on the hill outside the white house watching him give darshan. It was probably a week before he left his body. I thought, "Maharajji, I get the feeling I am going to be going back to the States soon, and I have two wishes. One, I'd like to get a good car and, two, I'd like to get a good job."

After he passed away, I went with Sita to Benares, where I got sick. I had to fly to the hospital in Nepal before I went back to the States. When I finally got home, my then girlfriend, who was quite wealthy, said, "Now that you are back in town, you probably need a car." She pulled out around $8,000 in cash, gave it to me, and told me to get myself a nice Volvo.

Then my cousin who was in the trades called me up and said, "You need a job? I'll get you a job." So right away I got a brand-new car and a job.

I was thinking, "Duh, what if I had said, 'Maharajji, I'm going back home soon. It would be nice to go to a little higher state of being than I am now'?" But instead I asked for a car and a job.

There had been intimations that Maharajji would not be around forever, but still, no one expected what happened in September 1973.

16

Dropping the Blanket

Fall 1973

Ram nam satya hai, satya bol, satya hai.
The Name of God is truth, sing the truth, the truth is.

—CHANT ACCOMPANYING
A DEAD BODY TO THE BURNING GHATS

W e were in Allahabad at Dada's one evening in January 1972. During darshan, an Indian man with bad gout did puja to Maharajji, then sang *Sri Ram Jai Ram*. He repeated a sloka that translated as: "All suffering is nothing to me, as long as I never forget your name." He asked Maharajji for his grace to utter his name at his last breath. It was very, very powerful, followed by a long silence. I was sitting with my eyes closed and suddenly a thought flashed into my mind about the possibility of Maharajji's death. It shocked me, and I got up in tears. I didn't realize Maharajji had already left the room. When I stumbled out, I saw that Maharajji was sitting in the courtyard. I ran over and fell at his feet. He shooed me away by putting me in the care of a regal Indian woman. The thought of his death left my head completely. He was eternal, wasn't he?

JANAKI: The last day that Maharajji was in Kainchi, many buses had come, and there were throngs of people in the courtyard. It was a fun and festive atmosphere. He had a little show that he did with me and Krishna Tewari, who used to like me to sing *Mere Guru Dev* and then he would go into samadhi. In a film Draupadi shot that day, Krishna Tewari is in samadhi, Maharajji's got his blanket over Tewari's head, and he's hitting him to wake up. We were all in a really great space.

Then Maharajji went inside to take his lunch, so the whole place emptied out. I was in an elevated awareness. I couldn't eat or talk with people, so I stayed down at the Devi mandir. Maharajji was in his room having his lunch, and the window was open. Maharajji sent for Tewari. Maharajji evidently told him that he was supposed to teach the Westerners; I could hear them laughing. I was singing, and when I stopped to get some tea, Maharajji leaned out the window, "Janaki, keep going." So I did. I stayed there singing, singing, and hours passed while he was in the room with Tewari and the mothers.

Then he got up and whacked those doors open hard against the wall. It was a huge sound, because I hadn't been paying attention to what was going on in the room. He was shouting, "You people are useless. You don't know anything. You don't know how to manage this place. It's all going to ruin. There's not enough food there"—he was pointing to where the food storage was. He was verbally abusing everybody.

He came to the Devi temple, so of course I stood up. He pranaamed to the Devi, then went into each of the mandirs. We walked out the gate with him. Maharajji shouted at me, "Janaki, you're going to forget me, but I'm never going to forget you." He was looking at me with the meanest look, like laser beams right into my eyes, and I'm like, "Oh my God. What did I do?"

He was very agitated. There was clearly something going on. His blanket was falling off. Ravi was fussing with the blanket. Maharajji said, "Stop that. It's useless. I'm leaving Central Jail."

RAVI KHANNA: He had been complaining of problems, and the doctor came from Nainital to take a look at him. They all thought he was fine, but he wanted to see a heart specialist in Agra. Maharajji sent for Indar Singh, who had a farm in Haldwani and supplied most of the grains for the puris. He drove down in his car.

Out of the blue Maharajji said, "Ravi, come. We're going." I knew not to ask where. We went to the train station. There were rainbows on the way down, and he commented on that. He sent Indar to get two first-class tickets to Agra. I assumed it was for Indar and him, but then he sent Indar off. It was unusual. Indar had been with him forever, and I was this fairly new kid. I wasn't even twenty.

We were in one of those two-person first-class booths on the train, those tiny little rooms. He was down on the bottom part, and there was no way I was going to get up on the top and be above him, so I spent the night on the floor. He didn't sleep all night. He kept talking about how things were deteriorating, how religion was lost in this country, and things were not pure anymore. He seemed very disturbed, not about his health, but more about the state of things. He kept getting rid of his stuff. We had a thermos of Ganges water. He said, "Give it away."

"But Maharajji, this is your water."

"No, no, no, I don't want it. Give it away." I gave it to someone who was walking by in the train station.

We got to Agra. We got out of the train station, and he was bargaining with the rickshaw driver. I thought that would be my job. We got to a devotee's house in Agra. From there he visited the doctor, and when he came back, we thought he was fine. Devotees found out he was there, so there was a steady stream of people all day.

The same evening we were going back to Kainchi. He got on the train, and Dharm Narayan, who I didn't know was Maharajji's son, joined us. That same train goes through Mathura on its way to Kathgodam. When we got on the train, he asked me to sit in another compartment for a while. He wanted to talk with Dharm Narayan, so I got into another first-class compartment.

When I traveled with Maharajji, I used to wear a dhoti and no shoes. It was not respectful to be around him with shoes on. The people in the other compartment wanted to throw me out, because they thought I was going to steal from them, rob them in the night. I insisted on staying there. I could have gone and sat somewhere else, but I felt, hey, I didn't get to travel first-class that often. I had a ticket; I was entitled to be there. As the train left, they pulled the chain to stop the train. The conductor came, and they arrested me and took me off the train into a police car.

I said, "I have a ticket, and I'm with Neem Karoli Baba." Somebody came by who knew of Maharajji, and I told him to go check with Maharajji in the compartment. They took me back to him, and he was furious. "I am going to call the chief of police, I'm going to call . . . How dare you treat my son like this?"

When I was back in the compartment with him, he seemed uncomfortable. He decided to get off the train in Mathura instead of continuing to Nainital. We came out of the station. There are stairs before you get to the rickshaws. At that point he was sweating, and he seemed cold, which I guess is a sign of a heart attack or a stroke. Dharm Narayan and I went looking for a taxi. It was early in the morning, but we finally found a taxi. By that point it seemed like he was getting pretty sick.

We ended up in the Ramakrishna Mission Hospital in Vrindavan. There was no doctor on duty, so they had to go look for a doctor. They put oxygen on him, and he kept pulling it out. He chanted, *"Jaya Jagadish Hare* [Hail to the Lord of the Universe]" and passed away before the doctor got there. They pronounced him dead. They insisted that he had died before he got there, so they wouldn't have to take responsibility for his dying in their place. Then it was up to Dharm Narayan and me to get him to the ashram. It was pretty close by, so we put his body in the back of a taxi.

I was in shock, completely in shock. Dharm Narayan was the same. I think both of us were functioning because certain things had to happen. We got him to the ashram, and my job was to call people. I had to go to the post office, wake up the postmaster, and say I had urgent calls to make. Then I made like twenty phone calls. I called Kainchi, I called Dada's house, I called the Barmans and Soni, and I called the U.S. I went back to the ashram, and I spent the next day or two in a room crying.

Everyone came, and there were huge arguments about what to do. The people from Nainital wanted to take the body back up there, because they felt he was on the way there and that's where he should be cremated. The people in Vrindavan said that he couldn't leave there. People wanted to burn him at the river. People wanted to burn him in the ashram. It was chaos. I had nothing to do with that. I had no interest. It was totally him and him alone that I cared about . . . and he was gone.

Many devotees wondered why Maharajji went on his final journey with Ravi, a young Indian "hippie," instead of in the company of one of his longtime Indian devotees. But what they didn't know, and Ravi didn't find out till after Maharajji's death, was how far back their connection went (in this life).

RAVI KHANNA: After Maharajji passed away, it was in the papers all over India, and my name was mentioned because I was the one with him. My family hadn't known where I was, because I hadn't kept in touch with them. They came to get me in Vrindavan, so I went home for a little while.

My father grew up in Lucknow, and I was born there. My mother told me that my father was good friends with the Malhotras in Lucknow, who built the Lucknow temple. Malhotra was the main family that Maharajji used to stay with there. My family wasn't particularly into Maharajji. My father would go to see him at the Malhotras' only when he needed some help.

Apparently Maharajji showed up at our house one day, for the first and only time, and said, "Feed me." People came to visit him, and then he left. At that time my mother was pregnant with me. In a sense, he had gone to my parents' home and "reserved" me: "This one is mine." My parents had no connection with Maharajji after that one visit.

The Westerners who were living in the ashram at Kainchi, in the valley, or in Delhi heard the news and rushed to Vrindavan.

DWARKANATH: Kabir and I had been asked by Larry if we would like a job working for WHO, collecting stories of Shitala Devi, the goddess of smallpox. We had to go to Bhowali to send a wire. As soon as Maharajji went into his room at lunchtime that last day, we knew that he was going to be a while and now was our chance to go to Bhowali, do this errand, and come back in time for afternoon darshan. On the bus back to Kainchi, at the first hairpin curve, the bus came to a full stop to let another vehicle negotiate the curve. We're looking out, and see Maharajji in the car driving away. My first and last glimpses of him were through a bus window.

I was in the ashram two days later when Gita came up the path in the back and said, "Dwarkanath, something terrible has happened. Someone came in and told the mothers something, and they left the ashram wailing." Within five minutes, Draupadi, Mira, Gita, Mohini Ma, and I left the ashram. We went out on the road, and Gita waved down an army truck. We got in the back on top of gunny sacks and got into Bhowali, then continued on to Haldwani. There were a bunch of people from Nainital all negotiating taxis to drive them to Vrindavan; we became part of this fleet of five or more taxis in a convoy.

All the taxis stopped for a break along the way. We were sitting in the car when one of the taxi drivers came up and said to our driver, "So I hear that Baba's dead." That was the first I heard.

GITA: The very last darshan we had was amazing. Maharajji was in great spirits. After darshan we had lunch. Then I took a nap and had a dream. I was outside his office, and that hill right behind it was on fire. In the dream I went running to his room, knocked on his window, and said, "Maharajji, quick get up. Get out of here. The fire is coming, and it is going to get you."

He came to the window and said, "It's okay. Don't worry about it."

Then I woke up, and he was gone. He often went away for a couple of days, no big deal. Two days later the mothers are screaming and crying and leaving the ashram. That couldn't mean too many things. We got to Vrindavan just as they were getting ready to light the fire. I said, "No, no, please, let me touch his feet." They made room, I touched his feet, they put the last piece of wood on the pyre, and up it went in flames.

MIRA: Gita and I had a practice of going up to the roof at about four in the morning to meditate. Maharajji had left a day or two before, so the ashram was quiet. It was maybe about six, and we hear a blood-curdling sound, indescribably hysterical screaming from the Mas. In the mornings the Mas usually were really quiet doing their practice. We went down, and Mohini Ma told us, "Go

The Mas. Left to right: Mohini Ma, Siddhi Ma, Hari Priya Joshi, and Jivanti Ma.

Parvati Markus

to Vrindavan." That whole day is a blur to me. The only thing I remember like it was yesterday was Maharajji on the block of ice and then flames. And I remember being concerned about Siddhi Ma and Jaggati Ma; I felt like someone must be holding them back from jumping into that fire.

NAIMA: The morning before it happened, I came to the temple from my little mud hut. I had been doing my meditation, and for the first and only time I heard Maharajji speak to me in English. It was like the voice was coming from my chest, and it said, "Come, Naima, come." It was clear and compelling, unquestionable. I went down to the temple and told Siddhi Ma; she told me he had gone to visit some devotees in Agra and was not even planning to go to the temple in Vrindavan, but I felt like I needed to go because he told me to come. So I was on a night train headed to Vrindavan; I later learned he had been on the night train heading back up toward Nainital. Three hours before I arrived at the temple in Vrindavan, he had gotten off the train and was taken to the hospital. I was sitting on the train next to an open window, and the wind was rushing by; there was a sense of his presence and the feeling that Hanuman was out there in the wind. I got to Vrindavan at six in the morning and went straight to the temple. Ravi Khanna was just coming out on his bike to call Ram Dass to tell him that Maharajji had left his body.

When I entered the temple, there were three big blocks of ice with Maharajji laid out on them. First dead body I had ever seen. First person I had ever known who died. I felt so grateful that he called me to give me that teaching about death, because clearly that wasn't Maharajji. I could *feel* it. It's one thing to say we're not the body, but it's another to have that intense experience of a person you feel so close to. It's a blessing to be with that person's body—a meditation on impermanence unlike any other. I sat there all day fanning flies off his face.

The Mas were in one of the rooms crying hysterically. You know, we have such a dysfunctional relationship with grief in American culture. I was in awe that they gave themselves over so totally to their grief that they would literally lose consciousness; then they would wake up and remember that he had died. I didn't cry. I kept thinking that he told us he wasn't his body, that he's not gone really. I was so grateful to be there. That made a big difference for me. It wasn't at all abstract. It was just like there is his body and he's gone somewhere else, yet he's inseparable from all that is. That direct experience was life-changing for me.

RAMGIRI: Maharajji had become the absolute center of my universe, and to have any thought that he might be mortal was the farthest thing from my mind. How could the center of the universe disappear? On one level we were totally unprepared, but everyone had gotten a sign. Vishnu was in another town, and he had a vision of Maharajji's body in flames, being burned exactly the way he saw it a week later in Vrindavan. Maharajji prepared all of us, but consciously we didn't have a clue. It came as an absolute shock.

RAVI DAS: At the very end there came a time when I was called down, and Maharajji said, "Serve the poor and the sick. Serve the poor and the sick, and you'll be like Christ. Will you do it?"

I stammered out something like, "I'll do it with God's grace."

He kept saying, "Will you do it? Will you do it? Will you do it?"

I finally realized, "Wrong answer." So I said, "Yes."

"Jao."

That has stayed with me ever since.

We had laborers at Kainchi working on one of the temples, so I stayed when Maharajji left Kainchi. When he took his samadhi, a lot of people went down to Vrindavan, but it was not something I felt called to do. The ashram shut down out of respect, but I was cooking for the workers. I was very dry-eyed for three or four days, doing the kitchen. Suddenly, I don't know what set me off, but I started crying for hours. It all came out.

Before he died, Maharajji had said to a devotee from Haridwar, "You really ought to give us ten bags of flour." What he had done over about the six months prior to his samadhi was to set us up. We had all the staples that we needed, between what we got from the farm, the cows, the vegetables, the potatoes, and so on, plus all the stuff that had been laid up. We were good for about a year. At the end of that year, the devotees in India were getting organized, a trust was developed, and money was flowing in to keep the temple running.

DR. LARRY: Girija and I had found the perfect living arrangements in Delhi—a very small apartment and a very large air conditioner. One night at three in the morning there was a pounding on our door. Only one Indian knew where we lived, and that was Mr. Vaish; he would pick us up on weekends to go up to Kainchi. He was standing there crying. He said, "Neem Karoli Baba is no more." I didn't know what he meant.

We got in the car and drove to Vrindavan. When they brought his body from the Ramakrishna Mission Hospital and laid it out on slabs of ice, Girija and I spent a day waving away the flies over our guru's body. Talk about the distance between mystical beauty and the potential of humanity and then the death of someone you love so much. It was the hardest thing.

Then all that struggle between the hill people and the plains people happened over where to burn him—at the banks of the Yamuna or in the ashram. Pagal Baba came and he said, "You foolish people, the reason that ordinary people want to be cremated by the Yamuna is to be made holy by the Yamuna. Whichever place you cremate Maharajji will be made holy by his ashes. Cremate him here, because you will want to come and visit." So he was cremated. Dharm Narayan came and smashed his head with a large stick to liberate the spirit. I didn't realize at the time that that was because Dharm Narayan was his son.

Meenakshi and Saraswati were in Nepal, waiting to get new visas for India.

MEENAKSHI: Toward the end Maharajji sent me to Nepal, because my visa was done. Maharajji said, "I promise you are coming back. You will come to Vrindavan, and I promise I will be there. It's all taken care of." That was the last time I saw him.

I went to Nepal and lived up in the hills in Dhulikhel with no Westerners. Then Saraswati came to Nepal, because her visa was done too. We said, "Okay, let's do a trek." We had to get up in the middle of the night to get the bus to Pokhara, where the trek started.

I had a dream that night. Maharajji was sitting on a chair, not on the takhat. Many of the women who were with Maharajji were around him, massaging his head and shoulders, and the men were standing off to the side. There was a doorway, and Maharajji at one point got up, walked to the door, and said, "I'm going to a place you can't go with me now." And he walked through. That was the night he died, although we didn't know that then.

SARASWATI (from a letter to her parents): At the time he died, one o'clock in the morning, Tuesday, September 11, a beautiful bird awakened me just outside my window in Nepal with a clear, fresh flutelike call. Meenakshi and I got up and sang the forty verses in praise of Hanuman, Maharajji's favorite song. We had planned to leave that morning on the Jomsom trek, but it was raining, so we decided to do an all-day puja to Maharajji.

Walking to Pokhara to buy fruit and flowers for the puja, we both felt Maharajji's grace with us all the way; he seemed so close.

Once in Pokhara, at about the time that the devotees in Vrindavan were cremating his body, I happened to take out a photo of Vrindavan Hanuman, and in shock I said, "Meenakshi, look! He's crying!" Somehow the face in the photo had changed to grief, and you could see that he was weeping. We didn't know what to think.

Once we had all our goods gathered up, I went to pay, but the money was gone. The equivalent of $60, all gone! I had put all our money in my coin purse, as our room didn't lock. We looked at each other and said, "Maharajji wants us to go back to Kathmandu." I had a $20 traveler's check that Maharajji had told me to keep, which I had hidden in the room, and with that we traveled back to Kathmandu. We picked up our mail on Friday and read the telegram. By his grace we found the strength to contact all our fellow devotees in Kathmandu for an evening puja and feast, as Maharajji always insists: "Love them and feed them." Tears and song and support.

The following morning, Meenakshi and I boarded a plane back to India and, as Maharajji promised me, I was given a good three-month visa at the airport. For his own reasons, he sent me away during his last month in this body, but before, for a full month, he gave me *daily* private darshans and spoke to me a great deal about

my spiritual path. He warned me silently of his going. And now?
Nothing's *really* changed; the love that he is is still so, so present.

Daniel Garin first heard of Maharajji through Timothy Leary, who
had been staying in Avila, Switzerland. Daniel's friends went to visit
Leary. When Tim heard that Daniel was spending the time alone meditating, he sent him the book *Be Here Now*. Daniel came to Maharajji
as a barefoot and penniless wanderer; he was taken in and cared for.
He eventually went back to Switzerland and had just returned to India.
When he arrived in Vrindavan, Maharajji's body was out on parade on
top of a station wagon.

DANIEL: I arrived back in Delhi in September from Switzerland.
I had money now, so I went by train to Mathura, then boarded
the bus to Vrindavan. Some guy comes up to me and says,
"Maharajji's dead." What the heck is he saying?

At the bus stop in Vrindavan, a station wagon is driving down
the street at walking speed with a crowd of people walking
behind and around the car. Maharajji's body is on top covered
with flowers. [This "parade" all around Vrindavan, complete
with brass band, was done to give people a last darshan.] I follow
the car. After about a hundred yards of walking behind the car, I
suddenly feel like I am going to pass out, lost in despair. A little
Hindu kid right in front of me, a ten-year-old, turns around
and makes some hand motions, mudras, to me, and everything
suddenly changes.

I thought, "I'm sorry, Maharajji. I'm sorry to be so attached to
the body, to the form. I should have more faith in you." I look up,
and the kid has disappeared, but now I feel fine.

In the ashram, I couldn't relate to anyone, because I was
feeling so happy. I was not sad at all. I saw Dwarkanath crying

and Siddhi Ma crying. The fire was going. It was already sunset. There were two Hindu sadhus, old-time Shaivites, dancing around the fire and singing. Whew, at least I was not alone in how I felt. Then after the fire had finished burning, I bumped into Larry Brilliant. I said, "I just want to go to Delhi. There's nothing here for me." He talked to a doctor from Delhi who gave me a ride. *Poof.* The next day I took the plane back to Switzerland.

While Maharajji was "leaving Central Jail," Shivaya was still in it.

SHIVAYA: When Maharajji left his body, I was in Delhi Central Jail. Some years before I had helped some Westerners do a deal with hash. I didn't want any pay, but they couldn't leave me with nothing—they were going to be making a fortune—so they gave me a hard suitcase made out of 8 kilos of hash. I had left it with someone in Delhi while I was off being with Maharajji. After I had given away all of my money, I thought maybe it's time for me to sell this suitcase and go back to the States. The person I was dealing with turned me in to the police, so I wound up doing a couple of months in Central Jail.

We had great accommodations, a nice cell, a private cook for the Westerners. We had excellent food and service, and I had quite the outstanding time there. I was supposed to work in a factory making chairs, but I never really bothered with that. Beautiful gardens to sit in for meditation, and all of the hash we wanted. The guards provided everything we needed.

They said I was the only prisoner who ever requested an extension, but they wouldn't give it to me. I got out of prison around September 20. I had no money, nothing. There was a woman, Daniella, who was the only person I knew with an apartment in Delhi. I got there, and she had to pay the taxi. She told me that Maharajji had died. I responded with, "Oh yeah. I'm on my way to see him now."

She said, "You didn't hear what I said. Maharajji is gone. He's not in his body."

That didn't compute at all. I went into this interesting sort of grief and relief experience. I felt this grieving, which got to be even more and more later, but at that moment I also felt this relief that he was with me all of the time now and that I didn't have to go anywhere. I didn't have to go to Kainchi, but I had no idea what to do. She also told me that he said he was "leaving Central Jail at last."

I went to Morolli outside Delhi. I was sleeping out at the ruins, sitting at a fire, and I said, "What to do? Maharajji is gone." I took all of my clothes, my passport, and everything I had and threw it all into the fire. I kept a blanket, a lungi, and a *lota* [small pot for water] and burned everything else; then I started doing the sadhu thing. I figured I'd do this for the rest of my life and would never be back in America.

For those of us who were back in the West, the news spread rapidly. Many of those on the East Coast quickly gathered together at Ram Dass's father's house in New Hampshire, where we could both commiserate in our shock and sorrow and celebrate our Baba through storytelling and singing. Then before we knew it, twenty-seven of us were on a flight to India. In rather miraculous fashion, Raghu and I suddenly discovered a bank account we hadn't known existed that had exactly the amount of money we needed for the plane fare and three-week trip to India. There was no way I was going to believe he was gone until I saw that empty takhat.

And on the West Coast:

LSR Foundation Archive

Seated, left to right: Mohan, Parvati, Radha, Jagganath Das, Rameshwar Das, Lakshmi, Krishna Priya, "Little" Laxmi. Standing, left to right: Raghu, Mirabai (holding Owen), Krishna, Rukmini (Caroline), Ram Dass, Balaram Das, Anasuya (holding Govinddas), Krishna Das, Annapurna (holding Gita), Peter Brawley, Sunanda (holding Tara), and Danny Vishwanath.

JAI: When I got back to California, I lived for a while in Swami Muktananda's ashram in the Oakland hills. They basically hired me to sing kirtan for an hour a day in exchange for room and board. I thought that was cool! I was twenty-one by then, and a day didn't pass when I didn't think about going back to see Maharajji, but I felt I had all the time in the world. Then he died, and my world fell apart. I felt so awful about not having gone back to see him. We did an all-night kirtan, and cried and cried. I didn't go to India for the cremation, as I didn't have any money.

All these years later I see that in a sense it wasn't any different with him gone. I was in America worshipping him every day, in whatever way I could. Still am. His body died, but then all of these people started seeing him and being touched by him so deeply. And my life still revolves around him, like a planet around the sun.

ANJANI: When Maharajji left his body, I flew back to India with Ram Dass and others of the satsang. I walked into the ashram in Vrindavan, and there was still smoke coming from the funeral pyre. The feeling and vibration was so intense, you could hardly stay in your body. We were all in grief and disbelief, but being part of the ceremonies in the ashram made the unbelievable real. I had many dreams of Maharajji during that time; in some he was in a young body.

When we were leaving, there was a young man who had been there through the whole thing. He had a bottle of ashes and said, "I don't know what to do with these." He asked me to take them and put them in the river. I thought, "We'll go to Allahabad and

In India for Maharajji's mahasamadhi.

Rameshwar Das

put them in the Sangam." Uddhav and Revati and I took the train to Allahabad, and on the train the plastic bottle that the ashes were in cracked. I was afraid we were going to lose all of the ashes in the aisle of the train, so we emptied the ashes into a water bottle we had.

So here's the original bottle with all of this ash still left in it. I said, "Well, we can't throw it away. What are we going to do?" I put more water in it and drank it.

When we got to Allahabad, Dada took us out on the river in a boat, and we put Maharajji's ashes into the Ganges. It was a beautiful day. So peaceful.

KRISHNA DAS: After Maharajji died, I used to go around and ask babas, "How can I get close to my guru?"

They said, "What are you talking about? Your guru is looking out of your eyes right now. That's where Maharajji is."

17

And in the End

And in the end, the love you take
Is equal to the love you make.

—THE BEATLES, "THE END"

For Maharajji's Western devotees, the years following his death
were some of the hardest in their lives. Quite a few had no desire to
leave India and stayed for years; some spent time gathering stories
from Maharajji's devotees that were eventually compiled into the book
Miracle of Love,[1] while others became sadhus. Of those who returned
to the West, many were recently married and having children. Some
returned to school to learn a way in which they could serve the greater
good, while others were in such despair they turned for a while to drugs
to dull the pain. What was never lost was our connection to each other
and the way in which our lives were wrapped in a plaid blanket.

SHIVAYA: After Maharajji left his body, I did a couple of years of the barefoot sadhu thing. In '74 I was alone up a mountain in a cave, and a tiger came at night and was stalking me. Maharajji appeared next to me. I was in a state of terror, my body trembling and my mind racing God knows where, and he's laughing. He says to sing the Hanuman Chalisa. I knew that I was going to die, because I was looking right into the eyes of the tiger. I started singing really loud and, by the time I finished the first chalisa, all the spasming stopped in my body—that wrenching fear was gone.

I kept doing chalisas, and after some time the tiger started stomping through the brush. I figured, "Well, now it is coming," but it had just moved around me. Now it was in front of me. I kept singing. Twenty minutes or so later the tiger comes over on the side, and I am watching him and singing. I sang until I was totally exhausted. I couldn't even sit up. I figured it didn't matter if you got eaten when you were lying down or sitting up, so I lay down and decided that was it. I had said good-bye to everyone I had ever known. They all flashed in front of me, and I had all these visions. I lay down to die . . . and then I unexpectedly woke up the next day.

I have sung the chalisa every morning of my life since that day.

BALARAM DAS: Pangs of sorrow hit me like lightning bolts every so often, even though they're less frequent now. After all, he's everywhere. Krishna Das asked him, "When we dream about you, are you with us?"

He said, "I'm always with you."

But for a year after he left his body, I would burst out into tears while I was driving along. I'd get hit by this sense of loss that was almost paralyzing. For years I would hardly talk about Maharajji, because the loss was so painful. But everyone's saying we're not getting any younger. If there's going to be any record at all of what happened or what I could say about it, I might as well say it while I can.

I do have dreams regularly. In one I was walking uphill in a town in the mountains. I went into a building and down some hallways, and Maharajji was there. "Oh my God, what kind of bogus, horrendous mind cloud was this, when I thought he was gone all of this time? He's been here all along!" It's this wonderful feeling. Then the alarm goes off. Time to go to work. The dreams make me sad, but there's a message there too: what a fool I am to think he isn't here the whole time.

Now I'm content to just let things happen. I'll see him again. I'm getting close to the end of this life. My goals are staying out of trouble, always knowing Maharajji is by my side, and trying to say the name of God. In this Kali Yuga (the darkest age), as Maharajji would tell us, taking the name of God is the only thing to do.

BRUCE: I think Maharajji keeps me in place. If I get too dark, too nasty, or too cynical, I remember Maharajji, and I go, "Ahh, I'm going a little too far." I've been through two divorces and an amazing amount of pain where I thought it was the end of my life, where I felt Maharajji just wasn't there. Ten years ago I should have been dead, the amount of stuff I was ingesting. Now, my last couple of trips to India, I didn't ask for anything from Maharajji. All I asked is to go to his room by myself for five minutes, close my eyes, feel what I feel, and get on with going to the market, fixing up my room, and enjoying the people. I don't ask for anything anymore. He has given me enough.

DANNY: We run into Maharajji stories everywhere. Lama Norla has a retreat center just outside Poughkeepsie, New York. He was Kalu Rinpoche's retreat master in Tibet. He escaped the Chinese in 1958, found himself in India, had nowhere to go, and decided to continue his retreat somewhere near Haridwar. He found a broken-down kutir and started his retreat. One day this guy comes into his kutir and starts yelling at him. Norla doesn't understand what he's saying. This guy starts breaking his cooking things and then leaves. Lama Norla thinks, "There are crazy people around here. Maybe I should move."

A couple of hours later a kid comes with a *thali* [large plate] of food and indicates that he should come with him. He brings him into an ashram, and there's the crazy guy, who turns out to be Neem Karoli Baba. Maharajji gets him to understand that there are dangerous snakes in the place he was staying. Maharajji gives him a room in the ashram where he can continue his retreat. Lama Norla stayed with him for two years before Kalu heard where he was and sent for him. Norla was so sad to leave Maharajji. Maharajji didn't want to let him go until he heard it was his guru that was calling for him; then he said, "You should go."

LAMA SURYA DAS: In the late '70s, I helped start Lama Norla's monastery and three-year retreat center called Kagyu Thubten Choling in Wappingers Falls, New York. Lama Norla was the only Tibetan lama I ever met who knew Maharajji somewhat well. He likes to imitate Maharajji's voice. He told me that he used to call Maharajji Dudh Baba, because Maharajji used to send him milk [*dudh*] all the time. Maharajji used to call him Tibeti Baba. He was Tibeti Baba, and Maharajji was the Dudh Baba, which is extra funny in light of the great cult following of "the dude." And the dude endures.

JAI: Early one morning my friends and I were in the Buddhist village of Sarnath, meditating on top of a very large stupa, a constructed hill filled with Buddhist relics. I was struggling with this complex meditation practice I had been doing for some time, when suddenly I heard this thunderous explosion inside my head. Then I heard Maharajji's voice going *Ram Ram Ram Ram.* He was surrounding me and saying *Ram,* and with each repetition of *Ram* the so-called spiritual techniques I had been practicing were washed out of me. I felt like I was getting cleansed. Without doubt that was my mantra initiation. Maharajji gave me the Name.

I've read in Tulsi Das about the value of "disinterestedly" repeating God's name. For years I thought, "What does that mean? Why 'disinterestedly'?" When we were in India recently, I started to get a whole new glimpse of what that meant when I said to Siddhi Ma, "I sing all of the time, and people say I'm great, blah, blah, blah, but a lot of the time all I feel is effort, work, stress . . ."

Smiling, she said, "Jai Gopal, what does it matter what you're feeling? You're doing your service. You are serving Maharajji and touching people's hearts. You Americans think that service is eating a laddoo and blissing out under a tree. For us, service is often filled with a lot of worry and effort."

I started to see that the path of bhakti wasn't for ourselves, our own experience, our own bliss. Rather, it's for service, it's for guru, God, the devotees, the visitors, the universe of suffering people. I saw how the older Indian devotees around the temple served, and it had a profound impact on me. I pray to be blessed with that kind of devotion.

KRISHNA DAS: We got transmission from Ram Dass of what Maharajji felt like. I am doing it exactly the way Ram Dass did it, totally unconsciously, with no sense of doing anything at all. What comes through is what Maharajji wants to come through.

Every time I sing, people write to me and tell me how much this or that meant to them. They are feeling love, feeling Maharajji, feeling truth, feeling happiness, feeling whole, feeling faith. They say it helped them get through chemo, helped them get through this operation or the loss of a daughter, or son, or husband. No end of suffering and no end of his grace. Do I personally have any sense that I have done anything to make that happen? No. How could I? I am just singing the best I can to Maharajji. What happens is his doing.

I was in Bucharest, Budapest, Prague, Krakow, and Moscow. There were more people at the kirtan in Moscow than there were in New York. People are hungry over there. About fifteen hundred showed up in Moscow, and they actually knew the kirtans. Everybody's got YouTube, everybody's got downloads, everyone steals the music online, which is fine—let it get out there. Every place is exactly the same in terms of the feeling, what people want, what they are hungry for, what they are drinking in. The language is different, the clothes are different, the hairdos are different. The AC, the electricity might be different. Everything else is exactly the same. We went to the Balkans, Serbia, Croatia, Bosnia-Herzegovina. I guess this is what it is like for wandering sadhus. You never get really attached to one place.

I feel that Maharajji is touching the people it is his job and his grace to touch and planting seeds, because that is what the Name is. It is a piece of Maharajji, a seed of his love. Everybody who hears it is going to get a benefit in some way at some time or another. I am just planting seeds in myself, and anyone else who wants to listen is fine.

I must say how beautiful it is to see and to feel Maharajji's blanket envelop these people and me in these halls all around the world, to feel his presence so strongly. And to know that these people, whether they are aware of it or not, have been enveloped by him, taken under his blanket.

MEENAKSHI: Because my tradition was Christianity, what Maharajji was for me was like meeting Jesus, a much more real feeling of what it would have been like to be with Jesus. The fact that he would know something, the omnipotent part of Maharajji, was not important to me. What I loved about Maharajji was that you didn't have to do anything. There was no doctrine. I found it a more difficult path, but it suited who I am as a personality, not wanting to be taught anything. It wouldn't have mattered to me what tradition he had been born into. It didn't mean that that's what I needed to embrace.

Maharajji was a really beautiful mirror to show me myself, and the only thing that's really happening is my own, very individual path of getting there. Where he comes into that is in my connection with the satsang. It's still the people I'm closest to, with whom I still have the closest connection.

What I have come to at this point of my life with him is an honoring of the presence of that stillness and beauty that he represented. He was a beautiful example of where everyone can go. He was fraught with all of his humanness, and his humanness is the part that I loved the most. That is the beauty of who he was to me. Not his magic. Not my devotion to him. I don't even go to that place of unconditional love, because I don't think I know what that means. Enlightenment, I don't know what that means, and it really doesn't matter to me. For me he represented a stillness, an emptiness, yet everything there too. I honor that experience of getting to sit with him by myself, just quiet.

DR. LARRY: On one of our trips to Kainchi while working for the smallpox program, we were sitting by the takhat way in the back of the ashram. We were talking about different destinies, different dharmas, and he said, "Your own destiny, however humble, is greater than another's, however exalted"—a line from the *Bhagavad Gita*. We have early bloomers and late bloomers. We have people who like to slog it out in the world and people who like to sit in the quiet in a cave. Maharajji gave us all the sadhana, the dharma, the name, the plan, the nudge that was the best for us. You can't compare or judge or say my dharma is better than your dharma.

As we were sitting there with him, a line of Westerners came onto the road across the bridge, maybe fifteen Westerners who were all looking in on this scene, because Maharajji wouldn't let them into the ashram. Maharajji looked at them as he was talking about how everybody's destiny is different; his eyes went in the back of his head the way he did, and he looked at that row of Westerners like he was reading their akashic records and their futures. He knew that he was giving us what we needed, not necessarily what we wanted. He said, "So many different kinds of flowers. They bloom at the same time, but their fates are very different."

Suil Anna (or Scottish Annie) had a vision of Krishna in Scotland when she was sixteen, and at eighteen she went to India overland from Europe, first to Mathura, then to Vrindavan. When she got to the ashram, she was trying to stay in the back, and the next thing she knew she was sitting right in front. Maharajji looked at her and said, "Where are you from?" She felt it was a soul koan, not a question about the place where she was born in Scotland.

SUIL: When we went to Kainchi on the bus, we passed this house, and I went, "Oh, I want to stay there." It turned out the owners of that house, both doctors in Nainital, were from Scotland, from my same town. That was the house I wound up staying in. The flower garden there was almost like a nursery. You could go down the back road through all of those flowers, through the rivers, through the mountains, and end up at the rear of the ashram.

One morning I collected a bunch of flowers and came in through the back of the ashram. It turned out everyone had been *jaoed* except Larry and Girija. Maharajji called me over, and I gave him the flowers. What I heard him say to me, and what stayed in my mind for a long time, was, "Every flower blooms in its own time." I didn't have a very strong identity, and I wasn't really sure who I was in all of this. It was the first time I was living alone, in the mountains with the monkeys. So when he said that statement about all flowers blooming in their own time, I felt relief knowing that I didn't have to be concerned if I was okay, if I was going to be a saint or not.

Many years later at a bandhara I met Larry again. We were remembering that story with the flowers, and what Larry remembered was a completely different story. He had heard Maharajji say that all the flowers bloom at the same time. Really? I was sure he said in their own time. We talked about which version we liked better. I was glad that I heard my version, because that was very helpful in my whole journey. Even today, that idea that the timing of everything is really perfect, that there is a perfection in everything, and as the flowers bloom so shall we . . . There's been an ease that came in that story, and that was something I would never forget, in a very simple statement that other people heard differently, of course. We love that.

SITA: Even though I knew nothing about gurus or Hindu tradition, for me Maharajji represented the benchmark of the potential of human existence. Even though my mind could not conceptualize what that meant, there was no question that Maharajji was a perfected being and a true saint. I came to understand later, because I stayed in India for eight years and studied Hindu tradition, that there are three types of gurus: the *satguru*, the *diksha guru,* and the *upa guru.* The satguru is what Maharajji did for us. The diksha guru is the one who gives you a mantra and initiates you into a lineage. And an upa guru is one who teaches you practices. Because Maharajji is my satguru, every aspect of my life falls under his jurisdiction. He has made it clear that he continues to take care of the details of my life; he keeps me on track. My intention is to be reunited with Maharajji lifetime after lifetime, whatever it takes. What else could we ever want?

MIRABAI: Over the years it was always hard to tell people what happened, what we learned, what it was like there. Ram Dass says Maharajji gave us unconditional love, and he did, but that doesn't describe well enough what really happened. Recently there has been neuroscience research on mirror neurons in the field of social intelligence. It shows that when you are with another person, you are not only influencing each other by what you are talking about, but actually changing the cellular structure of each other, particularly when you're with someone who is very powerful. It's not just a psychological influence; it actually changes the brain. I used to say that I felt that my cells were being rearranged just by being with Maharajji. He didn't need to do anything to change me utterly. We were there, he was there. We just sat there, he loved us, and at the end of the day we were different from who we were before.

I always loved that line that Larry says in *Fierce Grace* [the documentary Mickey Lemle shot of Ram Dass six months after his stroke]: it wasn't that Maharajji loved us; it was that when we were around him, we loved him and each other so much. And that was true. The experience of the fully open heart—once you have that experience, you may not always dwell in that place, but you know it. That's been my life, knowing that possibility in every moment even when not fully being there. Through the work I've been doing, I see how much people respond to love. Maharajji said to love everyone. Even Monsanto. Even the army. It turns out to be the best teaching. Finding out how to do that, that's what it's all about.

RAMESHWAR DAS: The interesting part is just how the lila, his dance, continues in our lives. My daughter's death at fourteen has been one of the most profound as well as the most painful and difficult things that ever happened to me. Losing a child who is a part of you is so immediate. It also killed some of my attachment to how I think things are or how they were going to be. A child is so much a work in progress. You think, "Oh she'll take care of me in my old age," whatever your expectations are, even expecting you'll wake up the next day and she'll be there.

Mirabai's death has shown me some things about my relationship with Maharajji. Her death ripped me open. I was able to mourn for her in a way that I was not for him. I was with Ram

Dass in Franklin when we heard about Maharajji's death. I took it inside myself, which I did with her death too. But after she died, I realized I had never mourned him fully, that I didn't completely go through that process of separation from his body.

When he died a bunch of us went to India. His ashes were still smoldering, but his presence and the connection were still so strong, it seemed like he hadn't gone anywhere. I put her ashes in the ocean. There were only the waves and the light on the water.

Mirabai's inside me too. When I am quiet enough and my heart is open, I feel her. That love is still present; she became that love. If that is the teaching or the journey, I am grateful. Through her I feel more able to acknowledge Maharajji's love.

I guess I could have closed down, or just wished it hadn't happened, or wondered about what I could have done differently so it wouldn't have happened. But it did. I was working with Ram Dass in Maui when she died. She was home on Long Island and got run over while riding her bike. When we heard she had died at the hospital, I said to Ram Dass, "She didn't get to finish her life." He looked at me and said, "Yes, she did."

Her death pulled me inside more. I feel like I have been living with one foot in life and one foot in death. I guess it's preparation for my own death too.

There continues to be so much love from the people that she knew and are around us in the community and satsang family. We started a nonprofit, the Anna Mirabai Lytton Foundation. We are doing art and yoga and wellness programs in local schools, things she really enjoyed. Light on the water.

RAVI KHANNA: Maharajji started sending me off to Delhi to get cashew nuts. I said, "Maharajji, I can get cashew nuts from Benares."

"No, no, no. You go to Delhi and get cashew nuts from there."

I would go on the night bus, get there in the morning, get the cashews, and come back on the night bus. Then he sent me the next morning to get something else from Delhi, just useless errands. When I came back he would say, *"Kho gaya?* Are you lost?"

"Uh, no, Maharajji. I'm standing right here." I went on four consecutive trips, so it was like eight nights on the bus.

After he passed away, I ended up back in the Kainchi valley. I felt like I had lost my father. I didn't go to the ashram much. Then in a dream I saw him, and he asked me, "Are you lost? I haven't gone anywhere. I'm right here, and it's time for you to get up and get out of here." That's when I went to Delhi, talked to Larry, and started working with him.

Years later I was working at Oxfam as the information coordinator for the famine in Africa. This was before the Internet and e-mail. We had a telex machine, and every morning came these long telexes from country after country reporting how many children had died overnight. I was angry and frustrated. I couldn't stand people laughing or eating. I was at the edge of having a breakdown or quitting my job. I started remembering him saying, "Ravi, are you lost?" His voice would come into my head, *"Kho gaya,* Ravi?" It was a reminder that this was miserable, horrible, but it didn't give me an excuse not to do something about it; I just couldn't get lost in it.

I once saw him asking someone from America, "Why are you meditating?"

"I want to reach God."

"Why do you want to reach God?" he said. "You know, this is it. It's right here. There is no place up there. It's our job to make this a heaven for everybody."

RUKMINI: I see now that I indeed am both guru and disciple, creator of my own reality. When Maharajji said, "Love everyone, serve everyone, and remember God," I now know that what he was saying was that we are all God. When he said that I came to India searching for a guru and now didn't believe there were any saints, he was right. What I didn't know and what he told some of us later is that we are *all* saints. He truly was a reflection of who we all are. His admonition to construct no temples was saying, "Don't get it wrong. Don't worship me." He saw the danger of making him a religion, like was done to Christ. He saw the danger in dictating rules and restrictions through an established temple. He never taught what to do.

I got the message, loud and clear. We are all God, and to love everyone is to remember that. This now is my only prayer: *Let me remember.*

RAM DASS: Maharajji built temples, and I thought, "I'll build a temple in the United States." I wanted it to be the very hub, the center of the satsang. But some of the Westerners wanted bandharas on the West Coast, and those on the East Coast wanted them in the East, and few of the old satsang came to Taos. So I guess that was the end of my being commander in chief. I'm president of the board [of the Taos temple], yes, but I came to Maui and sort of abandoned my position. Now the satsang comes to see me here. It keeps me close to Maharajji.

The satsang really is a family. It's Maharajji's family. In a sense, the satsang has *become* Maharajji since he left his body.

I have a difficult time with the concept that some people were with Maharajji and others were not. People who have met him through their dreams or visions, through books or stories, they have golden hearts. He calls people, and certainly he still calls people now that he is out of his body.

Those of us who were there with him in India, we brought back the possibility of Maharajji. We brought back the possibility of what man can be. We brought back spirit, not in religious institutions, but inside our hearts. We brought back the familiarity of God, Ram, Krishna, Sita, Hanuman. We brought back the possibility of a culture where everybody can identify with their souls, not their roles. In India, I'd see the *chai wallahs* [tea vendors] and the train conductors having a conversation about the *Bhagavad Gita*. In the West roles are so important and souls are so unimportant, that we're thirsty for that kind of interaction. We brought back planes of consciousness the West didn't know existed. The West had science, but we didn't honor our hearts, our spiritual hearts. We brought back serving dying people. We brought back cross-generational living. We brought back an attitude of service. We brought back pure waters from the traditions, like Vipassana and kirtan.

In my eighties now, I'm a '60s icon. I'm a "leader of the New Age." The thing I want to be remembered for is bringing Maharajji to the West. I would also like to be remembered for introducing humor into the spiritual soup. Maharajji said to me, "Be like Gandhi." Gandhi said, "My life is my message." I like that. I like seeing souls as flowers that are opening up. That's a privilege, a privilege that Maharajji gave me.

Bios

The Westerners who had been with Maharajji in India were still quite young when he left his body. We had been privileged to have the darshan of a true siddha, to bask in the love that permeated his presence. But what now? How to live our lives, pay our bills, raise our children? What do you do when the brightest light you have ever known is extinguished from your outer gaze? You look inside to find the truth he has given you: the name you strive to live up to; the understanding that you are worthy to be loved; and the knowledge that the best way to find the Oneness of God, guru, and self is through service to humanity and through doing whatever you do in the most dharmic way possible.

By and large, the Western satsang, through all the ups and downs of our individual lives, has managed to find ways in which to serve, as we try our best to grasp the enormity of what it means to "love everyone, feed everyone, and remember God."

Anasuya (Teresa Weil)

Anasuya was the founder and director of the Tibetan Resettlement Project in New Mexico in the early 1990s. Then she graduated from the Shang Shung Institute School of Tibetan Medicine and the Qinghai University Tibetan Medicine School of Xining as a Doctor of Tibetan Medicine. It is her hope to acquaint Westerners with Tibetan medicine and its many healing modalities and benefits. She says, "For me, the study of

Tibetan medicine is a continuation and extension of my Buddhist practice." http://www.anasuyaweil.com.

Anjani (Joan O'Connell)

Anjani is a retired editor and analyst from the University of California at Santa Cruz. Earlier she worked at Columbia and UC–San Francisco and was able to take many leaves to travel to India (by now, fifteen times!). She spent a lot of time in Allahabad with Dada and Didi as well as at the ashrams in Vrindavan and Kainchi, but traveled around India mostly by herself. "I always felt completely protected, even in some frightening situations. After Maharajji left his body, I went to Amarkantak in Madhya Pradesh, because there was a story that he had been seen there in a young body. Of course, there was no finding him; it's just like the first time, he has to find you."

Badrinath Das, or Badri (Bruce Margolin)

Since 1967, Bruce has been an activist relentless in his efforts to legalize marijuana. As a criminal defense attorney, he continues to effectively represent his clients against all types of criminal charges and has successfully defended thousands of clients in marijuana cases. He was selected as Criminal Defense Super Lawyer and Criminal Defense Attorney of the year in 2014. Bruce was a candidate for governor of the State of California in 2003 and the U.S. Congress in 2012. He has helped establish the credibility of marijuana-legalization policies. He has served as chairman of the Ethics Committee for the NACDL (National Association of Criminal Defense Lawyers) and has been the director of the Los Angeles chapter of NORML (National Organization for the Reform of Marijuana Laws) since 1973. He was awarded the Certificate of Appreciation from the ACLU (American Civil Liberties Union) as well as honors for his work on behalf of the Constitution Rights Foundation. He is the author of *The Margolin Guide to Marijuana Laws*. http://www.1800420laws.com.

Balaram Das (Peter Goetsch)

After India, Balaram got a degree at UC–Berkeley in South and Southeastern languages— Hindi, Sanskrit, and Urdu—and then went to medical school and became an M.D. with a specialty in anesthesiology. He recently received a degree in law and now often acts as an expert witness in legal medical cases. "It's Maharajji's great blessing that I got this job, because I get to help people in a very real way." Balaram took many of the photos of Maharajji in this book.

Bhagavan Das (Michael Riggs)

Bhagavan Das is a spiritual teacher, performer, counterculture icon, and lover of God. He helped usher in the New Age spiritual movement as the first kirtan artist in America. Living as a sadhu in India for six years, Bhagavan Das studied the ancient science of nada yoga under the guidance and direction of Maharajji—the path of devotion to the inner sound current as a means to God realization. www.bhagavandas.com.

Bruce Granofsky

With a background in illustration and animation, Bruce next developed an interest in photography. Photography and the people of India have been ongoing passions of his. "I love getting on a plane with a bag full of cameras and lenses. Nothing's more fun than arriving in a place like China, Russia, the Ukraine, or India and having no idea what you'll do when you arrive."

Daniel Garin

Daniel worked as a house painter and tile layer, until a terrible motor-cycle accident left him without an arm and with visual and cognitive difficulties. Very motivated and always very athletic, he tried to retrain to work with others with handicaps, but wasn't able to, as his own handicaps were too significant. Today he lives on disability in Taos, near the Hanuman temple, and helps raise his teenage daughter.

Devaki (Louise Markus)

Devaki is a painter, writer, and multimedia artist. Although she shows in various galleries and conventional venues across North America and lately Turkey, she considers herself an entrepreneurial, renegade artist. She is the creator and writer of the blog www.65chevypickup.com, an account of her and her partner Grant Genova's travels as they maneuver through the world of art and architecture. Her current project is "Pages from the Book of Avalon," collage illuminations describing daily life in Pouch Cove, Newfoundland. www.louisemarkus.com.

Dwarkanath (Joe Bonner)

Dwarkanath is an artist who lives at 8,000 feet in the Sangre de Cristo Mountains outside of Taos, New Mexico.

"English" Sita (Heather Thompson)

"As I've grown older, I've learned that the greatest way I can pay tribute to my beloved guru is to serve. I've been doing hospice work for almost thirty years now. That, together with bringing spiritual care to the housebound and going into the state prison as a volunteer chaplain for three years, has taught me that the way to bask in Maharajji's blessings is to serve him—in *all* his many manifestations—as best as I can. To that end, I have also been blessed to write to prisoners. That is such a seva, to drop judgments and see the 'highest' aspect of each person. It is constantly learning to act on the principle that on some level all appearances are just a game: what is below that and fulfills that is Maharajji. It is all by his grace."

Frank and Jan

Frank and Jan are happily retired, living in California and raising kale, avocados, and koi.

Gangadhar (Mark Gerhard)

After graduating from UC–Berkeley and enjoying a lengthy career in art, 3-D animation, production, marketing, and design, Gangadhar joined the faculty of Gate Academy in San Rafael, California, as an upper-school instructor. He loves teaching kids and adults, which has included summers instructing animation in Sonoma's EXCEL enrichment program, specialty classes at Stanford summer camps, and college-level design visualization for engineers and architects. Gangadhar is also a professional musician and plays the Indian tabla. He spent a number of years in India, where he became fluent in Hindi and developed his expertise in Indian classical music. He also studied with the Bauls (ecstatic street singers) in Bengal and has recorded and performed with Jai Uttal, Uma Reed, Babukishan Das Baul, and others.

Girija (Elaine Brilliant)

Girija holds a PhD in social epidemiology and is an equal partner in many of her husband's enterprises. Cofounder of the Seva Foundation, she also participated in the WHO smallpox eradication program. "What Maharajji gave Larry and me is the ability to be comfortable in so many worlds—the corporate world, the philanthropic world, in groundwork epidemiology. Since Seva, most of the service I have done is in my hometown. I was on a local planning commission for six years and now serve on the County Commission on Aging, but supporting Larry in his work and raising three children was central to my life." She also serves on the board of Camp Winnarainbow.

Gita (Marci Gendloff)

Gita has been a real-estate professional in North San Diego County for more than twenty-five years. "I try to do my business with the highest integrity. I meditate every day, and it is the most important part of my day. Those years in India shaped my life and my values. The grace of the guru can never be underestimated!" http://gitagendloff.com.

Gopal (Paul Singer)

Before Gopal went to India in November 1972, he had earned an advanced degree in tax law. After returning to Rhode Island, he concentrated on tax planning and real estate, working with environmental entrepreneurs and emphasizing environmental legal advocacy, litigation, and land preservation. He also has worked extensively with foundations connected with Ram Dass as well as other nonprofit foundations and educational organizations. He sits on the boards of the Love Serve Remember Foundation and the Neem Karoli Baba Ashram in Taos, New Mexico.

Govind (Charlie Burnham)

Govind is a violinist and composer. He has married (a few times), raised two boys, and taken up residence in far-flung locales before returning to

Brooklyn, where he grew up and currently lives with his one-hundred-year-old mom and his wife. Govind's love of music and playing the fiddle turned into a professional career, and he has fiddled his way around the world. His playing can be heard on the recordings of popular jazz and pop artists. http://musicians.allaboutjazz.com/charlesburnham; http://en.wikipedia.org/wiki/Charles_Burnham_(musician).

Govind and Gayatri

Govind and Gayatri met on the road in Afghanistan in 1970. They traveled together to India, where they spent most of the next eleven years. When they returned, they settled in Santa Fe, New Mexico, where they have a clothing and jewelry boutique featuring Govind's jewelry.

Ira Rose

After Maharajji dropped his body, Ira went to Benares and spent time with the jewelry merchants, which is how his business started. Back home, he found a little cottage offset from the street, which his father had to cosign for, because he was seen as a hippie who was never going to pay the rent. Today Cottage Jewelry is one of the premiere sources for fine jewelry in downtown Evanston, Illinois. http://www.cottage jewelry.com.

Jacques Achsen

Jacques spent four years in India, mostly studying Indian classical music and Vipassana meditation. He returned to North America in 1974 with his music teacher and settled in the Bay Area, where the Indian music scene was most vibrant. He found his way to serve when he got involved in hospice work and went back to school to get his master's in Oriental

Medicine. These days Jacques has an acupuncture practice in San Anselmo, California. He still practices Vipassana and keeps his hand in music as much as he can. Jacques also served on the board of Maharajji's ashram in Taos.

Jagganath Das (Daniel Goleman)

Daniel ("Danny") is an internationally known psychologist who reported on the brain and behavioral sciences for the *New York Times* for many years. His 1995 book, *Emotional Intelligence,* was on the *New York Times* bestseller list for a year and a half and was reprinted in forty languages. Goleman is a cofounder of the Collaborative for Academic, Social, and Emotional Learning (www.casel.org) and currently codirects the Consortium for Research on Emotional Intelligence in Organizations (www.eiconsortium.org) at Rutgers University. A board member of the Mind and Life Institute, he organized a series of intensive conversations between the Dalai Lama and scientists. His book *A Force for Good: The Dalai Lama's Vision for Our World* was published in June 2015, upon the eightieth birthday of the Dalai Lama. "The experience of having been with Maharajji made me, as a psychologist, see that the potential upside of human development went way beyond what was in the psychology books, so a lot of my work since then is about bringing that news to the West."

Jai Gopal (Jai Uttal)

Jai Uttal's eclectic East-meets-West sound has put his music at the forefront of the world fusion movement. Jai's musical roots embrace everything from the hillbilly music of the Appalachian Mountains to the strains of Bengali street singers, from the rhythms and melodies of ancient India to contemporary electric rock sounds. In India, bhakti

yoga became his personal path. Jai has been teaching and leading kirtans around the world for more than forty years, creating a safe environment for people to open their hearts and voices. He calls kirtan his
"soul support system" and still marvels how his deeply private spiritual
practice became his very public profession. Jai's sixth CD, *Mondo Rama*,
received a Grammy nomination, and since then he has released over
ten more albums expressing his love and longing for the guru's grace.
www.jaiuttal.com.

Janaki (Rathod)

Creativity is at the heart of both who Janaki is and the work she does.
For over twenty years, she has made a name for herself as a designer,
producer, and artist with the skills and vision to deliver outstanding
results in a wide variety of environments—from web design and development to film production and as a commercial production manager.
Currently she designs and implements websites for individuals and
companies. "I just try to remember who I am all of the time. Practicing
only takes you so far. At some point you have to *be* that thing that you
are practicing." www.janakirathod.com.

Kabir Das (Jim McCarthy)

When Kabir Das first stepped onto Indian soil, he immediately felt that
he had found his true home. His first visit lasted four and a half years.
He learned the language and immersed himself in the ancient but living
culture of the Hindus, learning from Indian yogis and saints and sometimes living alone in caves in the Himalayas. In 1991, after many more
visits to India, he began to paint portraits of the ascetics and sadhus
and the poor widows of Vrindavan. Kabir Das lives today in Vermont
and continues to visit India whenever possible. His paintings hang in

private collections, in puja rooms, over entranceways, and in yoga studios and meditation halls around the world. https://www.flickr.com/photos/120267566@N06/sets/72157645153345842/.

Kausalya (Karen Pettit)

"My caretaking career started mainly when a dear friend had advanced cancer, so I took it on to be her personal assistant and help with her kids. Caretaking allows me to be right there with my own ideas of what life is, what death is, the fears involved in both living and dying, especially living. Service work has always been in the foreground for me."

Krishna (David Dobrer)

"Since I've been taking care of this eighty-seven-year-old woman, it's like everything I have learned in my life I am able to give her, and the essence of it is that unconditional love I got from Maharajji. And I've always been feeding people. I feel that I'm using everything that I've learned and am still learning."

Krishna (John Bush)

An award-winning New York filmmaker who began making films in 2001, Krishna's work, including his epic four-and-a-half-hour *Journey into Buddhism* trilogy, has been shown at major film festivals, theaters, and museums around the world as well as on nationwide television broadcasts on PBS and abroad. The themes of pilgrimage and journey have been constants in his work. Bush has also created a series of eight dance films that have played at more than seventy-five festivals and art museums in twenty-two different countries, including the Cannes Film Festival. Direct Pictures is releasing his new documentary feature, *Journey Om: Into the Heart of India.* www.directpictures.com/films.

Krishna Das, or KD (Jeff Kagel)

Krishna Das has been called yoga's "rock star." He has taken call-and-response chanting out of yoga centers and into concert halls, becoming a worldwide icon and the bestselling Western chant artist of all time, with over three hundred thousand records sold. His album *Live Ananda* was nominated for a Grammy in the Best New Age Album category. In February 2013, Krishna Das performed at the Grammy awards in Los Angeles, streamed online to millions of viewers. KD also cofounded Triloka Records, a world music label. The award-winning film *One Track Heart: The Story of Krishna Das* has been in over a hundred U.S. cities and ten countries worldwide and is available on DVD everywhere. www.krishnadas.com.

Krishna Priya (Florence Klein)

"Maharajji's the only one who runs his ashrams, including the one in Taos. He's had me on the board of the Taos ashram for many years. Exactly who he wants on the board, his staff, and his caretakers—everybody's learning their lessons using the temple as the vehicle. I love being on the board, because I have a built-in excuse to come to his ashram twice a year. It's a lot less expensive than going to India, and I've had more darshan of Maharajji in the 'office' in Taos than I've had anywhere else since he left his body."

Lama Surya Das (Jeffrey Miller)

Lama Surya Das is one of the foremost Western Buddhist meditation teachers and scholars. The Dalai Lama affectionately calls him "the American Lama." He has spent forty-five years studying Zen, Vipassana, yoga, and Tibetan Buddhism with many of the great old masters of Asia, including some of the Dalai Lama's own teachers. He is an authorized lama in the Tibetan Buddhist order, a leading spokesperson for Buddhism and contemporary spirituality, a translator, poet, meditation master, chant master, and spiritual activist. Lama Surya Das is the author of the international bestselling Awakening trilogy (*Awakening the Buddha Within, Awakening to the Sacred,* and *Awakening the Buddhist Heart*) as well as the recently released *Make Me One with Everything* and ten other books. In 1991 he established the Dzogchen Center and Dzogchen Retreats (www.dzogchen.org). In 1993, with the Dalai Lama, he founded the Western Buddhist Teachers Network and regularly organizes its international Buddhist teachers' conferences. Lama Surya Das teaches and lectures around the world, conducting dozens of meditation retreats and workshops each year, and is a regular contributor at the *Huffington Post*. His blog, *Ask the Lama,* can be found at http://askthelama.com. His lecture and retreat schedule is listed at www.surya.org.

Laxman (Douglass Markus)

As the owner of Cuba's Cookin', Laxman likes the idea of "feeding everyone" down in the Caribbean on the tiny island of Aruba, featuring a lot of Jewish soul food in his well-established Cuban restaurant. Laxman's primary business for over thirty years is as the publisher of tourist destination magazines that are available throughout the Caribbean—the ones you see in your hotel rooms with features on local life and listings for attractions, shopping, and restaurants. www.nightspublications.com.

Mahavir Das (Marty Malles)

"I was a garment center salesman, and now I have a doctorate in psychology. I don't know how that happened. The education that I have has nothing to do with the work I am doing. It's all Maharajji. That really is how I think."

Meenakshi

Meenakshi took to heart Maharajji's teaching to feed everyone. For her, "feeding everyone" comes from connecting with herself and others through kindness.

Mira (Karen Goetsch)

After graduating UC–Berkeley, Mira traveled overland from Europe to India. When Maharajji left his body, she returned to the Bay Area where she has raised two wonderful boys with Balaram Das. She has worked in residential real estate for the past twenty-five years in the San Francisco East Bay and travels to India as much as possible. http://www.mirahomes.com.

Mirabai (Linda Bush)

Mirabai is Senior Fellow and founder of the Center for Contemplative Mind in Society, which encourages contemplative practice and perspectives in American life (www.contemplativemind.org). The center has created the Association for Contemplative Mind in Higher Education, a network of scholars, teachers, and administrators, and introduced contemplative practices to lawyers, judges, activists, scientists, and business executives. Mirabai worked with Google on a workplace course called Search Inside Yourself and with the U.S. Army on a program for chaplains and medics. She formerly directed the Seva Foundation Guatemala Project (www.seva.org) and Sustaining Compassion, Sustaining the Earth, a series of retreats and events for grassroots environmental activists. With her ex-husband, John Bush, she cofounded Illuminations, Inc., whose innovative business approaches, based on mindfulness practice, have been reported in *Newsweek, Fortune,* and the *New York Times.* Mirabai is coauthor, with Ram Dass, of *Compassion in Action: Setting Out on the Path of Service;* coauthor, with Daniel Barbezat, of *Contemplative Practices in Higher Education;* and editor of *Contemplation Nation: How Ancient Practices Are Changing the Way We Live.* She is on the boards of *Shambhala Sun* and the Love Serve Remember Foundation. www.mirabaibush.com.

Photo's Mohan (Steve Baum)

After decades of being in the luxury steam/sauna business in New York, Mohan became a wandering sadhu of sorts, spending more than half his time in India, some time in Denmark (the country of his late wife, Swamini), and some time in the United States (once or twice a year). He put together a wonderful website of photos of Maharajji at http://imageevent.com/neemkarolibabaphotos.

Naima Shea

Naima began her Buddhist practice in Bodhgaya in 1972 and gravitated toward Tibetan practice over time. She has cooked as a volunteer for many meditation retreats over two decades and still maintains a small, private massage therapy practice. She finds that facilitating a quiet space for people to slow down and feel their bodies is beneficial and healing. She also manages a Facebook page for Mountain Stream Meditation Center in the Sierra Foothills. Her four years in India were fundamental to the entire foundation of her values in life and a very great blessing.

Parvati (Barbara Markus)

Parvati has been "midwifing" spiritually oriented nonfiction books and memoirs as a substantive editor/writer since her first efforts with Ram Dass's classic *Be Here Now*. Books she has edited have been published by, among others, Hay House, Inner Traditions, Simon & Schuster, Contemporary / McGraw Hill, and Lotus Press. She collaborated on the three books and two guidebooks in the initiatory journey of *The Box: Remembering the Gift*. She has also helped with spiritual organizations (as past president of the board of the Neem Karoli Baba Ashram and Hanuman Temple in Taos, New Mexico) and events (as a development consultant for the Global Peace Initiative of Women Religious and Spiritual Leaders, held at the U.N. in Geneva).

Premananda (Tom Forray)

Premananda is a licensed marriage and family therapist and certified drug and alcohol counselor. He is a case manager with the STAR Program (Support and Treatment After Release)—for folks who are right out of jail and suffer from mental illness and substance-abuse issues. The program takes individuals from jail to a life of sobriety; they get the treatment they need so they can work and live independently. They have their own mental-health court program. Premananda does whatever it takes to reconnect his clients with their families, get them drug and alcohol treatment, housing, and benefits, and take care of their legal and financial issues.

Radha Baum

Radha has combined East and West in her healing practice. Early on, she was taught healing work and prayer by Hilda Charlton. She became an acupuncturist, working with terminal cancer patients as well as those with other illnesses that Western medicine was not able to treat successfully. She later became a nurse, working with AIDS patients. To understand different perspectives on healing, Radha studied Chinese herbology; mind/body medicine with Deepak Chopra; Therapeutic Touch; Reiki; Imagery work with Gerald Epstein and Peter Reznik; Qi Gong with Master Wu; and various other pain/stress-reduction techniques. She then became a family nurse practitioner, combining allopathic and integrative medicine. Since 1998 she has been working with MIHR (Magnetically Influenced Homeopathic Remedies)—a revolutionary healing modality.

Raghvindra Das, or Raghu (Mitchell Markus)

Raghu has been involved in music and transformational media since the early 1970s, when he was program director of CKGM-FM in Montreal, and later worked as an independent producer for the Canadian Broadcasting Corporation. In 1974 he collaborated with Ram Dass on the LP box set *Love Serve Remember*. In 1990 he launched Triloka Records and Karuna Music. Triloka established itself as a critical leader in the development of world music and for seventeen years was home to such artists as Krishna Das, Hugh Masekela, Walela, and Jai Uttal and transformational media projects that featured Ram Dass and Deepak Chopra. Raghu is the executive director of the Love Serve Remember Foundation and also the cofounder of the podcast collective site www.mindpodnetwork.com.

Ram Dass (Richard Alpert)

Ram Dass has made his mark on the world by teaching the path of the heart and promoting service in the areas of social consciousness and care for the dying. Ram Dass has pursued an array of spiritual methods and practices from ancient wisdom traditions, including bhakti yoga, focused on the Hindu deity Hanuman; Buddhist meditation in the Theravadin, Mahayana Tibetan, and Zen Buddhist schools; and Sufi and Jewish mystical studies. His practice of karma yoga (spiritual service) has opened up millions of other souls to their deep spiritual practice and path.

Ram Dass became a pivotal influence in our culture with the publication of *Be Here Now* in 1971. "Be here now" has been a catchphrase in people's lives for over forty years. With the publication in 2011 of *Be Love Now,* Ram Dass completed his trilogy that began with *Be Here Now* and continued with *Still Here* in 2004. His newest book is *Polishing the Mirror: How to Live from Your Spiritual Heart.* Ram Dass now makes his home in Maui, teaches worldwide through his website www.ramdass.org, and continues the work of Neem Karoli Baba through the Love Serve Remember Foundation.

Ram Dev (Dale Borglum)

Ram Dev is the founder and executive director of the Living/Dying Project. He is a pioneer in the conscious dying movement and has worked directly with thousands of people with life-threatening illnesses and their families for over thirty-five years. In 1981, he founded the first residential facility for people who wished to die consciously in the United States, the Dying Center. He has taught and lectured extensively on the topics of spiritual support for those with life-threatening illnesses, on caregiving as a spiritual practice, and on healing. Ram Dev is the co-author, with Ram Dass, of *Journey of Awakening: A Meditator's Guidebook* and has taught meditation for the past forty years. His life's work and passion continue to be the healing of our individual and collective relationship with death and also using our mortality as an inspiration for spiritual awakening. www.livingdying.org.

Rameshwar Das, or Ramesh (Jim Lytton)

Rameshwar Das's principle vocation has been as a photographer, free-lancing for the *New York Times* and other publications. He has taught photography and photo-journalism and has also worked as an environmentalist and writer. Ramesh collaborated on several projects with Ram Dass, including the *Love Serve Remember* box set of records. He is the coauthor of Ram Dass's recent books *Be Love Now* and *Polishing the Mirror: How to Live from Your Spiritual Heart*. He is a board member of the Love Serve Remember Foundation and of the Taos Neem Karoli Baba Ashram. He lives with his family on the end of Long Island. Many of the photos in this book are his.

Ramgiri (Andreas Braun)

Because he was born in Germany in the aftermath of World War II and the Holocaust, Ramgiri's early years were difficult. It made him seek effective ways to end his suffering. In 1972 he met Maharajji, who showed him that enlightenment is his true nature and the nature of all beings. Ramgiri spent the next forty years learning from great masters and developing HeartSourcing Yoga, a contemporary way to enlightenment through the power of the heart, which he describes in his book *Heart-Sourcing: Finding Our Way to Love and Liberation*. Ramgiri is a spiritual teacher, lifelong yogi, and experienced psychologist. www.ramgiri.com.

RamRani (Yvette Rosser)

In 1973, Maharajji instructed RamRani to "return to America and study about India and help make Hinduism better understood and respected in the West." At the University of Texas at Austin, she received a BA in Indian

Literature and Language. She then taught world history at the secondary level and in her master's thesis investigated how India is represented in world history classes in American high schools; she published a number of papers on the topic, suggesting corrective strategies. Her PhD compared social studies textbooks in India, Pakistan, and Bangladesh—three countries with thousands of years of shared history, but very different contemporary perspectives on those historical events. She is currently working on a book, *The Politicization of Historiography in India,* which investigates influences that have impacted historical narratives in India through the centuries. http://en.wikipedia.org/wiki/Yvette_Rosser.

Ravi Das (Michael Jeffery)

Ravi Das received his law degree from Yale University, then spent almost five years living in India. He came to Alaska in 1977 as the first legal services attorney in Barrow and in 1982 was appointed the first (and only) judge of the new state Superior Court in Barrow. "The question for me was how did a Supreme Court judgeship fit with my promise to Maharajji to serve the poor and the sick. Turns out that most of the people I served were Natives, juvenile delinquents, all lower-income people, child-welfare cases, child-custody cases, and some civil litigation." At the end of 2014, he was legally required to retire at age seventy. He and his wife are remaining in Barrow for the foreseeable future.

Ravi Das spent considerable time addressing fetal alcohol spectrum disorders (FASD). He championed a change to state law in 2012 that enabled judges to allow lower sentences for people with fetal alcohol syndrome or related disorders. In general, he favored reintroduction into society over lengthy jail sentences, but imposed long sentences in serious felonies when required by facts and state law. Ravi Das feels he has the energy and legal skills to continue working for the community. He hopes to continue his efforts at tackling FASD issues.

Ravi Khanna

Ravi Khanna grew up in India and moved to the United States in 1977 at the age of twenty-three. Before coming to Resist foundation in February of 2011, Ravi served as the administrative director for PHENOM, the Public Higher Education Network of Massachusetts. Ravi has worked, consulted, and served on the boards of a number of progressive organizations, including Oxfam America, Peace Development Fund, Haymarket People's Fund, 1world communication, Grassroots International, the Men's Resource Center of Western Massachusetts, Movimiento Ciudadano por la Democracia (MDC), and Women's Rights International.

Rukmini (Linda Spiritoso)

Rukmini and her late husband, Murari, were named and married by Maharajji. She is a retired social worker, trainer, and an Interfaith minister as well as a runner and an animal-rights advocate. She still lives in Philadelphia, where she grew up and worked. The mother of three sons and grandmother to three boys, she says, "I feel blessed by all the love and teachings I have been given."

Sadhu Uma (Marcelle Hanselaar)

An oil painter and etcher, Marcelle is a figurative expressionist. Her images are about the conflict between the inner world and outer appearance, our inner beast versus our civilized demeanor. How strong is our moral stance when we find ourselves in conflict situations? Her work is in several major museum collections, and she is represented by galleries in the United Kingdom and Belgium. Remnants of the old sadhu appear as figures in her etchings.

Saraswati, or Sara (Rosalie Ransom)

Sara Ransom is the daughter and granddaughter of performing story-tellers. She has been featured in festivals and solo performances from New England to New Zealand. Sara received a National Endowment for the Arts Solo Performance Fellowship in 1991, and several of her recordings have received national awards. Over the years, Sara amassed a vast repertoire of tales, legends, and myths from around the world. Her dramatic portrayals of Kali, Shiva, and stories from the *Ramayana* gain an authentic feel from her years in India. She has also taught workshops tailored to different age groups (http://sararansom.com/). Sara formally retired several years back, but can sometimes be coerced into performing again. She also maintains a website of whimsical essays at http://sararansom.blogspot.com/.

Sita Sharan (Susan McCarthy)

Sita stayed in India for eight years, living in Benares as a Vaishnava sadhu, studying music, philosophy, and languages. She founded the Surya Incense Company and imports and sells her own "Surya" brand of hand-rolled all-natural incense. Her company is committed to the protection and preservation of the environment, the ingredients are grown in the clean air and water of the Himalayas, and the working conditions for the Indian employees exceed all current fair-wage, health, and safety standards. Ten percent of profits are donated directly to poor widows in Vrindavan. www.suryatrading.com.

Steven Schwartz

Steven J. Schwartz is the litigation director for the Center for Public Representation—a public-interest law firm dedicated to serving individuals with disabilities. He began practicing mental-disability law after graduating from Harvard Law School and served as the center's executive director for thirty-eight years. Steven has authored a number of law-review articles, testified before Congress on P&A-authorizing legislation and abuse and neglect issues, and served on the faculty of the Harvard and Western New England Law Schools. "Maharajji is part of my life every single moment. I have spent forty years trying to bring people with disabilities out of institutions and get them the support or treatments or whatever else is necessary to allow them to be at home." http://www.centerforpublicrep.org/our-organization/staff.

Suil Anna (Scottish Annie)

Suil trained in the Theravadin tradition before entering the monastery and being ordained as a Zen nun in the Korean Zen tradition. Currently she continues her practice in the Tibetan tradition. She came to America in 1982 as a translator with her Korean Zen master, Ku San Sunim. When Ram Dev started the Living/Dying Project in New Mexico, she had a shaved head and was in robes; Suil returned her vows and started working at the dying center. She is now the director of Asia for NLP (Neuro-Linguistic Programming) and teaches a certified coaching training program as well as executive mindfulness training programs. "When I was teaching meditation, people would come to see me, and their questions or challenges were not to do with meditation, but with personal issues. NLP is in really good harmony and very helpful with what I am doing."

Sunanda (Jeanne Markus)

As a business woman, Sunanda works as the managing director of Nights Publications, Inc., in Montreal, Quebec, along with her ex-husband, Laxman. On the philanthropic side, Sunanda works as grants program manager for the Mind and Life Institute, served as program coordinator for Contemplative Mind in Higher Education for twelve years, and has served on the boards of the Seva Foundation, Seva Service Society, and the Insight Meditation Society. She was an active member of the Seva Guatemala Project.

Subramaniam (Dr. Larry Brilliant)

Dr. Larry Brilliant is the president of the Skoll Global Threats Fund and senior adviser to Jeff Skoll (the founder of eBay). Prior to joining Skoll, Larry served as the inaugural executive director of Google.org and later as chief philanthropy evangelist, overseeing the Google Foundation, Google Grants, and the company's other major social-change initiatives. Larry, with M.D. and M.P.H. degrees, is board certified in preventive medicine and public health. He is a founder and director of the Seva Foundation and the author of two books and dozens of articles on infectious diseases, blindness, and international health policy. He played a key role in the successful World Health Organization (WHO) smallpox eradication program and more recently worked for the WHO polio eradication effort. Larry has received awards from the government of India and from WHO. In 2005 he was named International Public Health Hero by the University of California. In February 2006 he received the Sapling Foundation's TED Prize. In 2008, Brilliant was named one of *Time* magazine's 100 Most Influential People and also was given a Global Leadership Award by the United Nations. www.skollfoundation.org /staff/larry-brilliant/ and www.ted.com/speakers/larry_brilliant.

Tukaram, or Tuk (Jean Nantel)

On returning from India, Tukaram became the executive director of Alternatives, a pioneering free drug-rehabilitation clinic with a

cognitive-behavioral approach. Mindfulness training was a key compo-
nent of the program. Seven years later he returned to India with Kabir
Das as the representative of Canadian engineering firms. After a stint
working in Vancouver, BC, in corporate finance, he fell into a deep
depression. He returned to India and eventually met with Dada, who
helped him reopen to Maharajji's grace and constant presence. Today he
divides his time between India and Canada and pursues his practice in a
spirit of gratitude and astonishment.

Vidura (Francis X. Charet)

Vidura has a PhD in psychology and religion and coordinates the Consciousness Studies concentration in the Graduate Institute at Goddard
College, which brings together a number of fields to focus on the study
of consciousness and the development of an engaged practice. He is the
author of, among other publications, "Ram Dass: The Vicissitudes of
Devotion and Ferocity of Grace" in *Homegrown Gurus: From Hinduism in
America to American Hinduism,* edited by Ann Gleig and Lola Williamson.
http://goddard.edu/people/francis-xavier-charet.

Vishnu (Frank Hutton)

Vishnu's work on the board of directors of the Neem Karoli Baba Ashram in Taos is who he really is inside. He also feels Maharajji's presence
in his work as a guide and a medium in the Current room (meditation
space) of Casa de Dom Inacio, the healing center for the Brazilian healer
John of God. He travels to his home in Abadiania, Brazil, three times a
year and feels Maharajji's love strongly there. "One of the things that I
heard inside when I was with Maharajji was the question, 'What is your
deepest desire?' I said that if I could be allowed to be instrumental in

human beings coming home again, if even one person's heart could be opened, my life would be fulfilled."

Vishwanath (Daniel Miller)

Vishwanath and his wife, Uma, ran Buds, a flower shop in Taos, New Mexico, that provided flowers for the celebrations at the Hanuman temple. He and Uma then developed Blossoms, an organic garden center, which they sold to move to Santa Cruz, California. He now studies art and is active in environmental causes.

Vivekananda (Michael Attie)

"Maharajji asked me, 'What's your name?' I said, 'Michael.' He yelled at me, 'Vivekananda! What does Vivekananda mean?' I said, 'Bliss of discrimination.' He yelled at me, 'No.' He made me repeat three times: 'Vivekananda is a great teacher who spread the dharma in the West.' Okay, I'm the next Ram Dass! But the truth is it hasn't happened. Every once in a while I do a dharma event. I play the accordion—the 'squeeze-box swami show.' I've made CDs. I have written books of poetry. I hold four retreats a year. Every Tuesday night I have a sitting at my house in LA. Once a month I have an all-day sitting. Maharajji has given me a lifetime koan of letting go of my spiritual ego." http://www.jewishjournal .com/lifecycles/article/lingerie_and_meditation_20060203.

Vyed Vas (Ralph Abraham)

Ralph Abraham has been professor of mathematics at UC–Santa Cruz since 1968. He has a PhD in mathematics and taught at Berkeley, Columbia, and Princeton. He has held visiting positions in Amsterdam, Paris,

Warwick, Barcelona, Basel, and Florence and is the author of more than twenty texts, including eight books currently in print. Ralph has been active on the research frontier of dynamics in mathematics and in applications and experiments. He has been a consultant on chaos theory and its applications in numerous fields and is an active editor for the technical journals *World Futures* and the *International Journal of Bifurcations and Chaos*. In 1975, he founded the Visual Mathematics Project at UC–Santa Cruz, which became the Visual Math Institute in 1990. "The course of study that Maharajji put me on affected the work I do, and I've been interested in the applications to consciousness. In my book *Demystifying the Akasha*, I have expressed this connection between pure math, computer simulations, and contemplative practice." http://www.ralph-abraham.org.

In Memoriam

Death leaves a heartache no one can heal,
Love leaves a memory no one can steal.

—FROM AN IRISH HEADSTONE

Krishna Das (Roy Bonney)

ANNAPURNA (Georganne Coffee Broffman)

CARLOS VISHWANATH

DASARATHA, or DAS (Ed Markus)

MARIAM (Joanne Randall)

MURARI (Tom Spiritoso)

PETER BRAWLEY

PETER STRONG

SADHU MA ("Jesus Jenny")

SHIVAYA (Alan Cain)

SHYAMDAS (Stephen Schaffer)

SUDHAMA and SUNANDA (Ed and Kris Fleur)

SWAMI RAM TIRTH (Fred Blumfeld)

VISHNU DIGAMBAR (Andreas Hubman)

Notes

Introduction

1. http://www.alternativereel.com/soc/display_article.php?id=0000000017.

2. Jack Kornfield, "Sacred Journey," *Lomi School Bulletin*, Petaluma, CA (Summer 1980): 8.

Chapter 1: The Call

1. Ram Dass, *Be Here Now* (New York: Crown Publishing, 1971).

2. For more of Bhagavan Das's story, read his memoir, *It's Here Now (Are You?)* (New York: Broadway Books, 1997).

3. Krishna Das, *Chants of a Lifetime*, 2nd ed. (Carlsbad, CA: Hay House, 2011), 9–10.

4. The Hartleys (of the Hartley Film Foundation) filmed for a few days during "summer camp" in 1969. See their documentary *Evolution of a Yogi—Ram Dass*.

Chapter 3: The Early Ones

1. Krishna Das, *Chants of a Lifetime*, 2nd ed. (Carlsbad, CA: Hay House, 2011), 24–25.

2. ———. *Chants of a Lifetime*, 24–25.

Chapter 6: Christ and the Hanuman Are One

1. Krishna Das, Open Your Heart in Paradise Retreat, Maui, December 2013.

Chapter 10: Where the Sacred Rivers Meet

1. You can read Dada Mukerjee's own story with Maharajji in *By His Grace: A Devotee's Story* (Santa Fe, NM: Hanuman Foundation, 1990) and his stories about other devotees and Maharajji in *The Near and the Dear: Stories of Neem Karoli Baba and His Devotees* (Santa Fe, NM: Hanuman Foundation, 2000).

2. Raghu, Open Your Heart in Paradise Retreat, Maui, December 2013.

Chapter 11: Comings and Goings

1. From an interview with Pico Iyer on Super Soul Sunday.

Chapter 12: The Music of the Spheres

1. Krishna Das, Open Your Heart in Paradise Retreat, Maui, December 2013.

Chapter 15: The Summer of Delight

1. For more on Ramgiri's story, read his book *HeartSourcing: Finding Our Way to Love and Liberation* (Miami: Annapurna Institute, 2014).

Chapter 17: And in the End

1. *Miracle of Love* is no longer available as a paperback, but is now an e-book in Kindle and iBook editions: Ram Dass, *Miracle of Love: Stories about Neem Karoli Baba* (published by Love Serve Remember Foundation, 2014).

Glossary

All Hindi and Sanskrit words are defined in the text where they first appear. The following appear more than once or need further explanation.

AARTI (from Sanskrit *aratrika,* "something that removes darkness"), Hindu ritual in which light (usually from cotton wicks soaked in ghee) is offered to the guru or to one or more deities.

ACCHA, good; *bohut accha,* very good.

ASHRAM, a spiritual hermitage, traditionally in forests or mountainous regions, conducive to spiritual instruction and meditation.

ATMAN (Sanskrit), the essential unchanging self or soul.

BANDHARA, a feast where many people are fed.

BHAGAVAD GITA (Sanskrit, "Song of God"), the seven-hundred-verse section of the *Mahabharata* that is a dialogue between Krishna and Arjuna expounding the core beliefs of Hinduism.

BHAKTI, the path of devotion.

BRAHMIN (from Sanskrit *brahmana,* "he who possesses knowledge"), the highest level in the caste system, originally educators, scholars, and preachers; also known as the "twice born."

CHAI, Indian tea with milk, sugar, and spices.

CHAUKIDAR, gatekeeper at an ashram.

CHELA, disciple.

CHILLUM, a straight, cone-shaped pipe, usually made of clay, used by sadhus for smoking tobacco mixed with hash (*charas*) or marijuana (*ganja*).

DANDA PRANAAM, full prostration, indicating total surrender to the guru or God.

DARSHAN (Sanskrit, "sight"), having a vision of the divine or being in the presence of a holy person.

DHARMA, in Hinduism, the principle of cosmic order and the individual conduct that conforms with this principle; *dhamma* in Buddhism.

DHARMASALA, a simple building where spiritual seekers can stay.

DHOTI, a man's garment made of one long piece of cloth, wrapped around the hips with one end brought up between the legs and tucked into the waist.

GOPIS (Sanskrit, "cowherd girls"), the group of 108 cowherding girls who lived in Vrindavan and were famed for their unconditional devotion and playful relationship to Krishna during his youth. One gopi, Radha, is especially esteemed as having the highest form of unconditional love for God.

GURU (from Sanskrit *gu,* "darkness," and *ru,* "light"), one who removes the darkness; literally a preceptor who shows others knowledge (light) and destroys ignorance (darkness).

GURUBAHIN (sing., gurubhai), "brothers" (and sisters) who are devotees of the same guru.

HANUMAN, an incarnation of Lord Shiva who was embodied in the form of a *varana* (a member of the monkey race) in order to serve Lord Rama (an avatar of Lord Vishnu who embodies *dharma*, righteousness). Hanuman's exploits are told in the *Ramayana.* The Hanuman Chalisa is a hymn of forty verses in praise of Hanuman.

HAVAN, a fire ceremony.

ISHA (from Hebrew Yeshua), the name Maharajji used for Jesus. The Koran refers to Jesus as Isa.

JAO (pronounced "jow"), "Go!" To be *jaoed* is to be told to go, to be dismissed from one's presence.

JAPA (from Sanskrit *jap,* "to utter in a low voice, repeat internally, mutter"), a spiritual discipline that involves the repetition of a mantra or name of God. It may be done while meditating, performing activities, or in a group setting. Japa is frequently done with a mala, a string of 108 beads.

JHOLA, an Indian cloth bag.

KARMA (Sanskrit), the concept of "actions" or "deeds" and their consequences—the entire cycle of cause and effect. Karma is said to be produced through the thoughts, words, and actions we perform ourselves and actions others do under our instructions.

KIRTAN (from Sanskrit, "to repeat"), chanting the divine Name. Kirtan wallahs are the singers and musicians who do kirtan.

KRISHNA, an avatar of Vishnu, the embodiment of love.

KUTIR, a small hut.

LILA (Sanskrit, "sport" or "play"), the activities of God and his devotees.

LUNGI, a traditional men's garment worn wrapped around the waist.

MAHABHARATA, the major Sanskrit epic of ancient India narrating the Kurukshetra War and the fates of the two great tribes, the Kauravas and the Pandavas. The *Bhagavad Gita* is one part of this epic poem.

MAHARAJJI (literally, "great king"), in this book the honorific that refers to Neem Karoli Baba. It is more correctly spelled Maharaj-ji, but here it is rendered without the hyphen for simplicity.

MALA, a string of 108 beads made from various woods, seeds, or precious stones that carry spiritual vibrations; used especially for saying a mantra.

MANDIR, temple.

MANTRA, a sound, syllable, word, or group of words repeated to bring about a spiritual transformation.

MAST, God intoxicated.

MAUN, silent.

MELA (Sanskrit, "gathering" or "meeting"); the Kumbh Mela, a spiritual gathering held every twelve years, is the largest gathering in India. In January 2007, over seventy million people attended the Kumbh Mela in Allahabad over a forty-five-day period, making it the largest gathering anywhere in the world.

METTA (Pali, "loving-kindness"); the cultivation of metta is a form of meditation in Buddhism, the object of which is to love without attachment and to harbor no ill will or hostility toward others. It implies caring for another independent of all self-interest.

MUDRA, a position of the body, especially of the hands and fingers, that influences the body's energies.

MURTI (Sanskrit, "form," "embodiment"), the image of a deity used during worship.

NAHIN, "No."

NAMASTÉ, salutation meaning "I honor the light within you."

PRASAD (literally, "mercy"), anything that has been sanctified or blessed by being offered.

PUJA (Sanskrit, "worship," "adoration"), a rite of worship performed in the home, temple, or shrine to a murti or person, such as the satguru. Durga Puja is a nine-day ceremony in the fall that honors the goddess Durga.

PUJARI, a priest who performs a puja.

PURIS, deep-fried flatbread.

RAMAYANA ("Rama's Journey"), an ancient Sanskrit epic tale attributed to the Hindu sage Valmiki. It is the story of Lord Rama, his wife Sita, brother Lakshman, and devoted monkey servant Hanuman. Many versions of the story exist. The one most associated with Maharajji is the *Ramacharitamanas,* written in Hindi by Tulsi Das in the sixteenth century at the height of the bhakti revival. The heart of the epic is the chapter "Sundara Kanda," the detailed account of Hanuman's adventures.

RINPOCHE (from Tibetan, "precious jewel"), an honorific given to masters in Tibetan Buddhism.

SADHANA (from Sanskrit, "the means to accomplish something"), a specifically spiritual practice.

SADHU, a wandering monk, yogi, or ascetic.

SAMADHI (Sanskrit), the higher levels of consciousness. For bhaktas, samadhi is the complete absorption into the object of one's love. *Nirvikalpa samadhi* is the highest nondualistic state of consciousness, pure awareness. *Sahaja samadhi* is the state of staying in nirvikalpa samadhi and yet being fully functional in this world, like Maharajji. *Mahasamadhi,* the "great samadhi," is the term used for the intentional departure from the physical body at death by an enlightened being.

SANGAM (Sanskrit *sangama*), confluence; in Allahabad, the Triveni Sangam is where two physical rivers, the Ganges and Yamuna, and the mythical Saraswati River come together. Mahatma Gandhi's ashes were immersed at the Sangam in Allahabad in 1948.

SATGURU (Sanskrit, "the true guru"), an enlightened rishi or saint, as distinguished from other gurus like teachers or parents.

SATSANG (from Sanskrit *sat,* "true," and *sanga,* "company"), the assembly of people who come together to listen to and talk about spiritual teachings. In Buddhism, the satsang is called the *sanga.*

SEVA, service.

SHAKTI, the divine feminine creative power.

SHAKTIPAT, conferring spiritual energy upon someone.

SIDDHA, a perfected master.

SUB EK, "All is One."

SUTRA, a written aphorism or a collection of precepts.

TAKHAT (literally, "throne," "seat of power"), for Maharajji a wooden platform covered with a blanket.

THIK HAI, "It's okay."

TONGA, a two-wheeled horse-drawn cart.

UPANISHADS, a series of sacred Hindu treatises in Sanskrit, written between 800 and 200 BCE, that expound on the Vedas, the most ancient Hindu scriptures, believed to have been directly revealed to the early Aryan seers in India.

WALLAH, a person involved with or in charge [of a specified thing], like a chai wallah, rickshaw wallah, or kirtan wallah.

YATRA, a spiritual pilgrimage.

Resources

There are many methods of meditation, but Vipassana (insight, or mindfulness) meditation and metta (loving-kindness) meditation continue to be excellent foundations for quieting the mind and connecting to the heart. The Insight Meditation Society (IMS) in Barre, Massachusetts (www.dharma.org), was founded in 1975 by three Westerners who brought back this ancient practice from the East—Sharon Salzberg, Joseph Goldstein, and Jack Kornfield. Jack also founded Spirit Rock Meditation Center in Woodacre, California (www.spiritrock.org). These centers offer retreats, instruction, and guidance in insight and loving-kindness forms of meditation.

For audio files of Ram Dass's original lectures and
more Maharajji satsang stories, go to
www.ramdass.org.

For a full-page view of Maharajji quotes from Naima and
Mira journals, go to www.ramdass.org/loveeveryone.

For kirtan CDs, go to
www.krishnadas.com, www.jaiuttal.com,
and www.bhagavandas.com.
Shyamdas's CDs are available on iTunes and Amazon
and at the Taos ashram puja store.

To learn about the Neem Karoli Baba Ashram
and Hanuman Temple in Taos, New Mexico, go to
www.nkbashram.org.

To hear Shivaya telling many Maharajji stories,
go to www.shivaya.bandcamp.com.

To learn more about Shyamdas's contribution
to the path of devotion, go to
https://shyamdasfoundation.com.

Acknowledgments

I owe a tremendous debt of gratitude to Ram Dass for lighting my way to Maharajji's feet—a debt I could never adequately repay. Meeting Ram Das changed the course of my life and put it on a whole new trajectory. *Love Everyone* is my way to pay it forward.

I'd like to thank the readers of early versions who gave me useful feedback: Hanuman Tirth, Susan Ashman (special thanks to Susan for coparenting my cat!), Andrea Adler, and Kashi Frank.

Sincere thanks to Cecilia Montero and Robin Alexis for reading on a whole other level and keeping the energy flowing. And much credit goes to Radha Baum as the "bhav" barometer.

My thanks to Chris Morro for early transcribing efforts, and deep appreciation to Prema Michau for her exemplary transcription work.

Deep appreciation goes to Gideon Weil, my editor at HarperOne, for his enthusiasm and support for this project (and for "encouraging" me to make the book shorter and better!). And a big thank you to the whole team at HarperOne for their outstanding work and patience with me.

I could not have done this project—the years of gathering over seventy interviews around the country and compiling this book—without the support of the Love Serve Remember Foundation, especially the efforts of my ex-husband, Raghu Markus, executive director of the foundation. And I would like to acknowledge those I interviewed whose stories did not make it into this book (but will appear later in other formats).

Big thanks for their loving support to my wonderful sons, Noah and Shyam; Shyam's wife, Deborah; and my delightful granddaughters, Dylan, Zoey, and Willow.

And as always, deep love and abiding gratitude to Neem Karoli Baba. Thank you, Maharajji, for a love beyond imagining and a life wrapped in a plaid blanket. I am thrilled and humbled to be your "private secretary."

Index

Credits

Grateful acknowledgment is given to the following for the use of their work in this publication.

Gangadhar's story, pages 152–154, based on interview by Mahavir (Steven Newmark). Used by permission.

Endpaper photograph of Maharajji's blanket by Balaram Das. Used by permission.

Frontispiece by Krishna Das (Roy Bonney). Used by permission.

Photograph on the last page of the color insert, of Baba with aarti flame, by Balaram Das. Used by permission.

Photographs on pages v, xv, 54, 114, 122, 151, 164, 186, 198, 219, 225, 250, 262, 276, 286, and 355 from the personal collection of Krishna Das (Roy Bonney). Used by permission.

Photographs on pages xiv, 117, 119, 123, 143, 148, 173, 178, 184, 191, 197, 242, 257, 264, and 281 from the personal collection of Balaram Das. Used by permission.

Photographs on pages 6, 9, 46, 93, 214, and 309 from the collection of LSR Foundation Archive. Used by permission.

Photographs on pages 14, 20, 66, 100, 103, 112, and 310 from the personal collection of Rameshwar Das. Used by permission.

Photograph on page 26 from www.frontlineadventuretravel.com.

Photographs on pages 90, 213, 216, and 300 from the personal collection of Parvati Markus. Used by permission.

Photograph on page 207 from the personal collection of Naima Shea. Used by permission.

Photograph on page 230 from the personal collection of Premananda. Used by permission.

Photograph on page 248 from the personal collection of Sadhu Uma. Used by permission.